I0877499

THE FAKE PRISON DOCTOR OF AUSCHWITZ

THE FAKE PRISON DOCTOR OF AUSCHWITZ

UNCOVERING THE TRUTH BEHIND HOLOCAUST FRAUDSTERS

BOGDAN MUSIAL

In collaboration with Andrea Böltken
and Oliver Musial
Translated by Oliver Musial

Pen & Sword
MILITARY
AN IMPRINT OF PEN & SWORD BOOKS LTD.
YORKSHIRE – PHILADELPHIA

First published in Germany in 2019 by
Osburg Verlag as *Mengeles Koffer: Eine Spurensuche*

First published in Great Britain in 2024 by
Pen and Sword Military
An imprint of
Pen & Sword Books Ltd.
Yorkshire - Philadelphia

Copyright © Bogdan Musial, 2024

ISBN 978 1 39904 405 9

The right of Bogdan Musial to be identified as author of this work has been asserted by him in accordance with the Copyright, Designs and Patents Act 1988.

A CIP catalogue record for this book is available from the British Library.

All rights reserved. No part of this book may be reproduced or transmitted in any form or by any means, electronic or mechanical including photocopying, recording or by any information storage and retrieval system, without permission from the Publisher in writing.

Typeset in INDIA by IMPEC eSolutions
Printed and bound in England by CPI Group (UK) Ltd.

Pen & Sword Books Limited incorporates the imprints of Archaeology, Atlas, Aviation, Battleground, Digital, Discovery, Family History, Fiction, History, Local, Local History, Maritime, Military, Military Classics, Politics, Select, Transport, True Crime, After the Battle, Air World, Claymore Press, Frontline Publishing, Leo Cooper, Remember When, Seaforth Publishing, The Praetorian Press, Wharncliffe Books, Wharncliffe Local History, Wharncliffe Transport, Wharncliffe True Crime and White Owl.

For a complete list of Pen & Sword titles please contact:

PEN & SWORD BOOKS LIMITED
George House, Units 12 & 13, Beevor Street,
Off Pontefract Road, Barnsley, S71 1HN, UK
E-mail: enquiries@pen-and-sword.co.uk
Website: www.pen-and-sword.co.uk

or

PEN AND SWORD BOOKS
1950 Lawrence Rd, Havertown, PA 19083, USA
E-mail: Uspen-and-sword@casematepublishers.com
Website: www.penandswordbooks.com

FSC www.fsc.org MIX Paper from responsible sources FSC® C013604

Table of Contents

Foreword

Impostors are adept at weaving together lies and truth to deceive their audience. Their stories are both extraordinary and compelling, but when the deception is revealed, they often appear outright ridiculous. They challenge our ability to judge, doubly so if their lies touch upon the traumatic and unresolved. In these cases, we are often willing to accept the seemingly unlikely, and in the case of Auschwitz in particular, the crimes committed there are so mind-bendingly horrendous that even the actual history feels outlandish. This makes it even more important to get to the bottom of things. This we owe to ourselves and most importantly, to the victims.

This book recounts our search for the truth. In it, I write about the events and the way I viewed them at the time.

Bogdan Musial, August 2019

Chapter 1

An Unexpected Call

I hope that Magda will not read it, and if she does, then she will learn what a horrible person her grandfather was, or she will admire her grandfather and be proud of him. I hope the entire world will learn about the history of the doctors. In Auschwitz and in the German concentration camps... And the entire world will know [...] what a horror fascism was. [...] Yes, I will condemn it morally and legally, and indict this apocalypse!

Memoirs, page 117

'Hello Bogdan, Lisbeth has invited you to her Christmas party. Do you want to come with me?'

This seemingly harmless question by a doctor I was friends with marked the beginning of a scholarly odyssey that would keep me busy for over two and a half years. It would lead me through much of Europe, open up a new field of research for me – and nearly ruin my academic reputation.

On the phone was Dr Isabel Wassert,[1] a close family friend from a small town near Hanover. Wassert, in turn, was friends with Elisabeth Lothfels,[2] a wealthy heiress from Munich who had a very wide network of friends both within Germany and abroad. Every year, Lothfels gathered her family, friends and acquaintances at a restaurant in Tegernsee, a renowned spa town near Munich. The list of people Lothfels invited each year was as long as it was distinguished, and naturally I accepted the invitation even though it came as a surprise.

When we arrived in Tegernsee, Lothfels invited us to stay at her mansion, together with a few other guests. The villa was beautiful and offered a great view of the valley and the lake. Lothfels was an elegant lady in her late 60s and welcomed us with great friendliness and generosity. The party itself was very impressive. Held in the evening, it was attended by all kinds of prominent figures, ranging from the extraordinarily wealthy, to members of the German high nobility and notable figures from the business world, but also from politics and the arts. Most were from Munich, but many were from other parts of Germany as well; there were plenty of guests from Switzerland too, and even some from Asia.

Among the guests invited to stay at Lothfels' villa was a close friend of hers, a distinguished lady in her 60s. She was introduced to me as Professor Magdalena Nicoletta Kaiser-Szentágothay and was evidently well-aware of who I was as she greeted me as 'Polish professor' without any further ado. However, before I was able to articulate my astonishment, I noticed that she was speaking German with an accent. She mentioned that she was indeed from abroad, from Hungary in fact, and that she had excellent ties to Poland. We quickly began to talk and it rapidly emerged that Kaiser was a reputable virologist who had been a papal personal physician for the Vatican for decades. She had accompanied Pope John Paul II on his travels to Poland, which she spoke of vividly, adding anecdotes about his peculiarities and habits. Much of it I had already heard about; Pope John Paul II, born Karol Wojtyła, was the first Pole and indeed the first Slav to lead the Catholic Church and unsurprisingly, countless stories about him circulate within Poland.

However, it was apparent that she had actually known him well personally; she even dropped a few casual remarks about the inner workings of the Vatican. She then asked me which faith I belonged to. I did not want to discuss religion, so I deflected the question by pointing to the fact that I was teaching Central and Eastern European Studies at Warsaw's Catholic Cardinal Stefan Wyszyński University. This was enough for her and she moved on with our conversation, talking about the other guests and the usual gossip coupled with interesting anecdotes. It felt like the professor knew everyone, and everyone knew her. She moved among the guests like the proverbial fish in water. Overall, it was a very pleasant experience.

Several weeks later, Wassert told me that Lothfels and Professor Kaiser wanted to contact me. In mid-January 2014, both the heiress and the professor thus called me, but unlike at the Christmas party, where the professor had showcased her confident personality, she was clearly in great turmoil and Lothfels had to assist her during the call. After some back and forth they told me what was going on: Kaiser's grandfather had left documents to her which she was due to receive soon, decades after his death. This would not have been particularly exciting if not for the fact that her grandfather, then a renowned gynaecologist, had been in Auschwitz, where he was forced to work as a prisoner-doctor for none other than the infamous SS physician, Dr Josef Mengele. In Auschwitz, Mengele conducted a series of gruesome human experiments, and Kaiser feared that her grandfather may have been forced to participate. Kaiser herself did not know much about the topic or the documents her grandfather had left her, but what she did know was that these documents were locked away in the vault of a Swiss bank. They had been inaccessible thus far, but the blocking period was about to end on 27 January 2015.

Kaiser had been very close to her grandfather; indeed, he was the one who had raised her after her parents died when she was very young. This made matters very difficult for her. She was genuinely afraid of what the documents could reveal, but despite this, she felt that it was necessary to fulfil his wish to let the world know what happened. However, she knew she was not suited for this task at all; aside from her closeness to her grandfather, her work as a personal doctor for popes meant that she could not draw any attention to herself. Lothfels then took over the conversation and asked me if I was interested in examining the documents and making them accessible to the public.

Kaiser had told her friend about her predicament in the summer of 2013, but it had been Lothfels' idea to contact a historian working in this field. Kaiser thought this to be a good idea and agreed, provided Lothfels would handle this issue. It was now clear why I had been invited to Lothfels' Christmas party – it had been sort of a job interview.

The offer was as surprising as it was promising. Assuming they were genuine, receiving long-hidden documents from a Jewish prisoner-doctor in Auschwitz, who had likely participated in Mengele's experiments, would certainly be a sensational turn of events. The date of 27 January 2015 was likewise notable, since it was the 70th anniversary of the liberation of Auschwitz.

I asked Lothfels to give me some time to think about it, as well as for additional biographical information regarding Kaiser's grandfather, so that I could at least draw a rudimentary picture of the story.

Before long, I received the information I had asked for: Kaiser's grandfather was Salamon Ferencz Fülöp Grósz Chorin, born on 17 July 1879 in Szentágota in Transylvania, which was Hungarian then but is now part of Romania. Professor Grósz Chorin MD was a natural scientist specializing in anatomy, neuroanatomy, brain research and dissections, and had worked in Budapest from 1920 to 1936. Due to rising anti-Semitism, he changed his name in 1936 to Ferencz Kiss (Kiss is a common Hungarian surname that derives from the word 'kis', which means 'small', whereas Grósz is the Hungarian spelling of the German word 'groß', meaning 'big'). However, this was not enough, and he eventually emigrated. He travelled around and taught at several universities in Great Britain, the US and oddly enough, even in Nazi Germany, before settling in Basel, Switzerland in 1938. There, he was safe, but in December 1941 he travelled to Budapest to visit his family, where he was betrayed, arrested and eventually deported to Auschwitz. He somehow survived the hardships of the camp and after its liberation, he returned to Switzerland and added Szentágothay to his name. From 1946 he worked at the women's hospital in Zürich, officially until 1956 and unofficially until 1968, due to his advanced age. He died on 6 April 1977 in Küssnacht near Zürich.

He had been married once, to the professor and eye doctor Rebekka Lipot who had been born on 1 August 1880 into a renowned rabbinical family from Vienna. The couple had seven sons, but the four youngest – including a pair of twins – were murdered in Auschwitz, along with his wife. The other three survived the camp. Kaiser herself was born on 13 August 1950 in Zürich. Her mother, the Hungarian countess Krisztina Batthyány, died during childbirth and her father died in a car accident soon afterwards.

Kaiser warned me that she did not know much more about her grandfather; and she knew next to nothing about her family history. After all, her grandfather had always been a very secretive man who virtually never talked about his past, only hinting at it at times. The person who had known him the best had been his longtime housekeeper Elly Ostertag, but she had passed away in 1991.

This was indeed very little information, but it is very common that oral histories like this one are fraught with missing and sometimes even incorrect information, especially when serious trauma is involved. Nevertheless, this was enough to begin my initial research. Even though the documents were to remain sealed away for another year, I suggested that Lothfels and Kaiser visit the vault to see if there was anything there in the first place. Additionally, even a single look from the outside could help us estimate how many documents we were dealing with – just a few files, a suitcase or maybe even more?

In mid-February, Lothfels sent a message to me that Kaiser had travelled to the Swiss National Bank in Zürich, where she, accompanied by a bank employee, had looked at what was inside her grandfather's deposit box No. 268. She reported that six different packages were inside, each with notes attached to them,[3] which she had translated into German as follows:

1.
Note
Auschwitz
Auschwitz BII
1943-1944
Seal of Dr Josef Mengele and
Mengele's Signature
In Hebrew:
Handed to me on 13 January 1945
Signature Illegible

2:
Written in Hebrew:
Notes
With Otmar Freiherr von Verschuer
18 December 1941 to 31 December 1942
Signature Illegible

3.
Written in Hebrew:
Typhus fever
NOMA
Measles
Scarlet fever
Dr Wirth
January 1943 to 30 September 1943
Signature illegible

4.
Written in Hebrew:
May 1944
31 December 1944
Selections
Signature illegible

5.
Written in Hebrew:
Oblenz-Levi
Bertold Eppstein
Miklös Nyiszli)?????
Weisskopf
Robert Havemann
KWI Institute
1943-1946
Signature illegible

6.
Written in Hebrew:
Geneva 1949
Brazil – Araraquara 1964
Fam. Stammer
Meeting with Wolfgang Gerhard,
who had a tooth gap
Signature illegible

I could not believe my eyes. Between June 1943 and January 1945, Mengele had been a doctor in Auschwitz, first in the so-called Gypsy Camp in Auschwitz-Birkenau, in section Auschwitz B-IIe. In November 1943, he was promoted to the position of First Camp Doctor for the entirety of Birkenau. In this role, his primary tasks were to fight against the ever-present diseases that plagued the camp, and to carry out the so-called selections of prisoners for the gas chambers. What turned him into the 'Angel of Death' in the public imagination was something else, however, namely his far-reaching medical experiments and anthropological examinations.[4] In the course of these studies, he and his accomplices maimed and killed large numbers of prisoners, including children. Even though these experiments had been meticulously documented at the time, all the notes were considered missing – until now.

As the front approached during the final year of the war, the SS gradually scaled down operations in Auschwitz beginning in autumn 1944, but it was not until 27 January 1945 that the advancing Red Army finally reached the camp and liberated the remaining prisoners. As early as October 1944, the camp administration began to systematically hide any documents detailing the crimes committed at Auschwitz by either burning them or sending them elsewhere. This also included the documents from the infirmary block.[5] There was one exception, however: Mengele. According to several witnesses, he had kept his notes safe and took them with him as he left the camp in mid-January 1945. Unfortunately, these documents have remained missing ever since. There were no laboratory notes, no diaries, protocols or other manuscripts available. The only information regarding these experiments were the testimonies of survivors, but their knowledge of the full extent of Mengele's activities was naturally limited.[6] Now, we seemed to have these missing notes within our reach.

Mengele was born in 1911 in the town of Günzburg in southern Germany. Following a wide-ranging study programme that touched on both medicine and the natural sciences at universities in Munich, Bonn, and Vienna, he received his first doctorate in 1935 for a racial-morphological study on the anterior segment of the lower jaw. The following year, he passed the medical state examinations and earned his medical licence a year later. In 1938, he received his second doctorate on the heredity of the cleft lip and palate. By the time of his transfer to Auschwitz, he was considered to be a rising star in German medical science.[7] In particular, he had made a name for himself in the field of racial anthropology with his two dissertations, as well as numerous articles and scientific reviews.[8] He had a reputation for ambition and was known as a dedicated and efficient worker, and thus quickly established himself professionally. He soon found employment as a research assistant at the Institute for Hereditary Biology and Racial Hygiene at the University of Frankfurt, one of its tasks being to prepare 'hereditary-biological racial and family analyses' for the Reich Family Office. Afterwards, he worked at the SS Sanitary Inspection Office, the SS Race and Settlement Office, and the Office of the Reich Physician of the SS and the Police, Dr Ernst Grawitz. Beginning in 1940, his work was periodically interrupted by military service in the Second World War.

In Frankfurt, Mengele worked for Professor Otmar Freiherr von Verschuer, who was the head of the Institute for Hereditary Biology and Racial Hygiene at the time. Verschuer was an authority in the field of human heredity and his research on twins had won him widespread acclaim. It had also attracted the attention of the German government, which hoped to use his research to trace the heritability of certain traits and defects for eugenic purposes. Mengele was recommended to the institute by his first doctoral supervisor, the race hygienist Professor

Theodor Mollison, and Verschuer quickly took a liking to him. Verschuer thus not only became Mengele's new doctoral supervisor but also began to delegate more and more tasks to him. Even after Mengele left the institute, he would sometimes represent Verschuer in lectures. The close relationship continued during the war as well.

Prior to his transfer to Frankfurt in 1935, Verschuer had built from the ground up and headed the Department of Human Heredity and Eugenics, established in 1927, at the newly founded Kaiser-Wilhelm-Institute (KWI) for Anthropology. In October 1942, he returned to his old post at the KWI and soon reached out to Mengele. Mengele, who had been deployed on the Eastern Front as a medical officer at the SS 'Wiking' Division, returned to Berlin in January 1943. Since he was allowed to complete the rest of his military service with the SS Infantry Reserve Battallion 'Ost' in the capital, he was able to work with Verschuer again in his free time.

Beginning in early 1943, Mengele thus became Verschuer's de-facto assistant and likely a postdoctoral candidate. Mengele's twin experiments, which he conducted immediately following his arrival to Auschwitz in June 1943, were likely done not only to revive the KWI's twin research, which had somewhat stalled due to a lack of suitable test subjects, but also to supply Verschuer and others with specimens.[9] It is likewise probable that Mengele's activities were tied to his postdoctoral research and were therefore most likely meticulously documented for that reason. After the war, surviving prisoners reported that Mengele had been completely obsessed by his scientific ambitions.[10]

However, none of these documents were ever found. In 2003, the historian of science Benoît Massin lamented that, aside from a few lines of text in the surviving documents of the KWI, three very short reports by Verschuer to the DFG [Deutsche Forschungsgemeinschaft, a German research funding foundation], and a few sentences from Verschuer's letters, everything was missing.[11] A decade later, nothing had changed.

Package 1 was labelled: 'Auschwitz 1943-1944 Seal of Dr Josef Mengele' and 'Mengele's Signature... handed to me on 13 January 1945'. Was this real? Did Grósz Chorin truly receive Mengele's lost notes and keep them hidden for over half a century? The label of Package 2 was likewise intriguing: 'With Otmar Freiherr von Verschuer 18 December 1941 to 31 December 1942'. Had Grósz Chorin worked for Verschuer as well? His granddaughter had always said that Grósz Chorin was deported directly to Auschwitz in December 1941. Perhaps this only happened later?

The writing on Package 3, meanwhile, listed a number of diseases – typhus, noma, measles, scarlet fever – that commonly occurred in Auschwitz. It also mentioned 'Wirth', presumably Dr Eduard Wirths, who had been the chief SS medical officer for the entire Auschwitz complex from September 1942 and was therefore Mengele's direct superior there. The timeframe referenced on Package 4 was when the so-called Hungarian transports occurred. In March 1944, Germany had invaded the territory of its ally Hungary, toppled its government, and initiated the deportation of its Jews to Auschwitz. Between April and October 1944 alone, around 438,000 Jews were deported to Auschwitz, where most of them were murdered. It is known that during the selections, Mengele intensively searched these new arrivals for any twins he could use for his research. Being from Hungary, Grósz Chorin was likely conscripted by Mengele to assist him here.

Package 5 named several other well-known prisoner-doctors that had been in Auschwitz or had worked for the KWI. Dr Koblenz-Levi – actual name: Lévy-Coblentz – had been at the SS Hygiene Institute in Rajsko near Auschwitz. Professor Dr Berthold Epstein[12] had been a paediatrician of international renown, while Dr Miklós Nyiszli and Dr Rudolf Weißkopf had been forced to assist with Mengele's research. The title also mentioned Robert Havemann, a scientist and communist dissident. While not sent to Auschwitz, he was nevertheless persecuted by the National Socialists for political reasons and was made the head of the KWI in July 1945 by the Soviets. It was Havemann who then alerted the Allied authorities of the role of the KWI for Anthropology, Human Heredity, and Eugenics in the crimes at Auschwitz – including those committed by Mengele – and played a key role in exposing them.[13]

The labels on Package 6, meanwhile, were very vague. Did Grósz Chorin search for Mengele after the war in Brazil, where he had been hidden by Wolfgang Gerhard and his 'Kameradenwerk' as well as the Stammer couple? And what did 'Geneva 1949' mean?

Without exaggeration, each of the packages promised to be groundbreaking. Presented with this great treasure trove of documents, as a historian, I could not say no to this project. Although I had been researching Soviet economic history after the end of the Second World War as well as the reasons for its later collapse, I was very familiar with the history of the Holocaust. After all, I had written my doctoral thesis on the extermination of the Jews in German-occupied Poland and had continued to write on this topic later on.[14] There were personal factors as well. I was born near the town of Tarnów, from where the very first transport to Auschwitz arrived, and several prisoner-doctors were from there. Furthermore, one of my schoolteachers had been an Auschwitz survivor and in one class, two female survivors told us about life – and death – in the concentration camp as well as the medical experiments. Now it looked like I would revisit this topic once again, this time as a researcher. Together with Wassert, who offered to advise me in medical matters, we agreed to meet with Lothfels for an initial, in-depth discussion.

Chapter 2

First Moves

Time has passed like the twilight that pervades it. The details are veiled by the kind cloak of oblivion, only [...] the outlines [...] remain in the memories. [...] But since I have written my memoir only for my granddaughter, only for Magda as a memento, so [... I shall] not give the dates of the events everywhere, because [...] not the dates, but the experienced facts are important!!!

Memoir, pages 7 and 15

At the beginning of March, Isabel Wassert and I again travelled to southern Germany. Lothfels had invited us to her villa to meet with the professor. In the meantime, Wassert had been telling me more about the two women with whom she had been close friends with for years. She had been in close contact with Elisabeth Lothfels for over a decade; they called each other almost daily and Wassert regularly came to visit her. At one point, she was able to meet the Vatican doctor whom Lothfels had been talking about for a long time. The doctor was incredibly dedicated, Wassert explained, and together with Lothfels, they had engaged in several impressive charity projects. Among others, Lothfels and the doctor ran an orphanage in Romania, and were in the process of building a hospital in rural Kenya. In Kenya, Kaiser worked together with Father Florian, who was none other than Prince Franz-Josef of Bavaria, who had left behind his noble family to do missionary work in Africa three decades earlier. While Kaiser coordinated these projects on the ground, Lothfels financed them generously. I was also told that the Vatican doctor had given much comfort to Lothfels in a time of great personal crisis; overall, Kaiser was a tremendously empathetic and selfless human being.

Professor Kaiser was also quick to help with medical issues. Thanks to her vast connections within Germany and abroad, she was able to help many people to get in touch with the right doctor. Beyond that, she also taught at the University of Zürich, and had helped with the WHO – all in addition to her usual duties as a doctor in the Vatican. Her extremely busy schedule had both Wassert and Lothfels worried about her health for a long time and suspected she was suffering from some kind of helper syndrome. Yet, despite it all, Professor Kaiser seemed content, happy even. She also lived a relatively ascetic life; according to Wassert, Kaiser had even donated her late husband's fortune to charity.

In light of Kaiser's selflessness, it seemed that Lothfels was more than happy to be able to finally repay Kaiser for all the good she had been doing.

So, over the course of three days, we sat down with Kaiser and Lothfels and discussed the matter of her late grandfather; for more personal and delicate questions, Isabel Wassert took Professor Kaiser aside and interviewed her in private. In these three days, we learned a lot about Kaiser's grandfather, but also her own life story and the relationship between her and her grandfather. It turned out that Kaiser was in fact the last scion of the Batthyány dynasty, an influential noble family from Hungary, attested since at least the fourteenth century, which, over the years, had produced numerous counts, barons, and magnates. Her aunt on her mother's side had been unable to have children, while her brother had been a high-ranking figure in the Franciscan Order and therefore lived a life of celibacy. The Hungarian branch of the family – unlike the Austrian one – would thus end with Kaiser herself. Still, she was proud to be part of such an illustrious lineage and revealed to us her full name: Professor Dr Magdalena Nicoletta Krisztina Kaiser-Batthyány/Szentágothay MD. In 2013, she and Lothfels had travelled to Hungary to seek out what remained of the once-great Batthyány family. In contrast, the Szentágothay addition was much less ancient – she had only begun to use it a few years prior, in memory of her grandfather.

While her mother's side of the family had a very illustrious history, her father's side was somewhat shrouded in mystery. She knew that it had a long tradition of producing doctors such as her grandfather and herself. Personally, she had also been married to a doctor – a professor of neurology – until his death in 1991.

According to her, both of her parents tragically died the day she was born. Her mother, a dermatologist, died while giving birth, perhaps due to the haemophilia prevalent in her side of the family. Her grandfather was unable to save her but had been able to save her daughter, Magdalena. Meanwhile, her father, a neurologist, died in a car accident, presumably on the way to the hospital.

Her two surviving paternal uncles had emigrated after the war, one to Israel and the other to Toronto, and broke off contact with their father. Magdalena suspected that this was due to her grandfather's work as a prisoner-doctor in Auschwitz.

Magdalena was not even entirely sure about her grandfather's actual name. Even before the Second World War, her grandfather had changed his name to evade the rising anti-Semitism, and she strongly suspected that he had changed it again after the end of the war, this time out of shame.

She herself had been born in Zürich and was raised there by her grandfather, who began to study Catholic theology in order to honour his deceased daughter-in-law's wish to raise Magdalena as a Catholic. His Jewish faith therefore did not play a role in her upbringing, although she had to learn Hebrew. She also noted that she had never seen a tattoo on him; however, he had a scar on his lower arm – perhaps from her mother surgically removing the tattoo with the registration number from Auschwitz. Magdalena added that his feet were completely scarred and that he never laughed.

Magdalena also knew little about his relationship with Mengele. However, she knew that Mengele had enabled her grandfather's flight from Auschwitz. Apparently, Mengele had faked falling ill from an infectious disease in the autumn of 1944. He therefore had to leave Auschwitz and enter quarantine in a German hospital in nearby Kraków. He took Magdalena's grandfather there with him – as well as some of his notes – who then left at the first opportunity and found refuge with a Polish Catholic priest. While staying with the priest, he was given forged documents and joined a pilgrimage to Lourdes in southwest France before fleeing to Switzerland mid-way through the journey.

In the 1950s, while studying Catholic theology, her grandfather eventually met a certain Joseph Ratzinger – later Pope Benedict XVI. Magdalena believed that her grandfather was treating Ratzinger's ill sister at the time, and both men became such close friends that her grandfather asked Ratzinger to take care of Magdalena after his death. Truly a touching story of Jewish-Catholic friendship in the face of the Holocaust.

This made such an impression on Joseph Ratzinger that when he moved to the Vatican in 1982, he reached out to Magdalena – now a highly-qualified virologist – and she began to work for the Vatican in 1983. Eventually, she became Pope John Paul II's personal doctor, and after his death, she became the personal doctor of his successor, Pope Benedict XVI. She remained at the Vatican to this day and together with his private secretary, Georg Gänswein, took care of the now retired Pope, as well as the new Pope Francis I. Lothfels and Wassert said that over the years, Magdalena and Pope Benedict XVI developed a very close friendship; indeed, Gänswein and the pope had become somewhat of a 'surrogate family' for her.

Lothfels in particular had gained deep insights into this relationship and was herself – through Magdalena – in close contact with both the current and the retired pope. As a result, Lothfels and Wassert were very understanding when Magdalena informed them that Ratzinger knew about these documents and that he had to be consulted before every major decision. Even before she had opened the safe with the said documents, she had first gone to the Vatican to obtain his consent.

This was all we knew. Still, despite the very fragmented nature of her story, it was clear to me that we had enough information to begin investigating Grósz Chorin's story. His granddaughter wanted to help us and promised to give us important documents, such as her grandfather's death certificate and her own birth certificate. We also agreed to travel to Auschwitz with her and Lothfels.

Wassert and I thus got to work. One thing that struck me had been that the countess always claimed to know very little about the

Jewish branch of her family, particularly that of her grandfather, but in private conversations it became clear that she knew much more. I later learned that she had told Wassert her grandfather had worked together with Albert Schweitzer in Lambaréné; she also revealed more details about the flight of her grandfather to Wassert personally, as well as important medical details regarding her birth and the question of her grandfather's tattoo from Auschwitz.

It was clear that the countess trusted Wassert more than me, which was understandable considering they had known each other for years and were friends. Wassert and I therefore decided to let her conduct future interviews with the countess, while I would focus on the historical questions: the Auschwitz concentration camp, the SS doctors, the medical experiments and, above all, the other prisoner-doctors.

I soon realized that very little had been published about the prisoner-doctors, proper historical works on this issue are even more scant. Overall, the situation is very complicated: contemporary sources are very rare; instead, there was a host of post-war testimonies, reports and even pamphlets and books written by former prisoner-doctors. However, they have to be read with special caution, since following the war, prisoner-doctors and nurses were often blamed for the atrocities committed and were therefore frequently investigated and even tried in court. Most of these documents rest in Polish archives, in particular in the Archive of the Institute of National Remembrance (IPN) and are usually in Polish; some are in German, but the labelling suggests they are in Polish. As a result, they are barely read or even cited by Western scholars. The exception is the two-volume compendium *Auschwitz-Hefte*, which contains a German-language selection of texts published in Poland between 1961 and 1991, which includes several accounts written by former prisoner-doctors.[1]

A work dedicated to the issue of prisoner-doctors was absent in both West and East. While this made this project much harder, it also made it interesting from a historical perspective since I had to conduct original research. I soon decided to embark on a complimentary project: in addition to analyzing the estate of Grósz Chorin, I would also write a book about the prisoner-doctors of Auschwitz. That way, even if the documents we received did not yield anything, the research conducted was worth the effort in and of itself.

On 28 March 2014 we met again, this time in Kraków. While planning the trip to nearby Auschwitz the next day, the countess told us that she had already been to Auschwitz twice, together with her grandfather. Unfortunately, she did not mention what her grandfather had told her on these occasions and what the exact purpose of these visits was.

What she did mention, however, was that she had contacted the Auschwitz Memorial prior to our visit and had asked the archivists working there if they had any documents mentioning a prisoner-doctor by the name of Salamon Grósz Chorin. Lothfels, meanwhile, had suggested hiring a Polish cameraman to film our visit, to which the countess agreed.

As we arrived at Auschwitz, we were greeted by the cameraman as well as an archivist who expertly and in great detail informed us about the archival materials they had. Unfortunately, prior to the evacuation of the camp on 18 January 1945, the SS destroyed the vast majority of traces of the genocide, including virtually all the camp documents. The archivist told us he was unable to find any documents mentioning Salamon Grósz Chorin, but assured us that this did not mean much, as most prisoner records did not survive the war.

Undeterred by this not unexpected setback, we went on to visit the former main camp (Auschwitz I) and Auschwitz-Birkenau (Auschwitz II). In front of the ruins of crematoria II and III in Auschwitz-Birkenau, the countess surprised us with a several-pages-long letter by none other than retired Pope Benedict XVI. The letter looked very official and had both the seal and coat of arms of the Vatican; apparently, it had been typed out by the pope's private secretary, Gänswein. She then began to read out the letter, clearly moved, but still composed. However, when the retired pope began to directly talk about his personal relationship with her and her grandfather, she was overcome with emotion and asked her friend Lothfels, who had also been mentioned in the letter, to read out the rest.

I personally found this course of events rather strange. I was particularly surprised that the pope went on to talk about Zionism – twice – which seemed odd in this context. But the moment passed and the countess was very understandably touched by the situation; it was clearly important to her – and she was noticeably glad that it was being filmed. Previously, she had repeatedly mentioned her fears that our research would unearth horrible things about her grandfather and was anxious. Nevertheless, she handled this emotional situation with great dignity.

When we returned to Kraków, she relaxed as we walked through the city. It became evident that she knew her way around and she revealed that she had frequently visited Kraków together with none other than the late Pope John Paul II. She would go on to tell us many stories form their visits to the city.

In Kraków, we also agreed that Wassert would help me with the medical aspect of the research. Indeed, both Lothfels and the countess wished for this to happen, as did Wassert. After all, she was a medical doctor while I was merely a historian - the medical documents lying in Zürich would be incomprehensible to me. Beyond that, Wassert also wanted to research the countess' family history as well.

Before Wassert and I could begin our research in earnest, it was clear to me that we needed to secure the usage rights to the documents in the safe. Originally, the countess had transferred them to Lothfels, and now Lothfels transferred them to us on 6 April:

> Subject: Six packages with documents and written estate by a private person. Swiss National Bank Zürich Safe No. 268. To be opened first on 27 January 2015. Mrs Elisabeth Lothfels [...] was given, by the owner, the rights of disposal over the aforementioned documents/items. Mrs Elisabeth Lothfels stipulates that the power of disposal over these aforementioned documents/items and their contents are exclusively transferred to the following persons at the aforementioned date: Dr Bogdan Musial [...] Dr Isabel Wassert [...]. The evaluation and usage,

the textual work, public presentation and publication of the aforementioned documents/items lies fully, independently, and exclusively with the aforementioned persons. All named parties commit themselves to this agreement.

Munich, 6 April 2014.

This private agreement was notarized in Munich a short time later.

Since we did not have any medical documents at the time, Wassert began her research into the countess' family history as previously agreed. Together with the countess, Wassert thus travelled to Hungary and Switzerland to find out more about her family.

In the meantime, I began to investigate the histories and post-war biographies of the prisoner-doctors at Auschwitz. My first port of call was the archives of the Auschwitz Museum, followed by the Archive of the Institute of National Remembrance in Kraków and Warsaw, where, among others, the court documents for the trial of the camp commander, Rudolf Höss, are held.[2] Indeed, since most of the Auschwitz trials were held in Poland, the Polish archives contained a great deal of information on this topic, including on related issues such as the overall medical care in the camp, the activities of the SS doctors, and the differences in treatment between Jewish and non-Jewish prisoner-doctors.

The research in Switzerland, into the life of Grósz Chorin, was much more difficult. According to his granddaughter, he had worked at Zürich's women's hospital, which had been absorbed into the local university in 1956. However, the personal files for the women's hospital were neither at the university nor the state archive. When I called the personnel department at the women's hospital, I was promptly informed that personal files were only archived in special cases and generally destroyed after fifty years. This put a quick and disappointing end to all my research in Switzerland for the time being. Given that I also did not know the name under which he had published his works, I did not continue in this direction either – it would have been a waste of time.

Chapter 3

The Battle Over the Rights

January 1945: Mengele comes into my room with two suitcases. He hands me one and says: - Take good care of it my friend/ - get dressed, we need to leave/- he waits for us at the labour camp of the concentration camp – in his Opel car. He really came back to save me. 10 January – the Russian offensive has begun – I get dressed/should I go with him? Or should I stay? I went.

Auschwitz Notes

Instead of us finding our first leads, the summer of 2014 saw the emergence of a different issue that would preoccupy us for the months to come. In one of our discussions with Lothfels, she had raised the question of whether the documents we were awaiting could even legally leave Switzerland. After all, they were likely going to be very important and explosive documents. To clarify the situation, she suggested asking a friend of hers who was a lawyer specializing in such matters.

The lawyer she suggested was famous across Germany and had made a name for himself in several high-profile criminal trials; beyond that he also had very good ties to the German political and media elite. Having him on our side surely would be a great boon for our project. While I personally did not share Lothfels' concern regarding crossing the border with the documents, I did not think contacting this lawyer was a bad idea since we would likely need legal aid later anyway. Besides, he and his law firm had plenty of experience in dealing with archival documents.

On 25 June, Lothfels and I thus came to the seat of the law firm in western Germany and met with the lawyer in person. We told him of the estate of Grósz Chorin, its presumed contents, and that it would be released in January. During our discussions, it came out that he was also an acquaintance of the countess and knew of her work as a doctor in the Vatican and her close ties to Pope Benedict XVI – she clearly was very well connected.

Unfortunately, it soon became clear that his and my assessments regarding the usage rights went in opposite directions. In my view, the rights lay with Wassert and me ever since we signed the notarized agreement on 15 April 2014. In his view, it was necessary to first examine who had the rights to the estate; in case it contained documents from Auschwitz or even notes written by Mengele himself, Mengele's son or another family member could possibly assert his or her rights to the documents. I disagreed, pointing out that according to international law, official documents, research notes and so on belonged to their place of origin and the rights would thus be held by the Auschwitz Museum. The family could only claim purely personal records, but as long as we did not know the contents of these documents, any such considerations were superfluous anyway.

The discussion continued for a while and we also wound up talking about other issues, such as potential publishers and the other topics I had been researching. When I mentioned that I had originally wanted to write a book about the fall of the Soviet Union, he showed great interest and mentioned that he would be able to not only help me find a good publisher but would also be willing to use his extensive political ties to arrange interviews with high-ranking political figures who had first-hand experience with these events.

This all sounded very promising, but I still left the law firm with a bad feeling. The lawyer remained convinced that any legal claims had to be settled prior to the opening of the safe, and even suggested one of his partners in his law firm to us who could take over the case. In my opinion, he was simply trying to unsettle us. Either way, the word was out and news of the existence of Mengele's documents began to spread.

Over the coming weeks and months, I did not hear anything from the law firm, neither about the matter of Grósz Chorin nor any other projects. This was a good thing and allowed me to focus on completing archival research, mostly in Poland. I also continued to work through the historical literature on the topic and regularly met with both Lothfels and the countess. Particularly striking was an event in Budapest to which I had been invited by both ladies. The university was celebrating a project to sponsor students from Bhutan. This project had been initiated by the countess and Lothfels was using her own funds to finance it.

The Kingdom of Bhutan is located in the Himalayas between India and China and has around 750,000 inhabitants. At the time, its rulers were very interested in expanding its university system as the kingdom was in dire need of qualified personnel for the country's administration, tourism industry as well as its forestry and agricultural sectors. Countess Batthyány, meanwhile, had excellent ties to Budapest's renowned Szent István University, which, among other things, focused on teaching agriculture, environmental engineering, social studies, nutritional sciences and urban development. Lothfels, meanwhile, was good friends with the Bhutanese royal family, who are seen as the highest patrons of Bhutanese culture and education.

Together, Lothfels and the countess thus decided to establish a scholarship programme. Both the university and the royal family were very open to the idea, and the project proceeded smoothly. In January 2014, Lothfels and the countess visited the university president Dr Jánosz Tözsér and inspected the university's facilities and its English-language programmes, which would be open to between five and ten Bhutanese students without restrictions.

With these issues sorted out, Bhutan's Queen Mother Ashi Sangay Choden Wangchuck was to visit the university and ceremoniously sign a memorandum of understanding. We were invited for this reason.

It was a glamorous event. The Queen Mother had arrived together with a delegation that included a number of dignitaries, including His Excellency, Ambassador of Bhutan to the European Union Sonam Tshong, his wife, as well as President of the Hungarian-Bhutanese Society of Friends, Zoltán Valcsicsák. From the Hungarian side came the managing director of the nearby Gödöllö Castle, the director of Gödöllö's municipal library, a number of school principals, as well as several university dignitaries, namely the university rector, the vice-rector for research, the vice-rector for educational affairs, and the deans of three different departments, one of whom was responsible for managing the university's relations abroad.

In the course of the ceremony, the organizers lauded Her Majesty's contributions to charity, as well as Elisabeth Lothfels', who after all had financed the programme. Countess Batthyány-Szentágothay was likewise honoured since she had initiated the project, which also included several joint research projects. Once the memorandum had been ceremoniously signed, students from the Frederic Chopin Music School gave a concert. The Queen Mother then signed the university's guestbook, while a festive reception marked the end of the event.

The countess, both deeply touched and greatly satisfied, later took us to the mausoleum of the great Hungarian independence leader of the nineteenth century, Count Lajos Batthyány (1807-1849). After all, he was her ancestor and – as we had just experienced at the ceremony – was still revered in Hungary to this day.

Back in Germany, the date for the handover of the documents drew ever closer. In early December 2014, Wassert and I agreed to go to Lothfels' annual Christmas party together. Like every year, the countess was expected to be there as well and we could use this opportunity to discuss some of the questions that were still open. Unfortunately, however, while we did meet her, our conversation was brief and we could not settle anything.

Instead, I received a frantic call from Isabel Wassert just a few days later. Apparently, the German law firm had called and notified her that they had been given the rights for use of the documents we had been waiting for. She had objected, but Lothfels insisted that the rights of use had already been transferred to the law firm during our initial meeting six months earlier.

We were shocked. We had invested all this time and effort into this project, and now we had been outmanoeuvred just weeks ahead of the handover date. It soon became clear that following our meeting, the law firm had quickly moved to establish contact with the countess behind our backs.[1]

Kaiser, meanwhile, told us that the lawyers had pressured her so much that she felt she could do nothing but give them the rights to receive the documents in Zürich on 27 January 2015 and transport them to their seat in Essen. This had occurred on 5 July 2014, nearly half a year prior.[2]

The result was a very chaotic situation since we still held the rights of use. At any rate, neither Wassert nor I thought it was a good idea to start a legal fight with a powerful law firm over a collection of documents – whose contents were still completely unclear – was a good idea at all. To defuse the situation, I proposed a compromise: On 27 January, we would view the documents together in Zürich and then decide on the course of action. The lawyers, however, did not want to negotiate. In an email to Kaiser, they stated:

> As Your lawyers, we exclusively represent Your interests. We can only do this if we can view these documents first after You or together with You, before copies are made, and can advise You on the further course of action afterwards. It would not be expedient if an inspection already occurred together with Prof Dr Bogdan Musial and his colleague Dr Isabel Wassert, and if there were then a discussion on site in Zürich as to who would take or copy which documents. We can therefore not agree to such a course of action. We therefore ask You for a quick response and confirmation that You agree with us regarding the course of action laid out above.[3]

This was not the end of the story. Calls and negotiations continued and, two days later, the star lawyer personally contacted his friend, Lothfels, to convince her that the documents belonged in his care. She gave in and the next day, the co-founder of the law firm confirmed the agreement between the lawyer in an email to Kaiser:

> The documents in question, which are encased in steel mesh, will be received by us unopened in Zürich, transported to Essen and then opened by a smith/locksmith. After the opening, we will notify You to inspect the documents together with You and Prof

> Musial; then copies will be made for You, Prof Musial and us. The originals will be kept by us for the client.[4]

We protested again, pointing at the already existing agreement on the usage rights and our extensive preparatory research. This was the first time I had heard about the steel mesh but I pointed out that I was a trained mechanical engineer and was therefore more than able to remove the steel mesh on my own.

Just as our hopes appeared to have been dashed, 'the South' – i.e. the retired Pope Benedict XVI – intervened on our behalf. The Vatican, Kaiser informed us, wanted the documents to be inspected by a historian. The lawyers retreated. In an email to Lothfels, a lawyer confirmed: 'Your message sent today on behalf of Prof Kaiser-Batthyány/Szentágothay, that a lawyer [from that law firm; BM] and I shall not be present on 27 January in Zürich, but that You will contact us in the new year and after 27 January.'[5]

Crisis averted.

Chapter 4

The Research Continues: Experiments on Prisoners

My former good friend from Frankfurt University and the anthropology institute, Verschuer, destroyed all his correspondence with Mengele after the war and said that this was only scientific material. He will visit me here in Zürich before Christmas.

Memoirs, page 87

As mentioned earlier, we had spent the previous year doing wide-ranging research while we awaited the documents. Aside from investigating traces of Grósz Chorin and other prisoner-doctors, we also focused on the human experiments Mengele and other SS physicians had conducted in Auschwitz.

In the expansive German concentration camp system, the National Socialists sought to detain millions of real and imagined enemies, with the purpose of exploiting and exterminating them. Political enemies, 'asocials', 'habitual' criminals, homosexuals, but also persecuted people from other conquered nations, such as Poles, Sinti, Roma and, above all, the Jews, were thus subject to this inhumane system of forced labour and death.

As the concentration camp system began to expand rapidly, the SS doctors soon sensed the opportunity to tap into this pool of easily accessible and disposable 'human material' for all kinds of experiments. In the women's concentration camp of Ravensbrück, SS doctors, under the leadership of the surgeon Karl Gebhardt, launched a series of experiments on imprisoned Polish women to investigate possible improvements to healing wounds of injured soldiers via bone transplants and improved sulphonamides. At Buchenwald, typhoid fever vaccines were tested, while in Dachau, physicians such as Dr Sigmund Rascher exposed prisoners to low pressure and cold tests for the purposes of aviation medicine.[1]

Auschwitz soon became a major hub in medical experimentation as well, even though it had only been established in May 1940 for the purpose of detaining and murdering members of the Polish resistance, but also the clergy, military and civilian elites. The Polish resistance estimated that up to the end of 1941, around 25,000 people, most of them Poles but also around 2,000 Jews, had been sent to Auschwitz.[2] However, virtually none of the Jewish inmates survived this period, and even among the Poles, less than half survived. However, this was only the beginning and starting in summer 1941, the camp was continuously expanded both in size and function, and a sprawling complex of sub-camps was set up.

Prior to that, the camp commander, Rudolf Höss, had declared the surrounding area, around 40 square kilometres, to be a restricted area of interest – the '*Sperrgebiet Auschwitz*'. On 12 July 1940, Höss complained to Richard Glücks, the inspector of the concentration camps, that the local population was 'fanatically Polish and ready to take any action against the hated SS men. Every prisoner able to make an escape can expect immediate help as soon as he reaches the first Polish homestead.'[3] As a result, all Poles and Jews were expelled from the '*Sperrgebiet Auschwitz*' and replaced with German colonists as well as the families of the SS camp personnel. At the same time, several sub-camps were also established in the area.

In Monowice, just 6 kilometres east of the main camp, the chemical industrial giant I.G. Farben[4] built the Buna factory complex – together with an attached forced labour camp – for the purpose of producing synthetic fuel for the war effort. By late July 1944, the Auschwitz-Monowitz sub-camp housed around 11,350 slave labourers, most of them Jews.[5]

Three kilometres northwest of the base camp, in the former village of Brzezinka, arguably the most infamous of the sub-camps was built: Auschwitz-Birkenau. Initially, the plan had been to detain Soviet prisoners of war there, but as the persecution of Jews quickly turned into a full-scale genocide during the invasion of the Soviet Union, Auschwitz-Birkenau was repurposed to play a major role in the Final Solution and consequently became the largest of the German death camps. Around 1.1 million Jews, first from occupied Poland, and later from all of Europe, were murdered there, alongside around 123,000 non-Jews, over half of them Poles.[6] Most of the victims were gassed to death, and Birkenau had four separate gas chambers and attached crematoria – the main camp only had one. Those not sent to the gas chambers were confronted with starvation, a host of diseases, ruthless exploitation, mistreatment, total exhaustion, and sometimes medical experiments. After all, the steady stream of 'disposable' newcomers meant that the SS doctors had more than enough human material for their various experiments.

Between June 1940 and January 1945, at least thirty-six SS physicians are known by name to have served in Auschwitz as camp physicians,[7] and a number of them used the defenceless prisoners for their own needs. As early as 1941, young and inexperienced SS physicians who were 'eager to learn' made their way to Auschwitz. Particularly ambitious were the SS camp physicians Friedrich Entress and Horst Fischer, who – assisted by more experienced prisoner-doctors – practised difficult surgical operations on prisoners.[8]

Entress mostly practised surgeries of the stomach, while Fischer scanned the incoming transports for prisoners with hernias and herniated discs, who he would then use to try out the eighteen various surgical methods described in German medical textbooks.[9]

The professor of anatomy Professor Dr Johann Paul Kremer, from the University of Münster, was sent to substitute for another Auschwitz doctor between late August and mid-November 1942. There, he researched the effects of starvation on humans and 'reserved' for himself a number of prisoners in the final stage of starvation. After thoroughly interviewing the unlucky test subjects regarding their medical history and current symptoms, he ordered their immediate murder via an injection to the heart. They were then dissected and had their liver, spleen and pancreas removed, carefully preserved and then sent to Münster.[10] Dr Hellmuth Vetter, a researcher at Bayer

Leverkusen, worked in Auschwitz between October 1942 and March 1943, where he used the prisoners for deadly experiments with typhoid fever on behalf of I.G. Farben. Following his transfer to the Gusen concentration camp, SS camp physician Entress continued these experiments.[11]

Particularly infamous were Professor Carl Clauberg and Dr Horst Schumann, whose sterilization experiments had attracted the attention of Viktor Brack from the Reich Chancellery and even Reichsführer-SS Himmler. On 23 June 1942, as Operation Reinhardt – the extermination of the Polish Jews in the death camps of Bełżec, Sobibor and Treblinka – was already in full swing, Brack wrote to Himmler:

> Among the around 10 million European Jews, I feel that there are at least 2-3 million men and women who are very able to work. Considering the great difficulties we are facing with the labour question, I believe that these 2-3 million are to be extracted and preserved. However, this will only work if they are made unable to reproduce at the same time.

Since surgical 'sterilization, as is commonly done with the hereditarily ill, […] is too time-intensive and costly', Brack suggested to sterilize them via x-rays.[12]

On 11 August 1942, Himmler wrote back and attested his 'absolute interest to test the sterilization via x-rays in at least one camp in a trial'.[13] Brack then turned to Dr Horst Schumann. Born on 1 May 1906 in Halle an der Saale, Dr Schumann had already participated in 'Aktion T4' – euthanasia – and 'Aktion 14f13', the selection and murder of concentration camp inmates deemed either unable to work or incurably sick. For the latter, he had spent some time in Auschwitz in July 1942, participating in the selection of 575 prisoners who were then sent to the killing facilities at Sonnenstein Castle, where they were promptly gassed.[14]

A few months later, in late November 1942, Schumann then began the medical trials in Block 30 in Auschwitz-Birkenau's women's camp B-Ia.[15] Siemens had built two custom-made 'x-ray bombs' and trained Dr Schumann how to operate them. Once everything had been set up, Dr Schumann searched the camp for suitable young women, bombarded their ovaries with x-rays and then observed them. At the end of December, however, Dr Schumann had to interrupt his experiments – he had contracted typhoid fever and was out of action for several weeks.[16]

At the same time, Dr Clauberg arrived in the camp to conduct his own experiments in the same Block 30. Dr Clauberg was eight years older than his colleague and was a seasoned gynaecologist and the head physician at the women's hospital in Königshütte (today Chorzów) in Upper Silesia. An honorary SS-Gruppenführer, he had been researching sterilization methods since the 1930s. Already in 1940, Himmler had contacted Dr Clauberg and asked him in a personal conversation to come up with ideas of how to sterilize 'unwanted' population groups without surgery. At the time, Himmler was mostly thinking about Jewish and Polish women.[17] Dr Clauberg took on the matter and began his research with great zeal, and after a successful trial involving rabbits, he contacted Himmler in May 1941 and suggested trying out his method on concentration camp inmates.[18] A year later, he further detailed his proposal and asked 'to have the necessary experiments and facilities in the concentration camp in Auschwitz'.[19]

In December, he was then transferred to the same block in Auschwitz as Dr Schumann, on Himmler's personal orders.[20] He soon began his experiments, which focused on sterilizing women by treating them with injections that would seal their fallopian tubes shut.

In early April 1943, Clauberg moved his experiments from Auschwitz-Birkenau to Block 10 of the main camp. He was provided with two large infirmaries, one x-ray room, an operating room, a room for prisoner-nurses and one for female SS guards. Above, on the second floor, there were accommodations for up to 500 women who would be the human material Clauberg tested on. Within the camp, Block 10 was totally isolated, and it was strictly forbidden to enter without authorization.

Of the female prisoners in Block 10, around half were experimented on by Clauberg. By the end of 1943, 175 women had been affected. Clauberg often administered the injections himself, but also frequently delegated that task to August Büning, an SS paramedic he had personally trained, and later, Dr Johannes Goebel, a chemist. Even if done by professionals, these injections were extremely painful and triggered devastating side-effects such as peritonitis and fevers, vomiting and abdominal pain. At the very least, however, there were no deaths.[21]

Dr Horst Schumann also 'owned' a group of prisoners in Block 10, around thirty Jewish women from Greece, whom he had previously bombarded with x-rays in Auschwitz-Birkenau. In Block 10, fifteen of them had their ovaries surgically removed and sent as 'histological material' to Breslau (Wrocław) for further examination.[22]

Schumann also extended his experiments to men. Between May and November 1943, 159 male prisoners had their testicles removed. Many had been bombarded by x-rays before as well, but it is unclear how often this was the case; at least in some instances, amputations likely occurred following severe injuries at the hands of brutal kapos – prisoners given a supervisory role – or as punishment for homosexual acts. In most cases, the x-ray bombardments led to severe burns and purulent inflammations in both men and women, which were extremely painful and sometimes ended in death. Most of Schumann's victims, however, died from diseases that were common inside the camp, such as typhoid fever.

Schumann ceased his experiments in late 1943. On 29 April 1944, Hitler's Chancellery sent Schumann's final report regarding the effect of x-ray irradiation on human gonads to Himmler. In it, Schumann concluded that 'the castration of a male in this fashion is quite impossible or requires an amount of effort that is not worth it. Surgical castration, which, as I have seen myself, only takes 6-7 minutes, is more reliable and faster to carry out than castration via x-rays.'[23] The x-ray bombardment was likewise physically devastating for the women and rendered them virtually unable to work – and maintaining their ability to work had been the rationale behind these sterilizations in the first place.[24]

In contrast, Clauberg's experiments were more successful and he continued and even expanded upon his research until January 1945, when the camp was evacuated. In February 1943, he was also given his own x-ray machine to check if the fallopian tubes were indeed sealed.

While Schumann and Clauberg were researching how to sterilize 'unwanted' groups, such as Jews, in a cheap and efficient manner, the Wirths brothers used the research station in Block 10 to find new ways for the early detection of cervical cancer.

Dr Eduard Wirths had become the chief SS medic at Auschwitz on 1 September 1942 and was thus in charge of the camp's entire medical personnel. He was born in 1909 in Geroldshausen near Würzburg in southern Germany. After studying medicine and earning his doctorate, Wirths worked at the women's hospital in Jena before becoming a country doctor in 1938. An NSDAP member since May 1933, he had joined the SS in October 1934; in May 1940 he was an SS physician in the Waffen-SS and worked, among other places, in the sanitary inspectorate. In early 1942, he was written off as unfit for wartime service due to health reasons and was transferred to the Dachau concentration camp. In July 1942, he became First Camp Physician in the Neuengamme concentration camp before being transferred to Auschwitz soon after.

His brother, Helmuth Wirths – also a doctor – was five years younger and had been working at the general hospital in Altona, Hamburg, since 1938. There, he worked under the head of the department of obstetrics and gynaecology, Professor Hans Hinselmann. Over a decade prior, in 1924, Hinselmann had developed the colposcope, a camera that could be inserted into the vagina in order to screen the patient for uterine cancer, and under Hinselmann's guidance, Helmuth Wirths began to research this disease.

Soon after Eduard Wirths arrived in Auschwitz, he and his brother came up with the idea to use the facilities of Block 10 for their own purposes. In April 1943, the preparations were finished and so Helmuth Wirths travelled to Auschwitz for two weeks to initiate the experiments. According to the commandant of Auschwitz, Rudolf Höss, Himmler himself had authorized these experiments.[25]

Apparently, the main purpose of the experiments was to collect histological samples of tissue suspected to be cancerous, which would then be sent to nearby Rajsko, where the new SS Institute of Hygiene had just been opened in May 1943. After being histologically examined there, the samples would then be sent to Altona where Professor Hinselmann would examine them under his microscope.[26]

Compared to the experiments of Schumann and Clauberg, the experiments by the Wirths brothers were relatively 'harmless' and usually did not lead to lasting physical damage. Beginning in September 1943, they primarily focused on examinations with the colposcope[27] and it appears as if their activities completely ceased in early 1944.

In general, the human experiments in the concentration camps were intimately tied to the interests of those who had commissioned them. Himmler and the Führer's Chancellery sought ways to combine the exploitation of human labour with the extermination of unwanted groups. The Wehrmacht, meanwhile, sought to find new, better ways of healing wounds and combating epidemics, as well as testing the resilience of the human body. Pharmaceutical corporations were eager to use the unrestricted supply of human test subjects to research new medications, especially against typhoid fever and malaria. Finally, many of the SS physicians themselves used the opportunities Auschwitz provided to improve their skills and further their careers by practising surgeries, gathering specimens for medical collections or conducting their own research projects.

In the winter and spring of 1943, a number of changes occurred in Auschwitz that suddenly made the camp much more interesting for the Kaiser Wilhelm Institute of Anthropology, Human Heredity and Eugenics in Berlin-Dahlem (KWI). Founded in 1927, the Institute set its sights on three interconnected fields in the 1930s and 1940s, namely: 'racial biology', 'hereditary pathology' and 'phenogenetics'. Racial biology focused on the supposed biological differences between the human races and the resulting physiological and psychological manifestations. The hereditary pathologists examined various illnesses and deformities and sought to determine which were hereditary. Phenogenetics was, as Dr Eugen Fischer, its main proponent at the KWI, put it, 'the development "between the genome created by the fertilization of the egg and the complete phenom"'.[28]

In the 1940s, Fischer had established phenogenetics as the guiding paradigm at the KWI. The concept of phenogenetics was vague enough so that many different, previously unconnected and interdisciplinary research projects could be brought under the umbrella of the KWI.[29] In the mind of Fischer, the basis for this great phenogenetic project was to be an expansive collection. In 1940 he described his goal in this way:

> The phenogenetic research, in particular that on humans, requires […] a wealth of embryological material. […] Through the systematic collection of human and animal embryos from diseased lineages and from different races, a central collection shall be created, the research material of which will then be made available early on to external researchers.[30]

For the KWI, twin studies were the gold standard for research on the heritability of racial characteristics and heritable diseases. They could be used to determine if a particular disease was indeed heritable, and through subsequent family research, the exact hereditary mechanism could be deduced. Over 200 doctoral theses on twin research were written in National Socialist Germany.[31]

In October 1942, Eugen Fischer was replaced by Professor Otmar von Verschuer. Verschuer – an internationally renowned twin researcher – had been the head of the Institute from 1927 to 1935, when he moved to the University of Frankfurt to lead its Institute of Hereditary Biology and Racial Hygiene, which he turned into the foremost centre for twin research in Germany and indeed all of Europe. Upon his return to the KWI in 1942, he quickly reached out to hospitals, midwives, obstetricians, welfare offices, schools and other local authorities in the Berlin area to compile a database of around 4,000 twins. These twins were invited to be interviewed, medically examined, and – if they gave consent – x-rayed. While this yielded a host of good data, it also had its limits. Children under the age of 18 were barred from undergoing any more intensive tests involving injections and the like, for purposes that were not directly medical.

While this was allowed in adults, most were unwilling to consent to such experiments.[32]

Furthermore, it was completely out of question to intentionally infect twins who possessed German citizenship, which made studying the immunological and physiological reaction to diseases virtually impossible. However, this in particular was of great interest to hereditary pathologists such as Verschuer.

For this, the researchers also needed comparative histologic or anatomic studies, which in return required either highly invasive surgeries or dissections. In the case of dissecting twins, they also needed to have been infected and died at roughly the same time, so that the researchers could examine both similar and divergent reactions to the pathogens in simultaneous dissections. Under normal circumstances, this was only possible in stillbirths or prematurely born twins, but for older children or even adults, the likelihood of both twins dying at the same time was exceedingly low.

As a result, the twin researchers at the KWI were desperate to find new sources of 'material' to satisfy their needs, and the focus on phenogenetics only increased the demand for such human material. While he was still the head of the Institute, Eugen Fischer dreamed of building up a 'Hereditary Biological Central Collection' that included:

I. Twins:
- (1) Prematurely born babies and newborns, identical and fraternal
- (2) Organs of children and adults – identical and fraternal
- (3) Dual deformations of all kinds
- (4) Animal multiples and dual deformations

II. European Races: Premature babies, newborns and organs
1. From the races of the German people
2. From other European peoples
3. Jews

III. Non-European Races: As above [...]

IV. Hereditary diseases: Prematurely born babies, newborns and organs from families with certain hereditary pathological traits (ordered later by disease).[33]

Fischer had drawn up these plans in late 1940, after the defeat of France, which had left Germany in a state of relative peace. However, as the war continued to escalate and Germany's invasion of the Soviet Union dragged on, twin research in Germany came to a virtual standstill. Even in Germany itself, the war was tearing families apart. Fathers were conscripted into the military, while mothers had to contend with all kinds of other issues and simply did not have the time or energy to ferry their twins to the KWI in Dahlem for examination.[34]

This all changed when Himmler ordered the creation of the so-called Gypsy family camp in Auschwitz-Birkenau in February 1943.[35] At that time, the German leadership had not fully decided on 'the solution to the Gypsy Question' so in the meantime, Europe's Sinti and Roma – mostly Roma – were to be interned in the concentration camps. This had already been done in Germany and Austria, and was now extended to occupied Poland and the Czech lands, as well as Hungary, Croatia, Belgium, France, the Netherlands and even Norway. A total of 22,969 men, women and children were thus deported to Auschwitz between February 1943 and July 1944. Unlike the Jews, however, they did not undergo the dreaded selection process upon arrival and were instead crammed into a separate section (B-IIe) of the camp. They were also allowed to remain together with their families; and because Nazi racial 'science' had determined them to be unsuited for labour, they only had to perform relatively mild duties such as cleaning up the camp or collecting ingredients for the camp's so-called 'water soup' outside of the camp.

Nevertheless, living conditions within their section of the camp were appalling, and by the end of July 1944 around 13,600 – roughly half – had died from starvation and disease, most commonly typhoid fever. That summer the family camp was officially dissolved; of the survivors, around 5,600 were sent to the gas chambers, with the last being murdered on 2 August 1944.

When Verschuer and his men were informed of the Gypsy family camp's establishment, they felt they had struck gold. According to the most recent KWI research, the likelihood of 'gypsies' giving birth to twins stood at 2%, which was twice the European average. Furthermore, some of the soon-to-be test subjects had already been registered by the KWI.[36] The internment of entire families in that section of the camp also made it possible to augment the twin studies with family research, while the rampant diseases and starvation provided the hereditary pathologists with ample opportunities for their studies.

As mentioned earlier, May 1943 saw the establishment of the Hygiene Institute of the Waffen-SS and Police in Rajsko, just a few kilometres away from Auschwitz. This allowed researchers from the KWI to conduct serological and histological studies practically on site, without having to send the samples to Berlin first.[37]

Aside from the 'Gypsies' – who had been conveniently grouped together by clan – the number of Jews had also increased considerably by early 1943, and both groups were now at the complete mercy of the KWI researchers seeking to study racial biology and hereditary pathology. It was also the perfect opportunity to look for human material for the 'Hereditary Biological Central Collection'.

In late May 1943, Josef Mengele was sent from Berlin to Auschwitz-Birkenau, specifically to section B-IIe, the Gypsy family camp. There, he was to support the SS physician in charge, take part in the selection of prisoners, and conduct his experiments, which suspiciously matched with KWI interests.

On paper, Mengele was a perfect fit for this task. He had a doctorate in anthropology and medicine, and he had made a name for himself with his second doctoral thesis on the heredity of the cleft palate. This study had made a mark abroad as well and was even considered to be the standard reference on that topic until the 1960s.[38] Furthermore, he had previously worked as a research assistant for Verschuer at the University of Frankfurt and thus had experience with both twin and family research.[39]

Mengele was undoubtedly well-aware of the possibilities SS medicine allowed him and what its aims were, and approved of them. Although he had not been particularly engaged politically, it was clear where he stood ideologically. As a university student he had been a member of the far-right Stahlhelm and the Nazi SA; in May 1937, he joined the NSDAP and a year later, the SS. In June 1940, he then volunteered for the Waffen-SS.[40] There, he was trained as a military physician at the sanitary inspectorate of the Waffen-SS between August and November 1940, before being transferred to the Race and Settlement Main Office of the SS, specifically Department II of the Family Office, which dealt with 'care for hereditary health' and 'hereditary health checks'. In July 1942, he was again transferred to Berlin, to the office of the Reich Physician of the SS and Police, Ernst Grawitz. It is unclear, however, if Mengele even went there – he was fighting on the Eastern Front until the end of that year – although he did have ties to Grawitz' office. Grawitz oversaw the medical staff of the concentration camp system and as such had authority over the human experiments as well. His cousin, Siegfried Liebau, the personnel officer in the SS Medical Office, who signed Mengele's transfer order to Grawitz' office, had himself visited Auschwitz in early 1943 and had taken pictures of a 'Gypsy clan' with heterochromia – differently coloured eyes in the same individual – for Karin Magnussen at the KWI. Liebau had been a frequent visitor at the KWI since December 1942 and Verschuer even encouraged him to continue his medical education. It is not unlikely that Liebau and Mengele met there and talked about the opportunities Auschwitz provided for them.[41]

It is not entirely clear on whose initiative Mengele was transferred to Auschwitz – was it Verschuer or Liebau, or perhaps Mengele himself? What is clear, however, is that it was no accident. After Liebau, Mengele was the second SS physician with ties to the KWI to visit Auschwitz, and when Mengele fell ill in the summer and autumn of 1943, first with malaria then with typhoid fever, he was replaced by Dr Erwin von Helmersen, who had been with the KWI in Dahlem since 1942. Like Mengele, Helmersen was sent to work as a doctor in the Gypsy camp when he arrived in August 1943, and it appears that he briefly became Mengele's subordinate upon the latter's return.[42]

In early 1943, Verschuer initiated a research project to examine 'specific proteins' for the purpose of serological race tests. By August, he had secured funding from the German Research Foundation (Deutsche Forschungsgemeinschaft). In March 1944, he reported:

> As research partner in this discipline, my assistant Dr med. & Dr phil. Mengele was active. He is deployed as a Hauptstumführer and camp physician in the concentration camp Auschwitz. With approval from the Reichsführer-SS, anthropological studies are conducted involving the various racial groups in this concentration camp and blood samples are sent to be processed at my laboratory.[43]

The vein punctures this research project required were banned by law in the Reich at this point, and many of the racial groups, most notably Jews, Sinti and Roma, had been more or less annihilated within the pre-war borders of the Reich. They had even vanished from most concentration camps.[44]

When Mengele arrived in Auschwitz-Birkenau in June 1943, he was thus presented with a unique opportunity to conduct his experiments. In Auschwitz, his experiments were so deeply tied into what the KWI was doing that it appears as if he established some sort of field office of the Institute.[45]

After the war, the former commandant of the camp, Rudolf Höss, agreed with this assessment: 'He conducted studies on identical twins. […] He conducted them with the written approval of Himmler and together with a university professor, for whom he worked – whose name I cannot recall.'[46] It is likely that Mengele worked to further his personal interests in order to establish his own 'research fiefdom' that was tied to the KWI.[47]

Regardless of what exactly Mengele's plans were, he was intent on taking advantage of this opportunity, whatever the cost. Horst Fischer, the deputy SS chief physician in Auschwitz and thus one of Mengele's superiors, remarked: 'Mengele talked very enthusiastically about his "scientific" work in the "Auschwitz concentration camp", because the "material" that he had at his disposal here was apparently a one-off opportunity that would not be presented to a "scientist" ever again.'[48] The deputy head of the SS Hygiene Institute in Rajsko, Dr Hans Münch, had befriended Mengele. He put it even more dramatically. According to him, Mengele thought it would have been 'a sin, a crime […] to let pass the opportunities Auschwitz provided for twin research. When they were already going into the gas anyway. […] This opportunity will never appear again.'[49] Mengele would soon demonstrate what he meant by this.

Initially, Mengele had only been assigned to the Gypsy family camp, but he soon began to build up a kind of 'anthropological research institute'[50] in Auschwitz-Birkenau. Within a few months, he had recruited several 'research teams' composed of various doctors and specialists he had found among the camp's inmates; these teams were subordinate to him personally and conducted elaborate research projects, including experiments on their fellow prisoners. Among the prisoners he had recruited were ophthalmologists, otolaryngologists – ear, nose and throat doctors – paediatricians, gynaecologists, dentists and dissectors, as well as scientists, nurses, kindergarten teachers and secretaries.[51] In some cases, he even had specialists brought to him from other concentration camps. At least three of those cases are documented. The most important team was led by Professor Berthold Epstein, the former head of the children's hospital at the German University in Prague. He and his team worked on several different research projects that sometimes involved human experiments, initially in a special shack within the Gypsy camp. Another team was headed by the anthropologist Martina Puzyna; it carried out anthropological examinations in the women's camp. Finally, a team under Dr Miklós Nyiszli, a coroner, dissected the corpses from the experiments and prepared the 'specimens' for transport. The 'identification service' of the Political Department – the camp Gestapo – also helped Mengele and took pictures of everyone whom Mengele had shown interest in for various reasons.[52]

The work of Mengele's research teams was organized according to the ruthless logic of hereditary pathology. First a clinical and anthropological examination of the still-living subjects, followed by their murder at the hands of the camp personnel and then the dissection and pathological examination of their bodies in order to test assumptions and to draw conclusions. In case the test subjects were twins, they were killed quickly, one after the other, so that they could be dissected simultaneously. Auschwitz was the only place where such experiments were possible.

In the Gypsy family camp, Mengele quickly turned his attention to the twins there. In Block 29 and 31, he established a kindergarten for children under the age of 6; the kindergarten in Block 31 even included a fenced-in playground with a sandbox, swings, a carousel and gymnastics equipment. There, other prisoners took care of the children between 08:00 and 14:00 in return for better rations. Mengele himself also regularly visited 'his' children, gave them sweets and even toys. The children trusted Mengele and referred to him as their 'good uncle'.[53] For the adults, however, it soon became clear that Mengele's friendliness hid an ulterior motive: To attract children, make them compliant and use them for his experiments, which ended in many of their deaths.

This kindergarten thus became one of Mengele's favourite places to search for new human material. The children that piqued his interest were taken to a special room, where they were medically and anthropologically examined and experimented upon. The children had to endure frequent injections and had their blood sampled regularly, while also having their fingerprints taken, being photographed and sorted by hair and eye colour. Mengele was particularly interested in the at least seventeen pairs of identical twins he had there.[54] Together with the non-identical twins, Mengele had at his disposal at least around eighty pairs of twins.[55] Once he had run his tests on them, he had them killed or killed them himself, then he had them dissected and their body parts preserved for various purposes and interested parties.

In September 1943, a second family camp was set up in Birkenau (Section B-IIb) for the mostly Czech Jews from the Theresienstadt Ghetto. Until May 1944, 17,517 men, women and children were sent to the family camp, and like the Sinti and Roma before them, they did not have to undergo the gruelling selection process; while they were separated by gender, they were otherwise allowed to remain together as families. Mengele, since November 1943 the Head Physician of Birkenau, did not let this opportunity pass by and began his search for twins. Some of these twins were housed separately along with their mothers.[56] Like in the Gypsy family camp, he set up a special children's block that functioned as a kindergarten and school. Here, too, he soon became known as the 'good uncle' to the children.

As the pace of deportations to Auschwitz picked up, Mengele decided to screen all new Jewish arrivals for twins during the initial selection process. In 1944 alone, around 600,000 Jews arrived at Auschwitz.[57] Assuming that around 1% of all Jewish births were twins, Mengele could expect thousands of potential test subjects.

The highpoint of the deportations to Auschwitz came in mid-May 1944, when the deportation trains from Hungary began to arrive. During these times especially, Mengele – well dressed, elegant and with a riding crop in hand – stood at the infamous ramp, trying to spot any twins or people with deformities. According to one witness at the Frankfurt Auschwitz Trial, Mengele was 'always there'. Another one remarked: 'Mengele came to all the transports [...] And when he was busy, he sent a different, smart SS physician.'[58] According to the anthropologist Dr Martina Puzyna, a prisoner who had been previously 'recruited' by him, Mengele managed to pick out around 250 pairs of twins from the Hungarian transports.[59]

Beginning in May 1944, some of the twins were sent to a barrack in the infirmary of the women's camp (Section B-Ia). This group included girls between the ages of 2 and 16, boys under the age of 8, as well as mothers with babies under the age of 2. Older boys and men, including the disabled and so-called 'dwarves', were sent to Block 15 in Birkenau's men's prisoner hospital (B-IIf):[60] 'In the infirmary records they were kept as twin and dwarven material.'[61] People with physical deformities, especially those of highly unusual heights, thus became a secondary focus of Mengele's research.

Up until the summer of 1944, Mengele had thus established four different places where he kept 'his' human material – twins and people with disabilities: the Gypsy family camp (B-IIe), the Theresienstadt family camp (B-IIb), as well as in the men's (B-IIf) and the women's (B-Ia) camps. It is estimated that during his time in Auschwitz, he was able to utilize at least 900 twins for his research.[62] On 11 and 12 July 1944, the Theresienstadt family camp was officially dissolved by the camp authorities. Those who had survived until then were separated into two groups: Those deemed fit for work were sent to other concentration camps, while those unfit for work were immediately murdered. Thus, in just two days, 6,500 to 7,000 people were gassed. However, Mengele had made sure to make an exception: 'His' twins as well as 'his' prisoner-doctors were allowed to survive – for now.[63] When the Gypsy family camp was dissolved in the same fashion on 2 August, Mengele was unable to save 'his' twins. He was, however, able to have 'his' killed twins dissected.[64]

Mengele's first 'research project' went far beyond just twin research. In the summer of 1943, he was faced with two deadly outbreaks of disease in the Gypsy family camp: A typhoid epidemic that had been raging since that spring, and noma, a bacterial infection largely unknown in Europe at the time. Noma usually begins with ulcers in the oral mucosa; left untreated, it eats through both the surrounding soft tissue and bone, completely destroying the cheeks and face. To this day, it is not entirely known what causes the disease, but known risk factors are malnutrition, poor sanitary conditions and further infections – all present in the Gypsy family camp.

Mengele took this 'opportunity' to set up his first research team under the innocuous name 'Department for the Study and Treatment of Noma'.[65] Aside from the already mentioned paediatrician, Professor Epstein, he recruited Dr Rudolf Weisskopf, a specialist for skin diseases, in August 1943.[66]

Once he had established his team, he began his campaign to 'research and treat' noma. First, he organized better rations for the emaciated and, in many cases, the already completely disfigured sick. Once their condition began to improve, he cut rations again to observe how the disease progressed. In addition, he had drawings made of his test subjects. Those who died were sent to Rajsko to the Hygiene Institute of the SS to be dissected – Mengele did not have his own team for that yet. If a twin died, Mengele had the other twin killed immediately in order to conduct simultaneous dissections. In cases where only one twin suffered from the disease, Mengele made sure to infect the other twin with noma to test how their bodies reacted to the disease under living conditions entirely controlled by him.[67]

Very little is known about the other research projects Mengele assigned to Professor Epstein's team. Both Epstein and the other prisoner-doctors who had worked first in the Gypsy family camp and later – after the liquidation of the Gypsy camp – in Block 15 of the men's infirmary, kept their silence about their participation in the twin experiments after their liberation.[68]

As a result, little is known about Mengele's 'research empire', as Hans-Walter Schmuhl put it. In addition to the silence of the prisoner-doctors, Mengele himself had evaded capture until his death and his records have been lost. Meanwhile, the surviving test subjects by and large did not fully grasp what exactly was happening to them, while even the prisoner-nurses and many of the doctors as well, only knew what happened in front of them and had no knowledge of the bigger picture.

Aside from the experiments in treating noma, Mengele also studied the pigmentation of the iris. The exact anthropological and hereditary mechanisms of iris pigmentation were unclear to contemporary scientists, but German authorities were interested in learning more about it for the purpose of ancestry tests to distinguish Jews from Aryans. The causes for changes in eye colour during one's life were just as mysterious. To Eugen Fischer and his hereditary biologists, this was a research problem tailor-made for phenogenetics and twin research. At the KWI at the time, it was Karin Magnussen who – financed by the DFG (German Research Foundation) – researched these questions.

It was likely from her that Mengele received the substances he used to drip into the eyes of twin children in an attempt to change their eye colour. In several cases, this led to blindness and one newborn is said to have died afterwards. Magnussen was particularly interested in cases of heterochromia. During his visit to Auschwitz, Liebau had supplied her with photographs of twins from a 'Gypsy clan' that had an unusual number of members with heterochromia. Mengele continued to help her by removing their eyes and sending them to her as specimens, alongside the eyes of other inmates with heterochromia. Naturally, the victims had to be killed first.[69]

Verschuer, meanwhile, received around 200 blood samples from Mengele from people belonging to different 'races' for his project on race-specific proteins,[70] as well as the results from corresponding anthropological studies. The severed heads of Romani children with noma were preserved in Rajsko and then sent to Graz to the newly founded SS Medical Academy, which was in the process of setting up its own medical and anthropological collection.[71]

To the KWI in Dahlem, Mengele sent the skeletons of people of unusual heights – 'dwarves' and 'giants' – or with physical deformities such as hunched backs and clubfeet, in addition to embryos and foetuses that Mengele had obtained through forced abortions conducted in the men's infirmary,[72] as well as various preserved organs with all kinds of different illnesses. These deliveries suspiciously overlapped with what Verschuer needed for his Hereditary Biological Central Collection, which suggests that the search for these specimens was Mengele's main duty, together with the twin research.

Beyond that, it is likely that Mengele also carried out research on typhoid fever and/or tuberculosis as well as various pharmacological studies for I.G. Farben.[73] What is known is that Mengele selected twenty children to be infected with tuberculosis – a disease that can take years to fully manifest – and sent them to the Neuengamme concentration camp; they were killed shortly before the end of the war in nearby Hamburg in the infamous cellar of the Bullenhuser Damm School.[74]

Mengele almost certainly sought to use his stay in Auschwitz to work on his postdoctoral career. Hans Münch suggested this in his testimony and underlined Mengele's scientific ambitions.[75] Furthermore, Mengele had taken plaster casts of the jaws of many of 'his' twins, suggesting that he was preparing to continue to do research on jaw shapes and/or deformities.[76]

Both Verschuer and Höss mentioned that Himmler had approved of these research projects, and considering how much of an effect they had on the everyday functioning of the camp, it had to be approved by someone higher up. Prisoner-doctors, nurses, as well as other prisoner personnel working for Mengele, had to be relieved of their usual duties – usually heavy labour – and were even spared the gas chamber. In some cases, they even had to be transferred to Auschwitz from other camps. Mengele himself also had to be relieved of some of his duties as a camp physician, first in the Gypsy family camp, later in the entire Birkenau sub-camp.[77] Furthermore, Mengele's laboratories and dissection stations were equipped with state-of-the-art equipment. He was also able to select people for his experiments who otherwise would have been immediately sent to the gas chambers upon arrival, namely Jews deemed unfit for labour, including people with deformities or children. Instead, they were housed in special barracks and were supplied with food without having to do forced labour. They were thus seen as privileged by many other inmates, and some children lied about being twins to receive better treatment. 'For, us, for the twins, he was like dad, like mum', one of the surviving twins recalled 'and at the same time, he was a murderer' – but this only became clear later on.[78]

Virtually all of the testimonies highlight Mengele's two-facedness. He was described as elegant, handsome, friendly towards all children – but was not above killing them just moments later, in cold blood, to have them immediately dissected and study their corpses. Unlike many other SS physicians, he did not beat the prisoner personnel – yet he was universally feared inside the infirmaries because he was by far the most ruthless SS physician when it came to selecting sick prisoners to be discharged and killed. He sent tens of thousands into the gas chambers without batting an eye, but also saved individual prisoners for reasons that not even they understood. Mengele frequently hummed melodies from operas, even during the selections on the ramp and in the infirmaries, and flew into a rage when he felt that camp rules were being broken.

Mengele was also exceedingly meticulous when it came to science and documenting his experiments, yet none of his notes have ever been found. According to witnesses, he had hastily stuffed his research notes into a suitcase just ahead of the evacuation, and the suitcase has been missing ever since.[79] Likewise, all the material he sent to the KWI in Dahlem and the other institutes was destroyed and the cooperation was covered up.

All this had only served to fuel the popular imagination about the 'Angel of Death'. But now we were on the verge of uncovering one of the great mysteries of Auschwitz.

Chapter 5

Finally: The Handover

Trypaflavin – 6,3 Diamino-10-methylacriiniumchloride/1-10-1/ Building B-IIIe/B-IIf

Auschwitz Notes

The uneasiness brought about by the now-resolved legal fights lingered on past Christmas 2014 and into the first weeks of the new year. On my side, a lot of trust had been destroyed by Lothfels' and Kaiser's vacillating and potentially – for me – ruinous behaviour. But despite my fears, the situation remained more or less calm until late January.

On 27 January 2015, the date of the opening of the safe, Kaiser, Lothfels, Wassert and I drove to Zürich. We travelled together, but for the opening of the safe, Kaiser insisted on following the 'formalities' and requested to enter to the bank on her own. Naturally, we complied and went to wait at a local artisanal sweet shop.

Before too long, Kaiser called us, saying that she had received her grandfather's estate and that she was about to pick us up in her car. By half past one we were already on the way back to Lothfels' mansion in Germany. There, I picked up three completely sealed packages out of the trunk of Kaiser's car, which Kaiser ceremoniously handed over to Lothfels, who in turn handed them back over to me. Thus, the agreement from 6 April 2014, which had been fought over for months, had finally been honoured.

We were handed a leather briefcase, a small leather box, as well as a package with books and newspapers. As mentioned earlier, these packages were all secured from unwanted interference with a custom-made steel mesh. However, even before we had got past the steel protection, it was clear this was not entirely what we had been promised in February 2014. There had been no mention of books and newspapers, and instead of six, we only received three packages. The reason for the latter was as simple as it was frustrating: Kaiser explained us that during the opening of the safe, a representative of the Vatican had been present, who then took the majority of her grandfather's estate with him back to Rome. I was shocked but remained silent.

The next day, I drove home and immediately began to break down the steel mesh. After a few minutes, I was able to go through the contents of the packages. I quickly realized that we had not been handed the documents we were hoping for. Instead, we found a host of family pictures, various documents from the Third Reich, and more interestingly, old medical textbooks and a notebook – both filled with handwritten notes, some of them in code. After the initial review, I thought the following to be the most promising:

A *Hungarian medical notebook from 1936* with handwritten notes in Hungarian (around 95%) and German, of which around 80% were from the years 1942 to 1945, with the rest being written after the war. These appeared to be the notes Grósz Chorin made in Auschwitz. In total, the notebook contained around 100 pages (see Plate 1).

The *Trachoma Book*, a Hungarian medical textbook – 'A Trachoma' by Dr Emil Grósz, published in 1940 in Budapest. This book likely originally belonged to his wife, Rebekka Grósz Chorin, who had been an ophthalmologist and therefore likely had to treat trachoma – an infectious eye disease that can lead to blindness. According to Kaiser, Grósz Chorin had been able to keep the book with him in Auschwitz and used it to write down encrypted information, relating to, among other things, his research for the KWI and Verschuer. This was seemingly confirmed by a note written in pencil: '1942. January – 1942 – December, work in Kaiser-Wilhelm-Institut in Berlin was very successful. Dr Otmar Freiherr von Verschuer allowed me to translate his reports into Hungarian. Grósz Chorin.' The rest was encrypted with numbers (see Plate 2).

In total, the Trachoma book contained twenty encrypted entries, some of them several pages long. Another book with the title

Ítéljetek! Néhány Kiragadott Lap a Magyar-Zsidó Életközösség könyvéből [Judge! A few selected pages from the book of the Hungarian Jewish community], published in Budapest in 1939, also contained a smaller number of similarly coded notes.

Two *Gedeon Medical Notebooks* likewise contained handwritten entries, including a long series of numbers in one of them.

These encoded messages did not deter me. On the contrary: There were many cases of people in prisons and ghettoes writing down encrypted notes on the scant paper they could get their hands on. Old notebooks, books, everything that could be quickly picked up and smuggled past the guards was used for such notes.[1] A doctor like Grósz Chorin would surely be able to take medical textbooks and notebooks with him on his journey to Budapest, which had led to his arrest. Likewise, he also could probably have picked up various medical brochures at the KWI or even in Auschwitz; the medical notebooks in particular often contained lists of important medical terms. Considering that only very few notes from Auschwitz survived the war, the historical value of the documents we had lying in front of us promised to be extraordinary.

I quickly began to flip through the medical notebook from 1936, or the 'Auschwitz Notes' as I would call them from now on. While I did not and still do not speak Hungarian, I immediately noticed a slew of familiar words in the few pages: Auschwitz, Berlin, KWI, Institute for Anthropology, Professor Dr Otmar Freiherr von Verschuer, barrack, crematorium, Zyklon B, Sonderkommando. I asked a friend of mine, a historian from Hungary, to translate one of the pages for me:

> 18 March 1942: For the first time I had to take part in a gassing. 200 people were brought to the gas chamber. Afterwards, an SS physician ordered the opening of the Zyklon B canisters and to pour them through the grates. Death occurred after only 10-20 minutes. Poor, unfortunate humans – my fellow Jewish human beings. Oh my God.

My colleague was shaken, but it was clear that while grim, this was an authentic and promising source. Now it was time to translate the rest.

To my great surprise, Kaiser herself offered to do it on her own, even though she had always emphasized that she did not want anything to do with the contents of the documents. We ended up not taking her up on her offer, because of the great emotional turmoil it caused for her; I felt there was a very real chance of her unconsciously or even consciously mistranslating the words of her grandfather to protect his memory. However, while the materials were more or less comprehensible, we needed a reliable, accurate translation if we wanted to work with the texts in a scholarly way.

In February I thus sought out a certified translator in my area who was able to get to work immediately. While he had great difficulties in reading Grósz Chorin's handwriting, he was already half-finished with a preliminary translation of the Auschwitz Notes by March. The translated entries he sent to me confirmed that we indeed had a very extraordinary testimony in our hands. Among other things, they made clear that Salamon Grósz Chorin had been arrested 6 December 1941 and was sent to Auschwitz via Berlin. In Auschwitz-Birkenau, he participated in experiments for the KWI that included dissections, anatomical studies and experiments. The 'experimental and research station' was in the immediate vicinity of the gas chambers and the crematoria, in the area of the Sonderkommando responsible for burning the bodies.

Grósz Chorin and the others thus became direct witnesses to the gassings, were forced to infect other prisoners with pathogens and perform dissections; Grósz Chorin himself also had to participate in sterilizations. His writings contained both shorthand notes – usually regarding medication and experiments – as well as longer entries in which he wrote about various events or tasks, but also about his reactions to all of this. An example was this entry:

> Typhoid vaccine, only 500 shots for 25,000 people. Who should we give it to? Pregnant girls have to be infected. Me, as a gynecologist. What has happened to us? My God! My God!

He was clearly plagued by great feelings of despair and outright terror at the horrendous situation, but also guilt at his participation in it.

Aside from frequent invocations of the Almighty ('my God!') he often repeated sentences such as 'I am going insane here!' or 'My God, how deep have I fallen!' His notes also made clear that he had developed an addiction to Luminal, a powerful sedative.

His writings also confirmed that Grósz Chorin had been working closely with Josef Mengele, the latter even going so far as to force Grósz Chorin to participate in the selections during the arrivals of the Hungarian transports, which plunged the Jewish Hungarian prisoner-doctor into extreme turmoil:

> Selection, this crazy Mengele takes me with him to the ramp – the selection ramp. What would my children and my wife Rebekka say if they saw me there next to Mengele!!

Overall, Mengele was mentioned regularly in Grósz Chorin's notes and sometimes even quoted. Likewise, the first SS camp physician, Wirths (consistently misspelled as 'Wirth') featured frequently as well. Other SS functionaries such as Otto Moll, the supervisor of the Sonderkommando in Birkenau and later plenipotentiary for the extermination of the Hungarian Jews, as well as the crematorium supervisor Erich Muhsfeldt ('Mussfeld' in the notes) were also mentioned.

The entries from after 1945 were outright explosive. Apparently, Grósz Chorin and Mengele had somehow kept in touch after the war; Grósz Chorin had even helped Mengele several times during his flight from Europe and afterwards, albeit in a rather reluctant fashion. He also implicated the Vatican in helping Josef Mengele flee Europe after the war. In an entry, Grósz Chorin described his encounters with Mengele in 1948/49:

> [Mengele:] My friend, I have saved your life and the lives of your sons. I believe you know what you have to do. – Yes, Herr Colonel Dr Mengele. – Then I told him that I had got a Red Cross pass from the Swiss Guard in the Vatican. – He again left without saying goodbye. He came back in early April. – I gave

> him two addresses/Helmut Gregor is his new name/ Zürich – Günzburg/Zürich - Genoa – Rome – Genoa (Vatican Pius XII received him)/20 June 1949 aboard the ship *North King* he sailed to Buenos Aires.

The very last entry in the Auschwitz Notes, meanwhile, referenced Professor Dr Joseph Ratzinger.

This all raised many questions: Did the Vatican interfere in the transfer of documents, not only because of the friendship between Grósz Chorin and his theology professor, but also to erase any evidence of the Catholic Church helping Mengele? Were there more indications that Pope Pius XII – who was in an already controversial process of beatification – had been personally involved?

I quickly realized that I was not able to deal with the great flood of material and their implications on my own. Specifically, I needed additional funds to have the handwritten notes transcribed, appoint a second translator, and hire at least another research assistant for the necessary research in Germany and abroad. All of this could not simply be done on the side.

Lothfels had previously talked about providing the necessary funds. However, we had different views on how to proceed. She wanted to have the countess translate her grandfather's notes free of charge in order to limit costs. Kaiser had already agreed, and Dr Wassert thought this was a good idea as well. I did not and soon began to search for another source of funding. In April, I received a grant from the Hamburg Foundation for the Promotion of Science and Culture, a foundation I had already worked with in the past. Now we could truly begin.

To the disappointment of Dr Wassert, the Auschwitz Notes did not contain any medical documents she could analyze. She declared she would instead start working on a biography of Grósz Chorin; for this purpose, she wanted to continue interviewing the countess. I had no problem with that and only asked her to keep our findings confidential for the time being.

Another issue was that a proper forensic authentication of these documents was impossible. I contacted a Polish specialist who confirmed that the paper was without doubt from that time period. However, it was unclear if this was the case for the writing as well. The problem here was that the author had exclusively used pencils and copying pens, and the composition of pencil lead – a mix of graphite and clay – had not changed since the nineteenth century.[2]

As a result, I could only verify the authenticity of the notes through careful textual analysis and detailed research into the events described. This was going to be a lot of work, especially since in April, Kaiser announced that we would be given another batch of documents from the packages that had gone to the Vatican. If these notes were indeed authentic, they would most certainly cause a worldwide stir.

Chapter 6

The Pressure Rises

1964, when I was in the hospital and uncle Fritz visited my little granddaughter Magda and lied to her, ... she handed him [the Auschwitz Notes], because she did not know what was written in them. [...] Then Mengele again disappeared into the fog [...] But all my notes and the official notices from Mengele – they are lost – Dr Josef Mengele was the thief. [...] Him personally.

Memoirs, pages 181 and 183

Rumours around our unexpected discovery of new Mengele documents soon made the rounds. While I was still working on a research plan and going through the notes, the media caught wind of the story. On 26 April 2015, Eva Moses Kor appeared on the show of Günther Jauch, one of Germany's most famous TV presenters. Kor was a survivor of Mengele's twin experiments and made headlines after appearing in the Auschwitz Trial in Lüneburg. At one point during the trial, she reached out to shake the hand of the former SS-man Oskar Gröning, before hugging him and saying that she had forgiven him. This great gesture of forgiveness triggered a media storm, but it came with a condition. Eva Mozes Kor asked Gröning to testify earnestly to help uncover the crimes he and his comrades had committed at Auschwitz many decades prior.

She then used the ensuing media attention to call on the public to contact her if anyone had information regarding Mengele's lost notes. Even seventy years after the experiments, she did not know what kind of injections she and her sister had been given without their consent, and what exactly the long-term effects were. Her sister had likewise survived the experiments in Auschwitz, but had unfortunately passed away in the meantime.[1]

This turn of events reactivated the star lawyer we had fought off just a few months earlier. Before the talk show aired, he had contacted Lothfels, who then told me that Eva Kor desperately needed access to Mengele's research notes because she was suffering from chronic kidney disease. She was hoping that the documents we had received in January contained information on the kinds of experiments the twins were subjected to so that she could be helped.

However, what the lawyer did not know was that I myself had contacted Kor a year earlier, and had interviewed her at length regarding her experiences in Auschwitz and the physical effects of the experiments. Over the course of our conversations, she never mentioned anything about suffering from kidney disease.

In my opinion, this was nothing more than a ruse by the lawyer to find out more about the contents of the documents he was evidently still highly interested in. Jauch, the TV presenter, had likewise declared at the end of his show with Eva Kor that new documents regarding Mengele would soon appear.

A few days later, in early May, one of Jauch's colleagues thus tried to contact Kaiser directly. This was easier said than done: Even though she taught at the University of Zürich, her name was neither on the list of faculty nor on the list of lectures given. But this was to be expected; as the papal personal physician, she had to remain out of the spotlight and thus had come to an agreement with the university to keep her activities secret. This is not unheard of. I personally know academics who, for various reasons, do not or cannot make their teaching activities public. At any rate, it was clear to us that she did indeed teach; Dr Wassert had accompanied her on multiple research trips and Professor Kaiser was in frequent contact with her students. The two friends even discussed professional matters together at times, such as her academic career as well as when it came to treating the popes.

The Vatican likewise does not freely provide any information regarding its employees out of principle. Jauch's colleague thus had to find a way around it. In the end, he apparently found a report of the previous year's event at the university in Budapest, where the scholarship for the Bhutanese students was celebrated.[2] He therefore reached out to that university.

Kaiser was not pleased in the slightest. She complained to her friend Lothfels that she had been harassed 'in Rome' and shared her exasperation with Wassert and me. Shortly after this episode, I received a phone call from Jauch as I was going through the files of the Mengele case at the Hessian Main State Archive. We agreed to meet in early June.

This meeting remained pleasantly matter of fact. Having received permission from Kaiser and Lothfels, I explained to Jauch and his colleague that we had in our possession the notes of a former prisoner-doctor from Auschwitz. However, these notes still had to be translated first, their authenticity verified and then analyzed historically, before being made accessible to the public. This would be a long and labour-intensive process, I continued, especially considering the author's true identity had not been fully confirmed yet. Before all of that was done, Kaiser did not wish to be contacted by the media.

This was not the only inquiry. The ZDF – one of Germany's main public broadcasters – had also declared their interest in the story. We responded to them as we did to Jauch, but this episode left us with a bad feeling. How long would the press remain quiet?

Not wanting to waste any more time, I continued my research. I travelled again to Warsaw, where I went through the files on Auschwitz and especially those of the prisoner-doctors. In Berlin, I visited the Stasi Records Agency (BStU) since it contained files regarding the SS physician Horst Fischer, who was tried in East Germany in 1966 and executed. I also went to the Max-Planck-Society, the successor of the KWI. In Moscow, I went through the reports of the Extraordinary State Commission, which had been established in November 1942 to document the crimes the Germans had committed, and which had interrogated countless witnesses, including former prisoner-doctors from Auschwitz. In Heidelberg, we searched the university archives for any mention of Grósz Chorin, who had studied there. In Vienna, the school he had attended as a teenager was still open and even the old graduation report cards had been kept. However, in a twist of fate, the report cards from 1894 to 1897 were missing, which was precisely when Grósz Chorin had finished his schooling there. This was all very disappointing, but as a historian, I was used to this.

In the meantime, I had also reached out to Dr János Kemény, a young historian from the Corvinus University in Budapest, who spoke several languages very well. He would be able to help us with the transcription and translation of the Auschwitz Notes.

Kaiser was less than enthused when she heard about this and feared he would try to use this material for his own career. I did not share her concerns; Kemény had left a very positive impression and had been recommended to me by a fellow Hungarian historian I knew well. It was also clear that we desperately needed help, especially as pressure was beginning to mount from the outside, and Kemény had just the right skillset we needed.

Consequently, I chose to not tell the countess that we continued to work with Kemény after her intervention. Just to be sure, I initially only sent him excerpts that were short and unconnected enough so that he could not understand the greater picture and possibly publish the documents on his own.

Chapter 7

The State of Research

. . . why am I not being sent to the crematorium?

Auschwitz Notes

In the meantime, we continued our research on the medical system in Auschwitz. Up to 1942, it was strictly forbidden for any medically trained prisoners to work as prisoner-doctors in Auschwitz. The situation was similar in other concentration camps. The most important posts staffed by prisoners were held by the so-called revierkapos – i.e. kapos in charge of the infirmaries – or various block or infirmary elders. These were always ethnic German prisoners – either criminals or political ones – who had no medical training. The political prisoners in particular – usually communists – used their privileged position to shield politically aligned prisoners by giving them jobs in the medical system. As a result, those who fell sick were generally not treated properly. In the best-case scenario, the prisoner-nurses eased their pain or at least ignored them. In the worst-case scenario, the untrained medical personnel tried to conduct surgeries themselves, which often resulted in the death of the patient.[1]

Despite the ban, Polish prisoner-doctors worked in the medical system from the beginning. However, they had to lie about their background and were employed in subservient roles as prisoner-caregivers and support staff, which they gradually used to expand their influence. This was not the case for Jewish prisoner-doctors, because at the time Jewish inmates were not allowed to enter the infirmary, not even as patients.

In November 1941, during the expansion of the Auschwitz camp complex, the SS changed its policy. Due to the ever-growing number of prisoners as well as the frequent outbreaks of epidemics, the provision of rudimentary medical aid to the prisoners became a necessity. From then on, imprisoned doctors were formally allowed to work as prisoner-doctors and nurses.[2] Initially, this only applied to 'Aryans', i.e. Poles, but around May 1942, it was extended to Jews as well.[3]

The status of the prisoner-doctors rose rapidly during the fight against the rampant epidemics, especially typhoid fever. It further improved when it became obvious that only they could reliably treat injured slave labourers and make them productive again. In many cases, they were more qualified and experienced than the often young, SS camp physicians. As a result, the SS physicians successively delegated many tasks to the prisoner-doctors, such as making diagnoses, issuing medical reports, conducting surgeries and autopsies. As mentioned earlier, some SS physicians even took the opportunity to be trained by the prisoner-doctors.

In the second half of 1942, the SS then began to specifically search for doctors and other medical specialists among the prisoners. Mieczysław Kieta, an Auschwitz survivor, recounts that:

> During this time, special interest was given to the doctors and nurses in the infirmaries in Auschwitz and Birkenau. In November [1942], a heretofore unknown SS physician appeared in both camps who had the specialists in the fields of bacteriology, physical anatomy, biology and chemistry introduced to him. Sometimes, when they were free, he talked with the specialists one-on-one about their fields of expertise and their previous scientific work; sometimes, other SS physicians were called in as well. This interest in specialists was not limited to the camp infirmaries, by the way. They were also searching for them in the other commandos, certainly with the aid of the *Arbeitseinsatz* [the camp's labour office].[4]

Dr Eduard Wirths, in particular, who had been made the camp's first physician on 1 September 1942, chose to rely on trained medical-prisoner staff. At that time, mortality was high in all concentration camps, but Auschwitz was the worst. According to internal numbers, there were around 98,000 registered prisoners in the Reich's concentration system in July 1942, of whom 8,329 (8.5%) had died that month.[5] However, around half of all deaths, 4,125 to be precise, had occurred in Auschwitz. At the time, Auschwitz only had around 18,600 prisoners, or around 19% of the entire concentration camp population.[6] Naturally, these numbers were only for the registered prisoners; the Jews and Soviet prisoners of war that were murdered immediately upon arrival, were never registered and thus did not appear in this statistic.

The high death rates quickly led to complaints. Corporations such as I.G. Farben, which was in the process of setting up the Buna Works using forced labour from the other camps, were not pleased with the high 'turnover'. Himmler therefore ordered that the mortality in the concentration camps 'must be lowered'.[7]

The SS Main Economic and Administrative Office reiterated this in a letter of 28 December 1942:

> The First Camp Physicians have to use all tools available to them to make sure that the number of deaths in the individual camps is lowered significantly. The best doctor in the concentration camp is not the one who believes he must stand out by being inappropriately harsh, but he who keeps labour capacity as high as possible through monitoring and exchanging [prisoners] at work sites.[8]

With the help of these orders, Wirths was able to assert himself against the camp commander, Höss, who had preferred untrained political and criminal German prisoners over trained non-German prisoners.

One of the most prominent prisoner-doctors Wirths recruited was Stefan Budziaszek (after the war: Buthner). Born in 1913, Budziaszek saw his medical studies interrupted by the war and only finished his last medical exams illegally, under German occupation. He ended up working in a hospital in Kraków before being arrested in June 1941; after several months in prison, he was then sent to Auschwitz on 10 February 1942. An SS man broke his arm upon arrival and he was immediately sent to the infirmary – where he met one of his former colleagues from Kraków. Upon recovery, Budziaszek was first assigned to the laboratory, then to various other labour commandos, mostly in Buna/Monowitz. In late August 1942, his colleagues then helped him become a prisoner-nurse in the surgical unit of the main camp's infirmary.[9]

On 17 September 1942, Dr Wirths came and had all the prisoner-nurses and doctors stand in line. After briefly questioning the prisoners regarding their profession and reason for their arrest, Wirths picked out Budziaszek and had him personally brought to the sub-camp of Jawischowitz, where prisoners had to do forced labour in a coal mine. Budziaszek was made the infirmary elder with immediate effect. Apparently, he was able to combine medical expertise with organizational talent, and within just a few months, Jawischowitz had – by Auschwitz standards – a well-functioning infirmary.[10]

In June 1943, Budziaszek was then transferred to Buna to deal with the unacceptably high death rates. The prisoners there suffered from frequent pneumonia, phlegmons – purulent, diffusively spreading inflammation of the body's connective tissue – blood poisonings, starvation edema and diarrhoea, extreme emaciation, as well as from all kinds of cuts and injuries from falls and other workplace accidents. To make matters worse, 60% of those 'treated' at the infirmary died soon after.[11]

As in Jawischowitz, Budziaszek as the new infirmary elder began to search for trained doctors among the prisoners, while also 'organizing', through various means, equipment, medical instruments and other essentials for the infirmary. He also moved to undermine the influence of the unqualified German prisoner-functionaries in the infirmary.[12] With the approval of the SS camp physician, Horst Fischer, who was intent on practising his surgical skills, Budziaszek was able to set up a surgical ward as well. As a result of these changes, the mortality rates dropped, much to the satisfaction of both I.G. Farben and the SS camp administration.

Wirths acted similarly in Birkenau. In January 1943, Dr Otto Wolken had been deported from Vienna to Auschwitz. Initially, he was forced to do heavy physical labour in one of the outer commandos, before being transferred to Birkenau's men's camp, where he became a night guard. During his testimony decades later, Wolken recounted:

> In July 1943, a great typhoid fever epidemic broke out in Birkenau. To fight this epidemic effectively, all doctors were asked to report to the authorities, which I then did [...] and in an infirmary of camp B-IId, we were all gathered and were, so to speak, examined in a quite informal way by a prisoner-doctor from Poland by the name of Dr Senkteller [Zenkteller]. On this occasion, the SS camp physician, Dr Thilo, inquired about my medical career. After I had made known the training I had received, Thilo gave me the task of setting up a quarantine station in camp section B-IIa.[13]

Beginning in 1943, the general medical and hygienic conditions in the infirmaries improved dramatically. In some cases, the sick and injured prisoners were able to get proper medical care, including surgeries, after surgical wards were set up in the main camp and in Birkenau as well. In 1944, the prisoner-doctors finally won the power struggle against the unqualified German prisoner-functionaries. As the number of Jewish deportees skyrocketed in the summer of 1942, so did the number of Jewish medical personnel from all over Europe, primarily from Poland, France, Germany, Czechoslovakia and Hungary. A fair number of them were sent to work in the camps' infirmaries, and some were even made prisoner-functionaries. Aside from Jews and Poles, there was also a relatively small number of non-Jewish Czech, French, Russian and German prisoner-doctors.

In total, there were several hundred prisoner-doctors in Auschwitz and its various sub camps. However, it is hard to determine the exact number since the turnover was very high. Many died from disease, most commonly typhoid fever, while others were sent to other concentration camps. Some Polish prisoner-doctors were even released.

Inside Auschwitz, finding employment in the infirmaries radically increased one's odds of survival. Most ordinary prisoners died within months from exhaustion, starvation, disease or violence. Prisoner-doctors and nurses, meanwhile, were treated significantly better.

When Władysław Fejkiel arrived in Auschwitz on 8 October 1940, he weighed 75 kilograms. Four months later, he weighed only 41 kilograms. During the early days of the Auschwitz concentration camp, most of the prisoners were young and strong men but, as Fejkiel put it later, 'after a short stay in the camp, maximally after three months, these people were suffering from hunger atrophy'.[14] Fejkiel himself survived only because was sent to work as a prisoner-nurse shortly before he would have died from starvation; he later became a prisoner-doctor. Horst Fischer arrived in Auschwitz as an SS physician in November 1942 and made similar observations:

> Due to the [insufficient] number of calories, the general strength of the prisoners decreased more and more, and the typical symptoms of malnutrition appeared, such as hunger edema and cachexia – complete loss of subcutaneous fat tissue, muscle atrophy, skin dehydration. Inside the camp, these completely emaciated and malnourished prisoners who struggled to keep themselves upright were referred to as 'Muselmänner'. In my work as an SS camp physician, I [...] found that after three months at the most, the majority of prisoners were, due to the insufficient rations, in such a poor state of nutrition and physical strength that it was impossible for the prisoner to do labour.[15]

The emaciated and sick prisoners were regularly screened by the SS physicians and classified as 'unfit to work' and sent to the gas chambers.

Stefan Budziaszek was the first doctor among the prisoners who was given the position of infirmary elder, and he remained as such until the evacuation of the camp in January 1945. Dr Władysław Dering, also a Pole, was made the infirmary elder in the main camp in August 1943. After his release in January 1944, he was replaced by Władysław Fejkiel, another Polish prisoner-doctor. In Birkenau, this shift occurred somewhat later and the first medically trained infirmary elder, the

Polish prisoner-doctor Dr Roman Zenkteller, was only instated in March 1944. He was transferred to the Buchenwald concentration camp on 7 December 1944,[16] and Mengele appointed the Czech-Jewish prisoner-doctor Professor Berthold Epstein as his successor.

'An abnormal reaction to an abnormal situation is normal behavior' Viktor E. Frankl wrote in his book *Man's Search for Meaning* in 1946.[17] Frankl spoke from experience. He was a renowned Jewish neurologist and psychologist, who had been imprisoned, among other places, in Theresienstadt and Auschwitz.

Those who wanted to survive in Auschwitz had no choice but to do anything required of them. The German camp personnel, including Mengele and the other SS physicians, were very well aware of this. After all, they had created this situation in the first place, and now they intended to ruthlessly abuse it for their own ends. While Mengele and his colleagues usually relied on 'volunteers' in their search for medical personnel among the prisoners, this term was essentially meaningless in Auschwitz.

Mengele's 'staff' and the prisoner-doctors were 'privileged' among the camp inmates. They were so-called camp celebrities who did not have to perform the brutal slave labour that quickly destroyed every prisoner, no matter how strong. They were also housed separately and were given better rations, while also being shielded from the worst excesses of the kapos and SS guards.

In late autumn 1942, the prisoners in the Auschwitz main camp were told that a new research institute was to be founded nearby, the Hygiene Institute of the Waffen-SS, which began operations in the spring of 1943. Word of this quickly spread among the prisoners working in the infirmary. The Auschwitz survivor, Mieczysław Kieta, later recounted: 'Some even said that the prisoners working at the institute could, as specialists, be given the same rights as civilian employees, be allowed to have longer hair and their status would be significantly improved.'[18]

This was not entirely empty talk. Those doctors, scientists and medical specialists who found employment at the camp's infirmaries or at the SS Hygiene Institute, were frequently recruited from among the prisoners in Auschwitz who would have otherwise been certain to die from starvation and exhaustion. This was doubly true for older prisoners whose age meant they could not withstand the hardships of camp life for long.

As mentioned earlier, the first doctor Mengele 'recruited' was Professor Epstein. The internationally renowned pediatrician had been the chief doctor at the German University of Prague before the war and had left the country when the Wehrmacht invaded in March 1939, fleeing to Norway. However, Norway was conquered by German forces as well, and in October 1942 he and his wife were arrested by the Norwegian police on German orders.

After being handed over to the German authorities, he arrived in Auschwitz via Stettin on 1 December 1942 alongside 532 Jewish men, women and children.[19] His wife was immediately deemed 'unfit for work' and was gassed upon arrival. He himself was deemed 'fit for work' and was sent to Monowitz on 17 December. According to the German Jewish prisoner-doctor Lucie Adelsberger, who had worked with him in the Gypsy family camp:

> He never forgave himself that he had led his wife to her death. [When] the situation in the country became dangerous, friends offered to take him across the border. He refused because he was opposed to anything clandestine. Thus, he came to Auschwitz with the Norwegian transport.[20]

Epstein himself was spared heavy labour by a stroke of luck. While still in quarantine at the main camp, he was recognized by one of prisoners caring for the new arrivals, his former student, Dr Schattin. Schattin was able to help Epstein become a prisoner-nurse in Monowitz.[21]

Before long, word spread among the SS physicians that a famous paediatrician was working as a nurse in Monowitz. In March 1966, the Czech-Jewish Auschwitz survivor Karel Minc, who was a helper at the infirmary in Monowitz between January 1943 and the liberation of the camp, testified at the trial of Dr Horst Fischer in East Berlin:

> When Professor Epstein arrived, I still remember that Dr [Horst] Fischer, together with a few others from the SS, once asked: 'Where is Professor Epstein?' And they had a book or something with them, I had seen it from a distance, and they asked: 'Did you write it?' Then he said: 'Yes.'[22]

Mengele most likely was aware of this, too.

The second prisoner-doctor who 'joined' his 'staff' was the Czech-Jewish Dr Rudolf Weisskopf; he changed his name to Vitek after the war. According to his own testimony, Weisskopf became a 'sort of [...] personal assistant' to Mengele until the liberation of the camp.[23] Weisskopf was born in 1895 and had become an expert on skin diseases. He arrived in Auschwitz on 28 October 1942 as part of the first transport from Theresienstadt, together with 1,866 Jewish men, women and children, including his wife Eleonora, his daughter Susanne and his two sons Robert and Harry. His wife was immediately gassed upon arrival because 'she was short and weak'. His daughter was sent to the women's camp in Birkenau, where she later died. Weisskopf and his sons were sent to Monowitz, where both of his sons died as well. Weisskopf himself became a prisoner-nurse in Monowitz but fell ill and was transferred to the main camp to undergo surgery, before being transferred again in June 1943, this time to the Gypsy family camp in Birkenau, where he became a prisoner-doctor tasked with stamping out infectious diseases.[24]

In August 1943, Mengele approached both Weisskopf and Epstein and asked if they were willing to participate in the creation of the 'department for the study and cure of noma', which Mengele was in the process of setting up. After the war, Weisskopf emphasized that Mengele had assured them this was going to be purely scientific work and would not include experiments on humans.[25] Weisskopf believed that 'Mengele likely selected us from the great number of prisoner doctors due to our excellent knowledge of the German language.'[26] This was indeed most likely a major factor for Mengele. After all, they would have to write research reports and communicate well with him.

However, that Mengele categorically ruled out human experiments seems less believable.

Epstein and Weisskopf quickly became Mengele's most valued assistants. Epstein became the head of the 'research department' while Weisskopf became his deputy and Mengele's personal assistant. Both were treated better than the other prisoner-doctors under Mengele's command, since it was they who were largely responsible for conducting the 'scientific' research on noma and the twins Mengele and the KWI were so interested in.[27] Over time, Mengele continued to expand his research unit by recruiting other specialists among the prisoners.

One of them was the anthropologist Dr Martina Puzyna from Lviv, who survived only thanks to her working with Mengele on his twin research projects. Puzyna had been arrested in March 1943 for being a member of the Polish resistance. She arrived in Auschwitz in August 1943 and was assigned to several labour commandos working outside. As an academic, she was not at all used to the heavy physical labour and, coupled with the completely insufficient rations she received, she soon fell ill. After some time, she managed to be admitted to the infirmary, where she was treated for phlegmons and scabies. She slowly recovered, and some of the Polish prisoner-doctors, who knew about her professional background, helped her become a prisoner-nurse in the infirmary. However, she again fell sick soon after, this time from typhoid fever.[28]

Puzyna was treated by a fellow Pole, the prisoner-doctor Katarzyna Łaniewska, who knew that Mengele was searching for anthropologists for his twin studies and told him about Puzyna. Łaniewska introduced Puzyna as a talented anthropologist and the former assistant of Professor Jan Czekanowski 'who was a world-renowned figure in the field of anthropology. […] Mengele was familiar with this name.'[29] Immediately afterwards, Puzyna was told to come to Mengele the very next day.

> Because I was [too] weak to go on my own, two female prisoners had to lead me by my arms to another barrack in the women's camp, where Mengele had his office. […] Mengele asked me

> i[n] the presence of Dr König [an SS camp physician] if I was a student of Czekanowski, I affirmed this, then he asked me what I had been doing in the camp until then. Thereupon I responded truthfully that I had to carry stones, at which they both laughed. [...] Then I was sent back to the infirmary. Mengele ordered that I was to be given additional rations and that I was to be accommodated like the other prisoner-doctors. They were housed in a smaller section in the barrack that had four or five beds and a special fireplace. I was told that Mengele was very interested in having my ability to work restored as soon as possible. For me, this was, compared to my previous situation, heaven on earth.[30]

As soon as Puzyna had recovered, Mengele summoned her and said he wanted to conduct comparative studies on twins. Puzyna knew the importance of twin research for the field of anthropology, particularly when it came to heredity. Mengele made clear that he was interested in all types of twins:

> It was evident that the extraordinary conditions of a concentration camp the size of Birkenau offered otherwise unknown opportunities to have a large number of twins at one's disposal. [...] Mengele described to me the procedure to be followed. Special skull measurements were to be taken, i.e. the length and width of the skull, of course body height. There was also an examination checklist with several points, which included among others ear shape, nose shape, eye colour and similar characteristics. These points always had to be collected in the questionnaire.[31]

Mengele gave Puzyna special measuring instruments, as well as her own office and two female assistants. One of them had been an anthropology student and helped Puzyna take the measurements of twins and people with dwarfism. The second assistant meanwhile took notes. 'Measurements were taken practically every day. My work, if I recall correctly, began in early 1944, before the great transports from

Hungary arrived.' As they began to arrive in the camp in mid-May, Puzyna witnessed Mengele greeting the new arrivals by screaming: 'Twins out. To me, he seemed as if he was out of his mind when he ran around on the ramp looking for twins. At any rate, around 250 twin pairs were collected from the Hungary transports that way.'[32]

Mengele did not tell Puzyna what exactly he had in mind. 'However, I had the impression,' the anthropologist later recalled 'that he was clearly looking for the answer to questions in the field of heredity, which he seemed to want to solve by means of dissections.'[33]

The dissection of the dead 'test subjects' was the task of a third team, headed by the Hungarian-Jewish coroner Dr Miklós Nyiszli from Nagyvárad (now Oradea, Romania). In the 1920s, Nyiszli had studied medicine, among other places in Breslau (Wrocław), where he received his doctorate in forensic medicine. On 22 May 1944, he arrived in Auschwitz together with his wife and daughter. All three were deemed 'fit for labour' and admitted to the camp. Nyiszli himself was sent to the Buna works in Monowitz, where he was assigned to the concrete commando No. 197 after quarantine. For a 43-year-old doctor who had never had to do heavy physical labour before, this was essentially a death sentence.

Nyiszli had been working in the concrete commando for twelve days when the SS camp physician in Buna ordered all doctors among the prisoners to line up before him. Together with Nyiszli, this amounted to around fifty people. The SS physician then:

> commanded that those among us who were skilled coroners were to report for light labour. From the fifty doctors, two of us volunteered, all the better since I realized that I would collapse from the heavy concrete work sooner or later. After a thorough oral examination and questioning, we were both accepted. […] My hiring process went smoothly, as did that of my colleague, who was a doctor at the Strasbourg faculty.

The other doctor was probably Dr Jecheskiel (Josef) Körner, who had arrived in Auschwitz from Drancy, near Paris on 20 December

1943. On 27 June 1944, he was then sent to Birkenau to be Nyiszli's assistant.[34]

'It did not take an hour,' Nyiszli testified a year later 'when we were taken away by two armed SS men in a luxurious Red Cross car and that to my horror we were unloaded in the courtyard of Crematorium No. 1 in Auschwitz [Birkenau].'

The commander of Crematoria I and II, SS-Oberscharführer Erich Muhsfeldt, greeted both prisoners and explained to them 'what they were allowed to see here and what they were not'. Nyiszli and his colleague were not in the camp section of the Sonderkommando that had to prepare and clean up after the gassings, and which had to burn the bodies of the murdered.

> Then we were led to a neatly furnished room, which [...] Dr Mengele had placed at our disposal. The Oberscharführer then got a complete set of clothes and underwear from the possessions of the gassed. After a few hours, Dr Mengele appeared, also testing us for about an hour. Afterwards, he gave us work to do.[35]

Later, Mengele assigned two further assistants to help Nyiszli: Dr Dénes Görög, a Hungarian-Jewish doctor who had worked at the state hospital in Szombathely before his deportation, as well as Adolf Fischer, a Czech Jew who had been working as a dissection assistant for twenty years at the Prague Institute for Anatomy. Like the others, they had also been handpicked by Mengele.[36] At first, Nyiszli was astonished at the workplace assigned to him and his colleagues in the basement of Crematorium I. It was a proper dissection room 'of the most modern type': A red concrete floor, a dissection table with several drains; the equipment was likewise excellent and included, among other things, three microscopes. They were also provided with the most recent specialist literature. Nyiszli felt as if he was in a modern, well-equipped forensic institute.[37]

According to Nyiszli, Mengele told the SS crematorium personnel that 'his' prisoner-doctor only had to obey him and that the SS crematorium personnel had no authority over him whatsoever. Nyiszli received his food directly from the SS kitchen, and he was even allowed to go to the SS barber and did not have to appear during the morning and evening roll calls.[38] For a prisoner of Auschwitz, these were truly extraordinary 'privileges'.

Mengele quickly made clear what kind of work he wanted to see done. Nyiszli and his team thus soon began to dissect countless bodies. On 28 June 1945, Nyiszli testified:

> This work consisted of the medical examination of the (living) persons who had been selected from the transports due to their abnormal physical characteristics. We took the measurements, then Oberscharführer Muszfeld [Muhsfeldt] killed them with a small calibre, i.e. with a 6mm rifle, via a shot to the neck. Then we received the order to dissect the bodies and to make a very thorough protocol of the dissection. Afterwards, we dissolved the bodies of these abnormal persons with chlorinated lime and put the clean bones in packages and sent them to the anthropological institute in Berlin-Dahlem.[39]

Erich Muhsfeldt confirmed these events after the war – without mentioning his role, however.[40] In his testimony, Muhsfeldt brought up an incident which Nyiszli also mentioned, namely the killing of eight Gypsy twins:

> The SS physicians Mengele and Brand,[41] who conducted studies for the Race and Settlement Main Office, had their work room on the first floor of the first crematorium [...]. I recall that they killed eight gypsy children, twins. When I arrived for duty, I met three prisoner-doctors who were dissecting these bodies. I asked what sort of corpses these were. The doctors answered that the children were killed by Mengele via a lethal injection, because they had characteristics which Mengele was particularly interested in connection with his studies. He had in fact noticed that among these twin pairs, each twin had one blue and one grey eye. During

the dissection, the eyeballs were removed and sent to Berlin as exhibits.[42]

In addition to these dedicated research teams, Mengele also 'recruited' other prisoner-doctors in Auschwitz-Birkenau to carry out individual tasks. One of them was Dr Gisella Perl, a gynaecologist from Sighet (now in Romania). She had been deported to Auschwitz in May 1944 and while she was deemed 'fit for work' and thus admitted to the camp, the rest of her family was gassed upon arrival. After several weeks, Mengele ordered Perl to head the newly established infirmary in Block 15 in Birkenau. She testified that 'I had to gather several other prisoners from among the prisoners and take care of the sick people there. [...] Aside from me, there were two other graduated doctors, one dentist and several wives of doctors. We were all Hungarians.'[43]

Aside from caring for the sick, Mengele told her to 'acquire a living embryo' for his research; the embryo was then to be sent to Berlin. 'I therefore had to conduct a great number of abortions [on pregnant women] to get the embryos. [...] I want to say that I gave Mengele many embryos, not just one. These abortions continued for several weeks.'[44]

Perl was not the only doctor who had to conduct abortions for Mengele. In Block 2, in the infirmary of the men's camp (B-IIf), a special room for pregnant women was set up in the second half of 1944. There, the prisoner-doctor Wolken testified that 'on Mengele's orders, a premature birth or abortion was initiated. The women had to undergo these procedures voluntarily, because they would have to fear for their lives otherwise.' Wolken continued: 'All pregnant Jewish women were gassed. The detection of a pregnancy was a death sentence.'[45] In Block 2, the prisoner-doctors Stern, Herman, and Cohen[46] had to acquire the 'embryological material' which was then apparently sent to the Hereditary Biological Central Collection of the KWI in Dahlem.

Another of the prisoner-doctors was Dr Armin Sreter from Kisvárda. Sreter – who changed his name to Hajdu Arpad after the war – was deported to Auschwitz in May 1944 alongside his entire family. When they arrived, Mengele was personally selecting on the ramp where he noticed Sreter's twin daughters:

> He asked them: 'Are you twins?' My daughters – who spoke German – said, yes. He asked where their family members were. They said that they had arrived together with their family. Their mother was also quickly with them, but my mother-in-law had been assigned to those unfit for work and as we later learned, was already on her way to the crematorium. Then Mengele sent an SS soldier after the group of those unfit to work, who brought back my mother-in-law. Afterwards, my mother-in-law, Mrs Hartman Janos, as well as my wife and my daughters were – on the orders of Mengele – put into the FKL camp [women's camp]. From there, they went to anthropological examinations, which Mengele conducted in the outpatient clinic.[47]

Sreter himself was deemed 'fit for work' by Mengele and was sent to the Gypsy family camp. After three weeks, Mengele summoned Sreter and questioned him regarding his medical training. When Sreter told him he had studied at German universities, Mengele gave him the task of going through the files in the outpatient clinic in order to study the 'distribution of twin births in Hungary'. In an unusual turn of events, Sreter not only became a prisoner-doctor for Mengele but also an object of scientific curiosity as the father of twins:

> For reasons of research, he [Mengele] thought it was considered significant that they could simultaneously observe the ancestors of my twin daughters. During my stay there, I too was regularly examined in the internal, neurological and ophthalmological fields. Anthropological measurements were taken, various photographs were taken, my finger and footprints were taken and various drawings were made of me. Mengele's room was filled with anthropological measuring instruments.[48]

After Sreter had finished going through the personal files of the twins, Mengele transferred him to the camp infirmary in Birkenau's men's camp, where he worked as a prisoner-doctor. Sreter survived and was eventually liberated in Dachau by the Americans. His family survived as well; they were liberated by the Red Army in Auschwitz.

As mentioned earlier, Mengele and his colleagues also requested specialists and doctors to be sent to Auschwitz from ghettoes or other camps. However, this only applied to Jewish doctors. One of them was Dr Alina Brewda, a Polish-Jewish gynaecologist and obstetrician. She had been a prisoner-doctor in the Majdanek concentration camp before being sent to Auschwitz in September 1943, in order to take up the position of block physician in Block 10 – and to take part in medical experiments.[49] On 7 February 1943, four doctors and scientists from the internationally renowned Weigel Institute in Lviv were brought to Auschwitz alongside their families, namely the doctor and microbiologist Dr Ludwik Fleck, Dr Jakub Seemann, Dr Bernard Umschweif and Dr Owsiej Abramowicz. They were eventually transferred to Rajsko, where they had to participate in the development of typhoid fever vaccines.[50]

Another such prisoner was Professor Géza Mansfeld, a Hungarian-Jewish doctor and scientist of international repute. He had been arrested in Budapest on 24 March 1944 and sent to the Mauthausen concentration camp a few weeks later. In June, he was then transferred to Auschwitz – on the orders of SS headquarters in Berlin, as he was informed. He thus became one of the around fifty other prisoner-scientists who conducted research in Rajsko. Mansfeld himself participated in research projects on malaria and syphilis, but the renowned professor also penned a scientific paper on typhoid fever, which the SS physician Hans Delmotte promptly handed in as his own doctoral thesis.[51]

Henri Limousin, a professor of pathological anatomy and experimental forensics at the University of Clermont-Ferrand, was arrested in March 1944 for 'anti-German propaganda' and was sent to Dachau, where he was assigned to work in the morgue. In November 1944, he was transferred to Auschwitz where he was to work as a coroner. He was joined by fourteen other prisoners who were to replace the Polish prisoner-doctors and nurses sent to other concentration camps deep inside the Reich. However, Limousin fell sick before he could start his work.[52]

Nyiszli did not believe that Mengele and the KWI would let him survive considering what he had witnessed.[53] However, it appears as if nobody from the medical personnel was murdered for that reason, even though the SS was intent on erasing every trace of it. As mentioned earlier, the SS destroyed most of the documents detailing the crimes and even dug up the bodies of well over a million victims to have them burned, before getting rid of the ashes. The crematoria were likewise destroyed. Between October 1944 and the liberation of Auschwitz on 27 January 1945, around 85,000 prisoners – around 40,000 in the latter half of January – were marched off to be 'evacuated' to other camps. The last days of the camps were very chaotic.[54] Perhaps this was what allowed the prisoner-doctors to survive.

Mengele's 'research director' Epstein, the infirmary elder in Auschwitz-Birkenau, was left behind during the evacuation. He and a few other prisoner-doctors were to look after the around 3,000 prisoners who had been deemed 'unfit for transport'. On 27 January 1945 they were liberated by the advancing Red Army, which immediately set up a special commission to investigate the crimes committed at Auschwitz. Epstein and his colleagues became the commission's key witnesses right away. Moreover, Epstein was made a member of that commission, together with Max Grossmann, a professor of pathological anatomy from Zagreb. The commission soon got to work and in February and March 1945 alone interrogated around 200 witnesses.

Due to their extraordinary position, the prisoner-doctors had gained deep insights into the workings of the Auschwitz camp complex. They themselves were more than aware of this, and already prior to their liberation, several of them had risked their lives to gather evidence of the atrocities committed there by writing reports and copying or outright stealing documents. Many of these documents were hidden away, while others were smuggled out – after all, the infirmary in the main camp was one of the centres of the resistance within the camp.

Being trained doctors and academics, the prisoner-doctors were very familiar with writing down objective and precise reports. As a result, their writings and testimonies are very important sources, not just for historians. They were also key witnesses for post-war prosecutors and the testimonies of prisoner-doctors played a very prominent role in the Polish Auschwitz trials against former SS personnel.

On 4 March 1945, not even six weeks after their liberation, the four former prisoner-doctors: Professor Epstein, Professor Mansfeld, Dr Bruno Fischer from Prague and Professor Limousin, published an appeal to the 'international public'. Speaking as 'survivors of Auschwitz in Upper Silesia, the most infamous camp of human extermination' they wanted to give a 'brief overview of the horrors, killings and mutilations committed against innocent people of both sexes, of all ages, of nearly all nations, known to them.'[55] Over four pages, they laid out the crimes committed in Auschwitz: The shootings in Block 11 of the main camp, the killings via phenol injections, and the criminal medical experiments on living prisoners, who were treated like test animals. For the latter, they specifically mentioned the names of Dr Mengele, Dr Endress [Entress], Dr Klein, Dr Fischer, Dr Kitt, as well as SS-Sturmbannführer Professor Dr Klauberg [Clauberg]. They also stated that the greatest number of murders had been done via the gassings that had started in 1941.[56]

Throughout his testimonies, Epstein refused to talk about his role as Mengele's 'research director'. On 7 April 1945, the Polish investigative commission asked him about Mengele's medical experiments on children, he responded: 'I have no knowledge of this.'[57] He remained silent until his death – for very good reasons. Aside from forcing prisoners to participate in his experiments, Mengele, and many other SS physicians as well, sought to delegate the troublesome task of touring the infirmaries to select sick Jewish prisoners for the gas chambers. Some prisoner-doctors gave in to the pressure. According to the testimony of the Polish prisoner-clerk Tadeusz Joachimowski, Epstein was one of them; on Mengele's orders, he is said to have conducted repeated selections in the men's infirmary in Birkenau beginning in May 1944.[58] Epstein did not respond to such allegations.

Other prisoner-doctors, however, wrote about their experiences at length after liberation and published them. One of them was Nyiszli, Mengele's dissector-in-chief. Unlike Epstein, he had not been left behind in Auschwitz and was instead sent to Mauthausen, together with his colleagues, where they were later liberated by US troops. Physically and mentally broken, he travelled back home. However, his hopes of being reunited with his wife and his daughter were soon dashed. There was no trace of them. It was only in October 1945, six months after his own liberation, that suddenly and without warning they arrived at his doorstep. Their unexpected return brought back meaning into his life and helped him recover, although he did vow to never work with corpses again.[59]

Despite his extreme emotional pain, Nyiszli decided to write about his experiences in Auschwitz, including his work as a dissector for Mengele. He finished his book by March 1946 and published it the same year in Hungarian. His memoirs have since been translated into dozens of languages and are one of the most important testimonies 'of this dark time in human history'.[60] After the war, Nyiszli returned to work as a doctor at his local hospital until his death at the age of 55.

Epstein returned home as well. However, he was unable to return to his old position as the head of the children's hospital in Prague – the German University of Prague had been dissolved by the new Czechoslovak government as part of a wider de-Germanization policy that also saw the expulsion of ethnic Germans from the country. Epstein also had his academic titles revoked. He attempted to emigrate to the UK, but this failed when he could not find work as a paediatrician there.[61] Instead, he found employment at a private practice for the time being. In 1948, his academic titles were restored and on 1 October 1949, he was made the head of the paediatric department of the Bulovka hospital near Prague. He remained in this position until his death from a heart attack in 1962, aged 72.[62]

Many of the Jewish former prisoner-doctors decided to leave Europe altogether. Most went to Israel, while a substantial minority emigrated to the USA or to other countries. Some of the non-Jewish prisoner-doctors did so as well.

In 1961, several Polish former prisoner-doctors founded a magazine to give former concentration camp inmates – most of them Auschwitz survivors living in Poland – the opportunity to tell their stories. These *Zeszyty Oświęcimskie [Auschwitz Notebooks]* were published into the 1990s as a sub-section of the medical journal *Przegląd lekarski*.

Many tried to forget what they had experienced. The former prisoner-doctor Dr Lucie Adelsberger, for example, emigrated to the USA after 1945, where she was able to work as a doctor. She had published her experiences immediately after the war, but the memory of Auschwitz continued to take an increasingly heavy toll. In March 1970, the New Yorker lawyer Fritz Weinschenk contacted her on behalf of the German prosecutors, asking if she was willing to testify in the preliminary proceedings against the former prisoner-doctor Stefan Buthner (Budziaszek). She replied:

> I have to say that this name means nothing to me and that I have no recollection of it. Furthermore, I want to say that I am not able to give any further testimonies due to my health. In the afternoon of 21 March 1970, after the session with You and Mr Prosecutor Klein [,] I became so dizzy when I was on my way home that I could not walk on the street. That night and over the following nights I had constant heart cramps, no sleeping pills and tranquilizers were able to help me because I was re-living the events at Auschwitz in all their clarity. On Wednesday, 25 March, I had such a heavy, lasting heart cramp that I had to be admitted to the hospital as an emergency patient.[63]

Aside from trauma and ill health, prisoner-doctors also had to fear post-war prosecutors. Stefan Buthner was far from the only one, and in particular, prisoner-doctors who had been put in positions of authority or who had participated in medical experiments were often singled out by the justice system. Buthner had been the infirmary elder in Monowitz, before being transferred to Buchenwald during the 'evacuation' of Auschwitz, where he was liberated by the Americans. Buthner remained in Germany, passed his final examinations, earned his doctorate, and settled down in Hanover in 1951. Already in 1945, Polish authorities had launched an investigation into him that was quickly abandoned, however. Over ten years later, in 1961, West German prosecutors opened their own investigation against him. Like the earlier probe in Poland, most of the accusations were either demonstrably false or not verifiable and the case was dropped after fourteen years.

Dering, the former infirmary elder in the main camp, had fled Poland shortly after the war to escape the post-war Stalinist terror. He eventually immigrated to the UK. In the 1960s, he sued the author Leon Uris who claimed that Dering had participated in mass sterilization experiments in his international bestseller *Exodus*. These accusations could not be substantiated in court. Shortly before his death in July 1965, Dering was called into the German embassy in London where he gave testimony for the first Frankfurt Auschwitz Trial in the London embassy.

The infirmary elder in Birkenau, Zenkteller, also faced the wrath of the prosecution. In 1948, he was tried in front of the Kraków district court. The court acknowledged that he had been rough towards prisoners, including other prisoner-doctors, but that at the same time he had done his best to help sick prisoners. The court also did not find any evidence for him actively participating in selections, let alone him conducting selections on his own accord as he had been accused of having done, and he was acquitted.[64]

Enna Weiss, the head prisoner-doctor of the women's camp in Birkenau, is said to have been tried and acquitted in Czechoslovakia, before leaving for Australia. However, it is not entirely clear what happened to her afterwards. This is a common theme for many prisoner-doctors. For various reasons, including fear of legal persecution and public defamation, many prisoner-doctors tried their best to disappear. Indeed, it is notable that many went on to change their names after the war.

This was almost certainly the case with Grósz Chorin.

Chapter 8

Investigation Part I: Initial Breakthroughs

We received new medication for the sterilizations [...] I carried out the sterilizations with this triopan on twenty-six women from Bácska.
Auschwitz Notes

We were able to locate the environment Grósz Chorin was working in, but the man himself continued to elude us. Indeed, we failed to find any trace of him in both the documents and in the literature. We had to give up our research into his post-war life in Switzerland; nothing could be found regarding his school and university education, and Kaiser had still not given us the documents she had promised, such as his death certificate or even her own birth certificate.

This was most likely the result of his repeated name changes – and bad luck regarding missing files. Additionally, Kaiser herself may have had second thoughts about providing us with more necessary documents as well, which was not exactly surprising considering the circumstances.

What was particularly irksome was that not even his fellow prisoner-doctors in Auschwitz had mentioned him in their testimonies, neither to the commission nor to the Polish prosecutors later on. I thus began to suspect that Grósz Chorin had perhaps been in Auschwitz under a false name as well.

Such cases are known to historians and frequently appear in the sources. A well-known example is that of the Polish medical student Jerzy Tabeau (1918–2002). Following the German invasion and occupation of Poland in September 1939, he joined the Polish resistance and adopted the cover name Jerzy Wesołowski. In early

1942, he was arrested and deported to Auschwitz, where he was given the number 27273. He was initially forced to do heavy labour in the various outer commandos, but contracted pneumonia and was sent to the infirmary in the main camp, where he remained as a nurse following his recovery. In April 1943 he was made the barrack clerk of the Gypsy family camp, where he stayed until 19 November 1943, when he and another Polish prisoner successfully escaped the camp to rejoin the resistance.

As early as December 1943, Wesołowski began to work on a report detailing the realities of Auschwitz. He finished his work in early 1944, which was then sent to the Polish government-in-exile in London where it was translated into English and published as *The Polish Major's Report*. Wesołowski himself remained in Poland and fought against the Germans until the end of the occupation. After the war, he gave up his cover name and continued to study medicine under his real name, eventually becoming a respected cardiologist in Kraków. Only in the early 1980s was it revealed that he was the author of *The Polish Major's Report*.[1] Because of the post-war persecution of the Polish resistance by the new communist regime, Tabeau had resolved to remain quiet about his previous resistance activities.

However, Tabeau was not Jewish, and for Jews it was much harder to keep their true identities hidden. Still, this remained a possibility we did not want to rule out immediately.

We thus began to look for Jewish prisoner-doctors whose personal information and activities in Auschwitz roughly matched those of Grósz Chorin. We based our search on the preliminary translation of the Auschwitz Notes as well as Kaiser's information regarding her grandfather and the already examined sources and the literature on this topic. As luck would have it, we soon found someone.

Dr Maximilian (Max) Samuel was born in 1880, a year after Grósz Chorin (1879). This was important, since there were very few prisoner-doctors of a similar age in Auschwitz, such as Eugen Reach (1877),[2] Géza Mansfeld (1882)[3] and Erwin Valentin (1883).[4] None of them was known to have participated in medical experiments in the main camp or Birkenau – unlike Dr Samuel. He was an experienced gynaecologist who – like Grósz Chorin – had to take part in various experiments in Auschwitz.

Among the prisoner-doctors known to have been forced to participate in the experiments in Auschwitz, Dr Samuel was the only one above the age of 60. Before the war, he had been a gynaecologist in Cologne, but following the German pogroms in November 1938 he and his family had fled to neighbouring Belgium. In the summer of 1942, he tried to flee the now-occupied Belgium to Switzerland, but was caught on the way and imprisoned at the Drancy concentration camp in occupied France. Shortly afterwards, he, his wife and his daughter were deported to Auschwitz, arriving on 31 August 1942. His wife was murdered upon arrival, but their daughter and Dr Samuel were deemed 'fit for labour'. After several weeks in the main camp infirmary, he was sent to the sub-camp of Golleschau as a prisoner-doctor; according to some witnesses, he also worked as a prisoner-doctor in Monowitz. On 18 May 1943, Dr Samuel was transferred back to the main camp and became the prisoner-doctor-in-chief in Block 10.[5]

It was in that block that the infamous experiments on mostly Jewish women were conducted. As mentioned earlier, most of these experiments were about testing new methods of sterilization, but some focused on researching uterine cancer and other illnesses.[6] As the chief prisoner-doctor in Block 10, Dr Samuel participated in these experiments on the orders of Dr Wirths, Professor Clauberg and Dr Schumann. Wirths and his brother were focused on researching uterine cancer, while Clauberg sought to sterilize Jewish women by sealing their fallopian tubes via injections. Schumann, meanwhile, sterilized both Jewish men and women by bombarding them with x-rays.[7] Initially, Samuel's task was to take tissue samples for the Wirths brothers when they went beyond just colposcopies. For Clauberg and Schumann, Dr Samuel confirmed the damage the injections and radiation treatments had caused in the women. However, Samuel's skills as a doctor were apparently not up to par. According to the prisoner-doctor Dr Dobrosława Klein, even the minor procedures Samuel conducted such as simple tissue removal for the Wirths brothers 'very often' caused secondary bleeding. In October 1943, the Polish prisoner-doctor Dr Dering, an experienced surgeon who had by then been made the elder of the prisoner infirmary in the main camp, was given the task of carrying out all the procedures in that block. When Dering arrived, the women Dr Samuel had operated on were still suffering from infected wounds that would not heal until several weeks later.[8] Nevertheless, the name Dr Samuel did not appear once in the Auschwitz Notes, whereas all the others – Clauberg, Wirths, but also many of the prisoner-doctors – were mentioned by name. What was going on here?

Judging from the sources, it appears as if Dr Samuel was murdered in Auschwitz in either 1943 or 1944. However, the testimonies varied so widely regarding the date and circumstances of his death[9] that the United Nations War Crimes Commission put Dr Samuel on the list of wanted war criminals in November 1945, on the charges that he had 'performed experimental operations on female prisoners (March 1943 – August 1944)'. His presumed place of residence: 'Cologne'.[10]

The War Crimes Group of the US Army also included him on its list of perpetrators at the Auschwitz concentration camp with the following description: 'Subject performed ex-ray [*sic*] castrations on inmates of Auschwitz CC [Concentration Camp], and excision of ovaries. Subject participated in the sterilization [of] women inmates. [...] Subject was allegedly shot in September 1944. Present whereabouts unknown.'[11]

The question of what had actually happened to Samuel remained shrouded in mystery. Erna Fleig, one of the victims in Block 10, recalled that Dr Samuel had told her and other women that 'he wrote a book about his work [i.e. the experiments regarding cervical cancer]. Once that book was finished, he was shot. This was a rumour in Birkenau; nobody saw him since then.'[12]

This rumour raised our suspicions – perhaps our Grósz Chorin was none other than Dr Samuel himself, who may have survived his sudden disappearance? Or maybe he, Grósz Chorin, had assumed Samuel's identity early on with the help of Wirths and Mengele, the real Samuel having been killed much earlier.

Ordinary prisoners did not have access to the barracks of the Sonderkommando in Birkenau, where Grósz Chorin had worked for Mengele. This included many of the other prisoner-doctors as well.[13]

The former Polish prisoner-doctor Professor Jan Olbrycht testified during the trial of Rudolf Höss in March 1947 that Samuel 'had been chosen to found a new research centre in Birkenau. And in the evening, a message arrived [from Auschwitz-Birkenau]: "has died".'[14] This seemed very odd – perhaps someone had intentionally spread a rumour to cover his tracks? This incident would also have been the perfect opportunity for an identity swap. Turning Grósz Chorin into Samuel – or the other way around – would have been easy during such a transfer. This would also explain the odd issue of Grósz Chorin having been a specialist in the fields of neuroanatomy and brain research prior to his deportation to Auschwitz, before then turning into a gynaecologist, and not a very good one at that.

Both possibilities seemed rather adventurous – but research hypotheses are allowed to be wild. After all, their purpose is to widen one's perspective to also include the seemingly impossible, so that one does not commit too early to a particular interpretation of the sources that threatens to obfuscate the facts. In the end, what is decisive is which theses can be proven valid in view of the evidence, and which cannot.

When Kaiser then announced to us in August 2015 that we were soon to be given some of the documents that had been originally sent to Rome, we were filled with new hope. These documents, which were said to include her grandfather's post-war memoirs, promised to answer our most pressing questions. They would certainly confirm his true identity, as well as clear up some of the contradictions within the Auschwitz Notes.

Indeed, the Auschwitz Notes did contain clear mistakes. Many of them were likely due to Grósz Chorin's growing luminal addiction. For example, he wrote about Hitler visiting the Auschwitz concentration camp, which according to all known sources did not happen. Hitler never set foot inside a concentration camp, let alone a death camp like Auschwitz. Nevertheless, Grósz Chorin described in detail how the sick in Barrack 12 were to be cared for and made ready, how the camp was cleaned up under great secrecy, and the doctors were given new clothing that identified them as members of the Sonderkommando. And then it happened:

> The door opens: Generals and a Marshal-Colonel walk in with a marshal staff. 'The Führer'. Does this crazy Hitler feel no shame. […] The German Nazi-officers were greeted by Hitler with a raised arm and handshakes. He also shook my hand/he trembled, the handshake was wet and weak. […] – for a moment I wondered/ I looked at him, thinking that he was looking at me, but in his eyes, there was no glimmer anymore.

The delegation then visited Barrack 12. Mengele, whose penchant for singing is quite well-known, performed opera arias for Hitler. Half an hour later, the 'Führer' and his entourage crossed paths with Grósz Chorin again:

> When Hitler walked past me, he looked at me – his eyes were full of hate [*sic*] – he tapped me on the right shoulder and then I said 'Heil Hitler'/ I will never forgive myself for this, not even when I turn a hundred years old/ No, no, how low did I have to fall. I told him Heil Hitler and raised my right hand.

This account was as impressive as it is impossible.

However, as fate would have it, there were strong indicators that there was, in fact, a grain of truth in this story. In late May 1944, the air force general Erich Quade had visited the Auschwitz concentration camp. The camp commander's order No. 25/44 from 11 May 1944 states, among others: 'Wednesday, 31.05.1944, 20 o'clock: Lecture by the general of the airmen Quade: "German aerial warfare".'[15]

General Quade was five years older than the prematurely aged Hitler, had a similar moustache and wore a white general's uniform during his visit to Auschwitz. A civilian like Grósz Chorin could easily mistake his uniform for one of a marshal, and Quade for Hitler. As the photograph album of Karl-Friedrich Höcker shows,[16] the similarities were striking (see Plate 3).

Quade was not the only prominent guest at Auschwitz. Time and time again, high-ranking officials from the Wehrmacht, the party and other agencies visited the camp; some even toured the extermination facilities.[17]

The chance of such a mix-up was further increased by Grósz Chorin's addiction to luminal, which became obvious even during the cursory, preliminary translation. Prior to the supposed Hitler visit, Grósz Chorin had written in detail about how he had been taking the drug to escape the daily horrors of the camp. In his entry from 20 July 1943, for example, he wrote:

> I gather the leftover medication and glasses. With a fogged brain and trembling legs, I make my way home. As I arrive home, I stumble into my room. Today I do not classify any medication/ sort no glasses/I take luminal and lie down. Today's dose of luminal is 30 mg/ will it help against the funeral pyre illness?

And later:

> Luminal 40mg/luminal 50mg/ Depression! Depression!

Among the known side-effects of luminal are dizziness, concentration problems, drowsiness, disorientation and impaired judgement. At higher dosage, hallucinations and altered perception are common too. Given the trauma from the atrocities he regularly had to witness – and participate in – in Auschwitz, it seemed very plausible that he mistook the visit of the Nazi grandee for a personal encounter with the 'Führer' himself.

In the summer of 2015, we made yet another, albeit minor, breakthrough. The meaning of the mysterious columns of numbers in the 'Trachoma' book and the Gedeon notebooks had long eluded us. Now we had been able to crack the code of the first page in each of the books, but unfortunately nothing more. Aside from numbers, Grósz Chorin had also resorted to using special signs that were to encrypt his work (see Plate 4).

For us, only the numbers 5705-5706 as well as 5704 made sense – they conformed to the Hebrew calendar and stood for the years 1943-1944 and 1942, respectively. The signs, meanwhile, made no sense to us. We contacted Kaiser to help us, but even she did not know what these signs were. However, during one of our meetings with her that summer, she mentioned that her grandfather had been interested in medieval Hungarian writing systems.

I immediately set to work and soon found the origin of the symbols: the old Hungarian runic script. It is still known among interested circles in Hungary and there are letter lists available online,[18] with which I was able to decipher the writing on the cover page:

> Emil, Salámon Fri[t]z
> Grósz Chorin
> Professor Dr. med.
> 5705-5706 [1943-1944]
> 5704 [1942]
> […]
> Auschwitz

This discovery spurred me on. Emil and Frigyes (Fritz) were two of Grósz Chorin's sons, which he chose to mention on the cover page for some reason. After deciphering this code, I was also sure we could decipher the rest of it in due time as well. At this point I was genuinely excited about which new clues I would find in the documents that were to be delivered to us soon.

Chapter 9

'This is the Heart, the Central Piece.'

I had loved a Jewish boy very much – so at my request Dr Mengele did not harm him!! Primus Levi

Memoirs, page 73

As we eagerly awaited the arrival of the new documents, there came another unexpected delay. In August and September of 2015 the European migrant crisis was in full swing, and as a physician working for the Vatican, Kaiser was now working ceaselessly to provide basic humanitarian aid to the refugees and migrants coming to Europe. As a result, the handover was postponed again and again. By early September, Kemény had more or less finished transcribing and translating the Auschwitz Notes, but because we knew that the post-war memoirs would be able to solve most if not all of the discrepancies found in the Auschwitz Notes, we set them aside for the time being. After all, we did not want to waste our time with research that would likely soon be proven superfluous.

It was only by early October that Kaiser was granted a reprieve. I thus drove to Munich to pick up the released documents from her apartment. To my surprise, there were several people I did not yet know with her, namely her driver Attila, alongside his family. Considering how secretive she usually was, it was clear that she trusted them.

In Munich, I was given a sealed wooden box. The next day, with Wassert present as well, we opened it at Lothfels' mansion. Two notebooks came to light as well as a book from 1911 that was filled with written notes, alongside a number of other documents. The first notebook was from 1943 and contained several entries of varying length in Hungarian, written in pencil. The second notebook was from 1934; it contained brief shorthand notes in both Hungarian and German, written with a copy pen.

The most important find was something else, however. With the words 'This is the heart, the central piece', Kaiser took out a book from the pile of documents. *Útmutató Az Èlettani Gyakorlatokhoz* [A Guide to Biology Exercises] had been published in Budapest in 1911 and had a very curious feature – every double page is printed on one side only. The right page was thus always clear, which Grósz Chorin used to write down his words using a copy pen. In total, there were 108 pages filled with writing like this (see Plate 5). The last entry was from 18 November 1964. These were the memoirs we had been waiting for.

It was immediately clear the texts had all been written by the same person who wrote the Auschwitz Notes – which meant that they were authentic. However, the style was different this time. Some, such as the medical notebook from 1934, were written in shorthand, apparently during his time in Auschwitz. The notebook from 1943, as well as the book with his memoirs, were kept in a much longer style and were most likely written after the war.

This was great news: They most likely contained what we had needed to fill in the gaps of the earlier, very cursory notes. In my opinion, the earlier notes had probably served mostly to refresh Grósz Chorin's memory. But even that would have been extremely risky in the camp and especially in the Sonderkommando.

Now that we finally had access to more information, we hoped that we could also progress on deciphering the still-encrypted notes in the old books. At any rate, our information base had suddenly expanded considerably, and by comparing the newer information to what we already had, we hoped to fully trace Grósz Chorin's path. A cursory examination of the new materials confirmed our hopes. In the medical notebook from 1934, in particular, we noticed several familiar names of doctors and victims, as well as information hinting at experiments, which all coincided with what we knew from our preliminary research and the Auschwitz Notes.

To get a full picture, Kemény began to transcribe and translate the 'Central Piece' as well as the medical notebook from 1943. Meanwhile, I travelled to Kyiv, St Petersburg and Moscow for research.

The new information soon confirmed our suspicion that Grósz Chorin and Max Samuel were very connected. The old wooden box that had contained the documents even had a small brass plate with the initials 'S.M.' – 'Samuel Maximilian'?

While the Auschwitz Notes had named several doctors engaged in the sterilizations and had hinted at Grósz Chorin's participation in these experiments, the medical notebook from 1943 confirmed this and also suggested that there had been some kind of identity swap. Page 41 of the memoirs, for example, reads:

> I had to work together with Dr Schumann for two years. In 1941 he had arrived in Auschwitz – back then I was not there yet – and in 1944 he left Auschwitz.

In another passage on pages 79-81, he writes:

> Eduard Wirth and his secretary, the Austrian Hermann Langbein – I met with them as late as May (1950)! They were my elders i.e. my immediate superiors. [...] On the ramp, I witnessed Dr Wirth's first selections. He selected for research. He never exchanged a word with me, but he always sent the French doctor to me this Adelaide H. [Hautval]. She was a very beautiful woman, but she could never laugh.

In the medical notebook from 1943, the following entry caught our eye:

> 1958 Meeting with Wladyslaw Dehring!! In London. Brutal + arrogant.

As mentioned earlier, the sterilization experiments in Auschwitz had been conducted by two German doctors – Carl Clauberg and Horst

Schumann. They were assisted by several prisoner-doctors, but only two of them participated for a significant amount of time: Samuel and Dering – who had moved to Great Britain after the war. Clauberg had appeared repeatedly in the Auschwitz Notes, and the appearance of Schumann and Dering in the new documents – as well as the absence of Samuel – completed the picture. The only reference to him was on page 41 in connection with Schumann, when he wrote about a 'Prof. S. from Cologne' who 'also assists'. Given Grósz Chorin's diligence in naming everyone he met in his laboratory, especially the doctors, this was very suspicious. Even in the medical notebook from 1934, in which we immediately recognized most of the names since it was kept in German, the name of Samuel was missing.

As for Dering, he owed his survival to Clauberg. In 1944, Dering was released from Auschwitz and was conscripted to work at Clauberg's women's clinic in Königshütte (now Chorzów) in Upper Silesia.[1]

Dering's was not the only case of a prisoner-doctor being released from Auschwitz thanks to the intervention of an SS physician. Grabczyński was, like Dering, a Polish surgeon who was forced to conduct surgeries on behalf of Schumann and Wirths, including castrations. In late March 1944, however, he was released from Auschwitz on the orders of the camp's first SS physician. Following his release, Grabczyński had to remain in the town of Auschwitz (Oświęcim) at Wirths' disposal, who wanted to employ him in the new SS hospital that was being built there.[2]

Perhaps this is also what had happened to Samuel. Maybe one of the SS physicians intervened on his behalf? However, there were strong arguments against this: Unlike the Poles Dering and Grabczyński, Samuel was Jewish. Furthermore, neither Dering nor Grabczyński had been part of the secretive Sonderkommando. Such considerations were very important inside Auschwitz.[3]

Aside from their race and role within the camp, the most significant factor was the professional esteem the prisoner-doctors were held in by Wirths and the other SS physicians. Clauberg wanted Dering for his women's clinic in Königshütte and Wirths wanted Grabczyński for his hospital in Auschwitz.

Regarding the relationship between Wirths and Samuel, surviving witnesses made very divergent statements. Felicja Pleszowska, one of the prisoner-nurses in Block 10, testified that Wirths had treated Samuel very well, seeing him as an authority on scientific matters. The camp's SS first physician allegedly even tried to have the Jewish Samuel be reclassified as 'Aryan'.[4] This would have made releasing Samuel much easier. Jan Olbrycht, a key witness in the Höss trial, similarly said that his fellow prisoners congratulated Samuel that 'he enjoyed such a great deal of confidence' among the SS physicians; however, he thought this was fictitious, since to his knowledge, Samuel was murdered immediately afterwards.[5] The French prisoner-doctor Adelaide Hautval, who had been mentioned by name in Grósz Chorin's writings, testified that Samuel had been able to leave the camp with a special permit personally given to him by Wirths.[6]

On the other hand, Wirths' secretary Hermann Langbein, an Austrian communist imprisoned for political reasons, remarked that Wirths had a low opinion of Samuel. Many prisoner-doctors did not think highly of him either. The prisoner-doctor Klein criticized him in a report that was smuggled out of Auschwitz in late 1943. According to her, during the shoddy surgeries he conducted for the Wirths brothers, 'this Samuel developed such a speed (3 or more a day) that was not required of him' and that even after the cessation of these experiments, he was torturing these women with daily gynaecological exams and colposcopies without any need, simply 'to keep his position'.[7]

Tadeusz Paczuła, another former prisoner who was the infirmary report writer, as well as Dering, remarked later on that Samuel was 'covered with wet eczema' and that he had a 'festering face', and thought that the disgust of the SS for him directly led to his death.[8] In a way, however, this matched Grósz Chorin's earlier Auschwitz Notes – he had repeatedly complained about open wounds and 'boils on the face'. There was also another factor: According to the Auschwitz Notes, Wirths' wife had arrived at Auschwitz already sick, and that it had been Samuel who healed her of her affliction in November 1942. If this was true, Wirths likely felt indebted to him.

To make matters even more confusing, it may not even have been Samuel's relationship with Wirths that was decisive here, but his relationship with Mengele. According to Olbrycht's testimony in the Höss trial, Samuel was transferred to Birkenau in May or June 1944, just when Mengele was searching for prisoner-doctors to staff his new research station there.

Already, the Auschwitz Notes had made it clear that Grósz Chorin's relationship with Mengele was both close and highly complex. Perhaps it was he who had been responsible for protecting Grósz Chorin/Samuel in the camp, helped him disguise his identity and then flee the camp. I had found out earlier that the escape story Kaiser had told me was not true. The former German hospital in Kraków had kept its files from the period – and they recorded no admission of a patient with the last name of Mengele during that timeframe.

In early December, I finally returned from my research travels abroad. In the meantime, Kemény had finished transcribing the documents I had sent to him, so I decided to send him additional passages from Grósz Chorin's memoir for him to transcribe. I picked up the 'Central Piece' once again to search for more passages that seemed to be of particular interest due to the names of relevant people or other similar clues. Suddenly, towards the end of the book, on page 165, I saw a peculiar set of numbers: 0048 33 8448015.

A seven-digit Polish telephone number!

Chapter 10

Investigation Part II: The Search for the Source

The […] lie will win, the story will be distorted!

Memoirs, page 135

As soon as I saw the phone number I knew this was a forgery. According to the memoir itself, Grósz Chorin had finished writing it on 18 November 1964. However, the country code for Poland – 0048 – was only introduced in the 1960s, the area code (0)33 in the 1970s, and seven-digit phone numbers were first introduced in Poland in 2001.[1] By 2001, Grósz Chorin had been dead for twenty-four years, according to his granddaughter.

For the time being, I did not share my suspicions. I did, however, change my approach regarding the translation. Instead of bits and pieces, I now sent Kemény longer passages of up to ten pages from different sections of the memoirs. Before long, he too voiced his own concerns – the text apparently contained a series of highly suspicious style breaks.

This was very alarming. I immediately contacted my colleague from Kraków who I had already talked to earlier regarding the forensic verification of the documents. Like the Auschwitz Notes, the documents we received later had been written on paper from that time period, either in pencil or copy pen. It was therefore impossible to confirm or reject their veracity on that account. Nevertheless, the expert was able to give me valuable advice. The key to his considerations was the aforementioned episode where Hitler was said to have visited Auschwitz. A forger, my colleague theorized, would likely not include such an easily disprovable story. But what if this was intentional? Indeed, one of the most convincing things about Grósz Chorin's story had been that it contained seemingly impossible things that began to make sense upon close inspection. Another thing my colleague pointed out was the inconsistencies in the handwriting. As I drove home, I therefore resolved to have the handwriting analyzed by a professional.

Several days after my return, Kemény came as well. As soon as he arrived, I asked him to look at the passage with the telephone number and to translate it. This was the result:

> I had a very nice patient from Hungary – from Budapest. Dr Gyula Motorcza had nearly become prime minister of Kanada [likely the storage barracks in Auschwitz, not the country]. His telephone number in Poland was 0048 33 8448015 – the number of Mengele!

Regardless of whose telephone number it was, it absolutely was not Mengele's. And who was this Gyula Motorcza? After a quick search, Kemény had found the answer. In 2011, Motorcza had privately published a book titled *Keresse Dr. Menegelét! Tel.: 0048 33 8448015* [Call Dr Mengele! Phone: 0048 33 8448015] (see Plate 6). The telephone number was the same as the one in the memoir and belonged, as Motorcza stated in the foreword, to the Auschwitz Museum. Motorcza had picked the number as he could not think of a better title.

Did 'Grósz Chorin' plagiarize Motorcza's book? Did he plagiarize others as well?

Kemény and I now began to search for more evidence. On the page with Mengele's supposed phone number, we spotted several plagiarized sentences. They were all lifted from page 13 of Motorcza's book and were either slightly paraphrased (shown in italics in the below translation) or outright copied (underlined):

> Even though he [Mengele] saved my life and the lives of my three sons, I cannot forgive him for what he has done in Auschwitz! I <u>detest him. With unquenchable hate I think of him. The gracious God will forgive me for this.</u> *He played the piano very beautifully*

> *and sang very well, I got from him* South American motifs he had carved out of wood by himself. He was a precise, exact, pedantic and masculine man, on his pleasant face one could not find any criminal features.
>
> Aside from me, he also saved hundred/50 other doctors from the camp.
>
> He never yelled at his children and his patients. Calmly, with his [...] method, he killed them, not he himself, he only gave the sign.

This was everything that had been plagiarized from Motorcza's book, but the similarities were stunning. What was also clear was that the person or the persons who had written this evidently had not read the original very closely, otherwise the blunder with the phone number would not have happened.

As we continued our investigation, we quickly found that the passages copied from Motorcza's book were only the tip of the iceberg. Indeed, a whole slew of exclusively Hungarian publications – books, articles, internet posts – had been plagiarized, in some cases even going on for pages. No wonder Kemény had noticed so many style breaks.

Over the coming days, the supposed memoir thus revealed itself to be a colourful collage of non-fiction texts such as the book *Emberkisérletek a náci haláltáborokban* [Human Experiments in the Nazi Death Camps] by the journalist Attila Kirády, various literary texts and poems, and – perhaps most egregiously – Simon Wiesenthal's autobiography *Justice, Not Vengeance*. By far the most plagiarized text was Kirády's book, which had been first published in 2004 and has since been re-published several times, with the latest edition having come out in 2015, just months prior to the hand-over of the 'Central Piece'. We found that the author – or the authors – of the memoirs had plagiarized from pages 9-10, 13, 16-17, 23-4, 64, 76, 77, 108, 125, 143, 148, 157, 167-168, 183, 203, 208-209, 214, 223, 235-238, 269-70 and 273. At times, only a single sentence or subclause was lifted from the original text, sometimes it was just a name, sometimes an entire paragraph.

Pages 235 to 238 in particular had attracted the attention of the forger. They dealt with medical experiments in Imperial Japan between 1936 and 1945, and were nearly completely copied. Only a few changes (shown here in italics) had been made to make it appear more 'authentic', as an example on page 67 of the memoir demonstrates:

> Dr. Ken Yuasa, a Japanese surgeon – *he was even worse than our Mengele* – worked in a hospital in China during the war…[2]

Simon Wiesenthal's memoirs had been plagiarized in a similar fashion, with an omission here and an addition there. His autobiography had been published in Hungarian in 1991,[3] and from it, the forger had copied content word for word from pages 437-9, 503-504 and 508. They were found scattered across Grósz Chorin's memoir, specifically on pages 119, 121, 123, 125 and 127.

In terms of literary plagiarism, the memoir exclusively focused on the works of well-known Hungarian poets and authors who were either Jewish or of Jewish origin. On pages 143-55, we repeatedly found passages from Imre Kertész' *Fatelessness,*[4] as well as the poems 'Admonisher' and 'Preface' from the novel *Voronezh* by István Örkény,[5] and a haiku from Zoltán Zelk's collection titled *Meszelt égbolt* [Whitewashed Sky] published in 1976. Another source of inspiration was the preface of Frigyes Karinthy's poetry collection *Nem mondhatom el senkinek* [I Cannot Tell Anyone], which was partly copied as well. Among the more recent literary works that had been copied was a contribution by the poet Stefánia Mándy that appeared in the newspaper *Múlt* és *jövö* [Past and Present] in 2000; the memoirs had lifted excerpts from the introduction and the epilogue, as well as the poems 'Egy halott álmaiból' [From the Dreams of a Dead Man] and 'Kíntorna' [Hurdy Gurdy].[6] The latter had been first published in 1992 as part of a poetry collection with the title *Az ellopott történelem* [The Stolen History] – which was rather amusing considering the circumstances.[7]

In the end, we found that over 60% of the 'Central Piece' had been plagiarized. The rest had evidently been made up freely in such a way that during a superficial reading, the disparate stolen works would merge into a complete narrative of a tormented man, who wrote down the different entries at different points over the course of his life, with changing priorities and perspectives.

In December 2015, we were still not aware of the scope of the plagiarism. However, we knew already that the memoir was not an authentic document. Nevertheless, Kemény finished the transcription of the memoir and translated it alongside the pocket diary from 1943. After all, we needed a solid textual basis to verify our suspicions. At the same time, Kemény started an internet search to find evidence of the books we had been given in the first and second deliveries from Grósz Chorin's supposed estate. Once again, he quickly found what he was looking for. On the website of a Hungarian internet antiquarian bookstore – www.antikvarium.hu – he found listings of every single book we had received. Although it was not clear if Grósz Chorin's books had been bought there, this was certainly a hint to a possible source. At the same time, this reinforced our belief that we were dealing with a forgery.

With all these pieces of evidence in our hands, I contacted the foundation funding the project and asked for a meeting. Additionally, I wrote to the handwriting expert I had been recommended and sent her writing samples from the Auschwitz Notes, the memoirs, the pocket diary from 1943 and the medical calendar from 1934. Indeed, our suspicions had since spread to all the documents we had received, even the seemingly authentic ones we had received back in January.

In late January 2016, we received the results of the handwriting analysis. The expert, Professor Dr Ewa Gruza, was a former judge at the Polish Supreme Court and now held the chair of criminology at the Institute of Criminal Law at the University of Warsaw. She had analyzed the general typeface and line work, measured the width and height of the writing, taking into account the various type sizes, analyzed the topography of the writing regarding the horizontal orientation of the lines of text and the spacing, both between the lines and words, as well as to the right and left edges of the pages, in addition to eighteen different letters to find consistent features. Her verdict was unambiguous: All four texts had been written by the same person.[8]

Everything had been a forgery: The memoirs and the pocket diary from 1943, but also the Auschwitz Notes we had spent so much energy verifying, with seeming success. The shorthand notes with the names and medical notes in the medical diary from 1934 were likewise fake.

In the meantime, we had also analyzed the notebooks from 1934 and 1943 and found serious issues there as well. Thus, Professor Gruza's report did not really surprise us. We had already known that much if not everything had been fake, but it still snuffed out all remaining hope.

The writings in the pocket diary from 1943 that were meant to supplement the memoirs were structured in the same way as the 'Central Piece'. Again, it was a collage of multiple Hungarian texts taken from various books, newspaper articles and internet posts, intertwined with self-written passages. As in the memoirs, the original parts were supposed to give the impression that the author was an elderly, first person narrator who tried to bundle together his often very elaborate trains of thought – here mostly about the history of Judaism and the persecution of Jews in Hungary. While the sources were different from the memoir, the system was the same.[9]

This was not the case for the medical diary from 1934, which was not a coherent text but rather a collection of very brief shorthand notes that did not really seem to make sense at first glance. As a result, I had initially believed them to have been nothing more than scribbles meant to help Grósz Chorin remember things later on, when he was writing down the full story in more detail. We had therefore thought these entries to be hard to decipher but overall harmless.

One of the key figures in the Auschwitz Notes was Dr Dénes Görög, a coroner from Szombathely in Hungary. He had worked at the local hospital since 1929 before being deported to Auschwitz in May 1944. In the camp, he was assigned to Nyiszli's team and was forced to participate in the dissection of murdered prisoners. Görög did not survive the war, but he nevertheless played a major role in the narrative.

However, our research quickly found that even the notes on the first page had been plagiarized, this time from a work by Dr Ferenc Garzuly. Born in 1937, Garzuly became a neurologist and neuropathologist at the hospital in Szombathely, where he developed an acute interest in the history of that hospital. He had since published his research in a book,[10] as well as in an article, which is freely available online.[11]

In said article, Garzuly writes about the history of the hospital's coroner's office between 1920 and 1946. He frequently cites the remaining autopsy records, and since Görög was the hospital's chief coroner at the time, he is often mentioned. As we went through the article, we could not help but notice the many similarities between it and Grósz Chorin's supposed notes in the medical diary from 1934:

Excerpt from Dr Garzuly's Article	Page 1 of the Medical Diary from 1934	Translation
Az elmeosztályon **1932-ben** kitört **hastífusz** járványt dr. Tanka Dezső főorvos írásából ismerhetjük meg. […] Az osztály »megfigyelőjében« ***51 beteg*** volt összezsúfolva, ezek közül 25 kapta meg a betegséget, közülük hét meg is halt. [12]	Dr Görög Dénessel dolgoztunk együtt **1932-ben** **Hastífusz 51 beteg**	We worked together with Dr Dénes Görög **in the year 1932** **Abdominal typhoid fever 51 sick**
1937-ben a **boncolás**ok száma **179**, 1938-ban visszaesik 107-re, majd fokozatosan újra emelkedik, **1942-ben** éri el a maximumot, 406 boncolást, de még 1943-ban is jelentős a szám, **320**. [...] Ismételten felüti a fejét a **Heine-Medin kór, skarlát, szamárköhögés, diftéria, tetanusz, vérhas, hastífusz.** [13]	**1932-ben 179 boncolás 1942-ben 320:**[14] **- Heine-Medin kór skarlát** **- szamárköhögés** **- diftéria** **- tetanusz** **- vérhas** **- hastífusz**	**1932 179 Dissections 1942 320:** **- Polio Scarlet fever** **- Whooping cough** **- Diphtheria** **- Tetanus** **- Dysentery** **- Abdominal typhoid fever**

We had thus discovered one of the main sources of this text as well. However, there were also pages containing lists of names (see Plates 7 and 8). After a brief search, we found that these were the names of the Auschwitz survivors that had been honoured with a photo series by the German newspaper *Süddeutsche Zeitung* on 27 January 2015. These were also found online together with brief accompanying profiles.[15] All of the persons named in the medical diary appeared there:

> *Janina Reklajtis* was deported from Warsaw to Auschwitz along with her mother as a 12-year-old and was registered there with the number 83043. Later she was sent to Berlin to do forced labour. She was liberated there.
>
> *Stefan Sot* came to Auschwitz in 1944 and was given the number 192705. Later, the Pole was sent to a labour camp as a teenager, where he had to work in the kitchen where the food for the SS was prepared.
>
> *Jacek Nadolny* is 77 years old. The Pole came to Auschwitz as a 7-year-old. Later, he was sent to a labour camp in Germany.
>
> *Danuta Bogdaniuk-Bogucka*, née Kaminska arrived in Auschwitz as a 10-year-old together with her mother. The girl was abused by the infamous SS physician Josef Mengele as part of his human experiments.
>
> *Bogdan Bartnikowski* from Warsaw is 82 years old. As a 12-year-old boy he was registered under the number 192731 in Auschwitz.

Other people mentioned in different parts of the medical diary also appeared on the same list, namely: Golda Pollac, Zofia Wareluk, Halina Brzozowska, Dr János Forgács, Erzsébet Brodt and László Bernath. From a similar list that was published in the Hungarian newspaper *HVG* on 27 January 2014, the forger or forgers lifted names as well: Danyi Béla, Fischhof Endre, Gáti György Karcag, Rados Anna, Szigety Imréné, Goldschmied Erzsébet and Varsáni Imre.[16]

Now that we had established that three of the texts we had received were forgeries, it was safe to say that the Auschwitz Notes, which had been written by the same hand, were forgeries as well. We thus did not even attempt to check them in detail. Likewise, we also discounted the notebooks with the long rows of numbers – trying to crack the code was too much work considering we already knew it was all fake.

At this point, we knew that these were forgeries and how these documents were forged. However, we neither knew who was behind this nor who had actually forged the documents, or for what purpose. Clarifying this was our next task.

It was evident that the person or group behind these forgeries had a great deal of expertise and criminal energy. Our first suspect was Professor Kaiser herself. After all, she had been the one who had given us all the documents in the first place.

Isabel Wassert refused to believe our suspicions about her long-time friend. On the contrary, when I shared my doubts about the documents with her before the end of the previous year, she believed that both Kaiser and Lothfels were victims of some kind of intrigue and sought to warn them immediately. I urged her to not do this and instead continued our investigations discreetly to uncover the supposed conspiracy against her friends. At any rate, I did not trust her judgement after that and asked the remaining team – János Kemény and my son Oliver – to not tell her anything about our investigation lest she warn her friend – and our prime suspect – about it.

Looking back, I recalled how odd it was that Professor Kaiser had been able to immediately locate and pull out the supposed 'Central Piece' in the second delivery – even though she supposedly knew nothing about the contents of the package. As I began to think more about it, other odd behaviours of hers began to pop into my mind as well. This all solidified my suspicions – but we still needed solid proof. Since we already had the handwriting analysis, the next logical step was to obtain a sample of the countess' handwriting and to compare it to the forgeries.

We soon found what we were looking for. In July 2015, Kaiser had gifted her friend Dr Wassert a porcelain doll that she had received from

'Uncle Fritz' in 1956. This 'Uncle Fritz' was none other than Mengele, who – according to both the Auschwitz Notes and the memoir – had repeatedly visited Grósz Chorin and his granddaughter after the war. Together with the doll, there had been an envelope that contained the eyes of the doll,[17] and this envelope had been labelled by Kaiser herself (see Plate 9).

Back then, I had barely paid attention to it and instead focused my efforts on analyzing the documents we had been given. But half a year later, in February 2016, I took the envelope and sent it to Professor Gruza for analysis. Given that both the words 'Fritz' and 'Uncle', as well as 'Engelberg' repeatedly featured in the forgeries, I hoped that this was enough for a comparison.

In the meantime, Wassert and I travelled to Budapest to meet with Kaiser in March 2016. There, Kaiser had organized a get-together of Holocaust survivors for us. Afterwards, we travelled to Oradea in Romania, where, thanks to her help, we were able to meet with Holocaust survivors and members of the Jewish Orthodox community.

She had taken care of everything. Her chauffeur Attila, who we had already met when we picked up the second batch of documents the previous year, drove us around, and rooms had been booked for us under the name 'Professor Dr Batthány-Szentágothay' in the luxurious Kempinski Hotel in Budapest.[18]

On the way to Oradea, we were offered a glimpse into Kaiser's charity network when we made a brief stop at an orphanage she had been supporting with funds from her friend Lothfels since 2013. When we arrived there, Kaiser was greeted with genuine gratitude and happiness. The warm welcome impressed everyone, including Dr Monika Reichenbach, a local Hungarian politician and lawyer, who was accompanying us on the trip.

Throughout the trip, I never brought up my suspicions regarding the forgeries. As long as we did not know who was behind this, it was best to keep the investigation a secret. Instead, I talked to Kaiser about our progress: The publication of the memoirs and the notebook from 1943 were well under way; the publisher had responded to the material with much enthusiasm, and the editing process had nearly been finished.

However, I noted that the publication of the Auschwitz Notes and the medical diary would take extra time, since the scientific processing of the documents required considerably more effort. The countess was very happy about the first message and expressed understanding regarding the second. In addition, she later informed us that an additional batch of documents had emerged and that we would receive them soon.

Kaiser had orchestrated the trip to Oradea for us to investigate a theory she had voiced earlier, namely that the famous report the coroner and Auschwitz-survivor Miklós Nyiszli had published in 1946 was not in fact his, but her grandfather's. According to her theory, Nyiszli had either died in Auschwitz or another concentration camp. By meeting with members of the Jewish Orthodox community and visiting their cemetery to seek out Nyiszli's grave, Kaiser hoped that we could this clear up.

While the documents we had been given had been very clearly fake, there were indeed similarities between Nyiszli's report and the Auschwitz Notes. For example, Grósz Chorin states at one point:

> That I/dissect/a head/I remove the skull cap/I remove the pituitary gland/ - everything is full of blood/ on the outer wall of the left heart chamber a small needle hole/- strong smell of chloroform/ - injected chloroform causes heart paralysis/'Phenylnutren/Phenyl injections'/ my knees shake with pąin/ heterochromia/ small eyes/ pairs of eyes, scraped out/I dissect./Dubois' abscess.

In his book, Nyiszli describes the dissection of four pairs of twins under the age of 10. According to him, they had been selected from the so-called Gypsy family camp due to their extraordinary physical characteristics – heterochromia – before being killed by an injection of chloroform to the heart. Nyiszli also noted the presence of the rare Dubois' abscess.[19] What a coincidence!

At another point, Nyiszli writes about a Jewish father with a hunchback and his disabled son. Nyiszli first had to examine both of them when they were still alive, before dissecting them after they were murdered and then having to make them 'ready for transport' to the KWI in Dahlem.[20] The Auschwitz Notes reference such an event as well. Indeed, there were several such coincidences, and finally there was this passage:

> Nyiszli is dead, but his/ data are with me/everything – everything.

In Oradea, we did not find Miklós Nyiszli's grave. The local Jewish Orthodox community knew about Nyiszli and his courageous report, but they knew nothing about him as a member of their community. Nevertheless, they agreed that Nyiszli had lived there.

While in Oradea, I witnessed a rather memorable event. As we entered the Jewish Orthodox synagogue, we had to hand our passports to a security guard who then wrote our names into the guestbook. Ever since realizing we were dealing with forgeries, I had grown suspicious of Kaiser's identity and made sure that I would be the one to collect the passes afterwards so that I could look at hers. Before I could do so, however, she stepped out of the synagogue and turned towards the neighbouring community centre. As soon as she saw me with the stack of passports in my hand, the elderly lady charged towards me with the words 'This is my passport!' and snatched hers. She was clearly very intent on me not getting a look at her passport.

Back in Budapest, I sought to involve Kaiser's driver Attila in a casual conversation without Kaiser present. On 12 March, the opportunity finally arrived. During a car ride through the city, we began to talk about all kinds of things when I asked him how long he had known the countess. 'For twenty-five years', he replied. 'I always drive her around when she comes to Budapest.' 'And Gänswein too?' I followed up. He confirmed: 'Yes, he always comes with Nicole.' I tried to dig deeper and asked him how often Pope Benedict's secretary was visiting, but Attila evaded the question and I changed the topic.

Another thing that perplexed me was that during one of our walks through Budapest, Kaiser recommended the very same online antiquarian bookstore to her Hungarian friends – www.antikvarium.hu – that Kemény had determined to be the source of some if not all the books, newspapers and so on, that we had received. We took this as further confirmation that the materials had indeed been bought there.

The website keeps the listings of items even after they have been sold. In some cases, some of the documents we received even included sales notes from the bookstore on their title pages and in other parts of the book (see Plates 10 and 11). The bookstore also listed the prices of the items. Books and the pocket diaries similar to those we had received were usually sold for a price of around 4,000 Forints, which was around 12.85 Euros at the time.

On the following day, we left Budapest by plane. However, on the way to the airport, Wassert noted that Kaiser had given her passport to her driver without any fuss so he could check in for her. This was very suspicious – he was clearly allowed to see something that was to be hidden from the rest of us.

In early April, we received the results from the second handwriting analysis. Aside from simply comparing the handwriting within the different texts, Professor Gruza also examined the time intervals in which the supposed Grósz Chorin had written down 'his' notes. According to the information we had received, he started writing about his experiences in 1942 and had continued for around three decades until the early 1970s.

Professor Gruza explained that a person's handwriting usually stabilizes around the age of 30, and people who write a lot and do so frequently, commonly develop many unique features. Afterwards, the handwriting does not change much, unless the writer becomes ill or their motor skills decline with age. Typical changes caused by aging that appear after 60 are the increased size of the writing, as well as that of the spacing, due to failing eyesight, and the writing thus becomes less fluid and more erratic, which affects both individual strokes as well as the entire style.

At the end of her analysis, Professor Gruza stated that 'In my more than twenty years of experience, I have never encountered handwriting that had not changed over the course of twenty to thirty years' – but this case was different. Despite having been in a concentration camp, experiencing extreme trauma, a growing luminal addiction and finally old age, the author had written as cleanly and consistently in the last entry as in the first. The conclusion was clear: The text was written in a relatively short timeframe, by someone under or around the age of 60. It was also evident that all the texts had been penned by the same person who had written on the envelope we had received from Kaiser.[21]

Could this really be true? Why would she a – highly respected physician who had served under three different popes, worked for the WHO, taught as a university professor and was also a very well-connected benefactor from a noble family – personally forge the documents? Even worse, why would she betray her close friends Lothfels and Wassert like that?

It was hard to fully grasp the implications of this at first. Her friend Wassert oscillated between acceptance and denial. The initial suspicion that we were dealing with a forgery had shaken her to the core and the realization that her friend had played some role in it made it even worse. Despite my insistence, Wassert had already implied to Lothfels back in January that we had our suspicions regarding the documents. However, we agreed that it was best to not tell Lothfels of this new revelation; that it had been Kaiser who had forged them. This would simply have been too much of a shock for her, and we decided to delay telling her until we had incontrovertible proof.

My relationship with Kaiser had always been more businesslike, so my reaction was relatively calm. Especially after the last trip to Budapest, I would have been surprised if she had not been behind the forgery. However, there were still plenty of questions to be answered: Did the Vatican physician forge everything on her own, or did she have the backing of a criminal network that helped her forge this rather impressive body of fake stories? The latter seemed very plausible, considering that the forgery required a great deal of specialized historical knowledge. Indeed, they even contained references to documents hidden away in archives such as one in the Jewish Museum in Budapest.

Another question arose as well: Namely, who exactly was she to begin with? Did the deception go much deeper than we knew? Before we discovered the answer to these questions, Wassert and I resolved to remain quiet and to pretend to everyone else – aside from Kemény and my son Oliver, who were both working with me – that we were continuing to work on our project as before.

In a way, we just did that. The more we transcribed and translated the memoirs – the book and the pocket diary from 1943 – the more we saw how the entire construct of lies had been set up. Aside from the many instances of plagiarism, we also found plenty of faked circumstantial evidence – someone clearly knew what she or they were doing. The passages not copied from other works were often meant to either reinforce our prior conceptions, explain something that had seemed puzzling at first, or to redirect our attention to something new. The memoirs went into a fair amount of detail regarding the relationship between Grósz Chorin and Mengele, more so than the Auschwitz Notes did. Curiously enough, the memoirs also contained plenty of hints that Grósz Chorin and Max Samuel were one and the same person.

According to the memoirs, Mengele had saved Grósz Chorin's three adult sons. To his shock, he ended up recognizing one of them – Albert, Kaiser's father – during a visit to the 'medical research and experimental barrack':

> … we pretended as if we did not know each other, I only revealed my secret to Dr Mengele when he promised that my son would be allowed to live! I was thankful for this long after the war and the liberation. So thankful that I never said anything bad about Dr Mengele to anyone. [p. 25]

It remained unclear how exactly Mengele had managed to save Grósz Chorin's son Albert, and there was no mention of how the others were saved. Did this mean something? Oddly enough, neither of the other two sons appeared in the memoirs by name. Dr Samuel, meanwhile, was said to have had a daughter in the camp whom he cared for intensely, his former colleague Dr Hautval later testified.[22]

What was also noteworthy was the evolution of the story of Grósz Chorin's escape from Auschwitz. I had established very early on that the first version, according to which in the autumn of 1944 Mengele personally took Grósz Chorin with him to a hospital in Kraków, from where a Polish Catholic priest helped him escape the country, could not possibly be true. I had known this from before we even received the first documents. However, as it would later turn out, her friend Wassert had told her about my suspicions – upon which she had scrapped the story and replaced it with a new one in the Auschwitz Notes. There, the escape happened later, in January 1945, when Mengele was leaving the camp during the evacuation. The Kraków hospital, which as she now knew had kept the patient records, had disappeared, as had the Polish priest.

Legally speaking, the first batch of documents had been given to me not by Kaiser, but by Lothfels. On paper, the countess had nothing to do with them. As for the second delivery of documents, there had never even been a transfer of rights. As a result, we technically had no potential legal claim against Kaiser.

Wassert and I decided to change this. Already during our visit to Budapest I had brought up the topic of transferring the rights from the 'heiress' to us, claiming that the publisher required this to happen. She had signalled her agreement and asked me to send her a draft. On 27 April, we were ready to sign this document:

> Subject:
>
> Notes by Prof. Dr. Salamon, Ferencz, Fülöp Grósz Chorin, former prisoner doctor in the concentration and extermination camp Auschwitz, from 18 November 1964, in Hungarian, written down in the book *Útmutató az élettani gyakarlatokhoz*, Budapest 1911;
>
> Notes from Prof. Dr. Salamon, Ferencz, Fülöp Grósz Chorin (no date) in Hungarian, written down in the Hungarian medical diary from 1943 (Állatorvossi Évkönyv 1943).
>
> Dr. Magdalena Nicole Kaiser Batthyány-Szentágothay, born 13 August 1950, granddaughter of Prof. Emil [*sic*] Salamon Grósz

> Chorin declares that the right of use for the abovementioned documents/notes is transferred to the following persons: Dr. habil. Bogdan Musial [...] Dr. med. Isabel Wassert [...].

With this, I now had the first piece of incontrovertible evidence linking Kaiser to the forged memoir. She felt safe and did not even notice that we had intentionally changed her supposed grandfather's name by adding 'Emil' at one point. I also used the opportunity to secretly take a picture of her licence plate – perhaps we could find something out about the owner that way.

Over the following months, we continued our investigation into Kaiser, while she continuously tried to mislead us and send us onto the wrong track. The earlier visit to Oradea was just one example of many. Miklós Nyiszli's missing grave was supposed to suggest that he had died during the war and that Grósz Chorin had been the true author of his famous report. However, when we revisited Oradea in June, we did in fact find his grave – not in the Jewish Orthodox cemetery where she had led us, but in the Jewish Reformed cemetery. Nyiszli's supposed death was featured in both the Auschwitz Notes and the memoir; with him being cared for both times by a devoted Grósz Chorin who could not save him in the end.

In the Auschwitz Notes, the author even gets confused regarding his own identity. According to an entry from the year 5721 in the Jewish calendar (1961 in the Gregorian), he wondered: 'I do not know for sure if I am Nyiszli [...] or if I am Grósz Chorin [...] I do not know either.'

This is how the countess intended to keep us busy. These new developments – the announcement of new documents, the hinting at new cross-connections to other countries such as France, which we had to investigate immediately – all concerned the verification of the already existing, forged documents. At this point, she presumably already knew that I had my suspicions regarding the veracity of the documents, but she evidently did not know that I knew she had been the forger herself. Still, there were so many people involved in this project that I resolved to conduct the personal investigations on my own for the time being.

In May, I was invited to Kaiser's apartment in Munich where I caught a glimpse of Kaiser's personal ID and certificate of registration. I wrote them down in a quiet moment and when I returned home, I sent the details to my contacts in Poland and Hungary to find out who the countess really was.

It soon turned out that the countess had a penchant for speeding – she had been fined countless times in various different countries. Furthermore, the car was registered under her real name: Magdolna Kaiser, née Beretka, born in 1950 in the small town of Bečej in Serbia. Bečej lies close to the Hungarian border and the region has a significant Hungarian minority.

Unfortunately, the name Beretka is relatively common in the region and it took Kemény and me, as well as our contacts, a few months to locate her true family. After weeks of preparation, Kemény and I finally visited Bečej on 13 October 2016. We managed to find the primary school she had gone to as a child and were even able to find the address and telephone number of her mother. We called her, but she hung up as soon as we mentioned her daughter. She also did not open the door when we rang the doorbell at her house – we knew that someone was inside from the fact that the curtains were moving.

She was clearly not an orphan. According to the Serbian civil registry, Magdolna Beretka grew up with her father and her mother. Our contacts in Bečej told us that Magdolna had cut off contact with her parents years ago. Her father had since died, and her mother believed that she was living in Switzerland. According to the information provided by the primary school, her father was a civil servant, while her mother stayed at home. At any rate, they were not Hungarian high nobility.

In the meantime, I had found out from several sources that nobody with her name or appearance was known in the Vatican. Had she indeed been accompanying the popes as she had always claimed, at least one of the journalists or cameramen would have recognized her; she certainly did have a striking presence, but no one recognized her.

We also found out that her medical degrees were all fake as well. The reason she was not listed as a lecturer at the university in Zürich was simply that she never taught there. After graduating high school in Bečej at the age of 19, she did not go to university, even though she consistently had high marks ever since primary school. She had been particularly good in Serbian and Hungarian, but in German, the language she operated in, she never achieved anything above a B grade.

What was true was that she had been married. However, her husband had not been a professor of neurology as she had claimed, but most likely a window and building cleaner in Germany. In 1983, she had renounced her Yugoslavian citizenship. Family ties to Jews and Holocaust survivors: None.

Chapter 11

Feints

Throughout this investigation, I never confronted the fake countess about my suspicions. On the contrary, I always reassured her that the project was progressing well, that the publisher was enthusiastic and that the date of publication was drawing ever closer. This was the kind of news Kaiser was delighted to hear, and she reciprocated by announcing fresh document deliveries and new revelations to us. Lothfels likewise did not know what I knew, and I wanted to keep it that way until I had incontrovertible proof.

I had also kept my distance from Dr Wassert after her reaction to my initial suspicions, and only told her about the handwriting analysis in early August 2016. Unlike last time, however, she did not seem too surprised that it had been her friend Nicole who had been behind all the forgeries. Dr Wassert now declared that she wanted to support me in this investigation.

Upon realizing her friend's machinations, Dr Wassert began to tell me about the various other 'projects' the fake countess had been working on, as well as the supposed letters from the popes and the papal secretary Gänswein she had been delivering to Lothfels. During one of her visits to Tegernsee, she took pictures of some of the letters and sent them to me.

Among them was a greeting card from 20 June 2013, which 'your Nicole' (i.e. Magdolna Kaiser) had sent to her 'dearest Lisbeth' (Elisabeth Lothfels). I quickly compared her handwriting with that of the Auschwitz Notes, specifically with the entry on the page for 30 September, focusing on the words 'Juni', 'Rome' and 'Vatikan' (see Plate 12).

Once again, the similarities were striking. I also took a closer look at another greeting card with Easter wishes from the supposed 'quadriga' from Rome. That 'quadriga' consisted of the current Pope Francis I, the retired Pope Benedict XVI, Archbishop Georg Gänswein and Magdolna Kaiser. The text had been written by her, but Magdolna had also clearly forged the signatures of the three other members of that 'quadriga' before signing off with her own name ('and Your Nicole, who loves you very much') (see Plate 13).

I was again struck by the similarities in her handwriting; especially the capital 'D' in the half-sentence 'and Your Nicole, who loves you very much' was very similar to her capital 'Ds' in the Auschwitz Notes (see Plate 14).

At this point, I did not even bother to send these samples to the handwriting expert – they were obviously from the same person. I also realized that Magdolna Kaiser was not simply a forger, but also a career fraudster. All of this called into question her other 'charitable' activities, in particular her patronage of the orphanage in Romania seemed very suspicious now.

We thus began to slowly unravel her web of lies and fraudulent projects. I soon found out that Magdolna Kaiser had been frequenting the circles of southern German, moneyed and high nobility since at least early 2010, claiming to be a papal personal physician, a professor of medicine and a member of the Hungarian nobility.

She started off on a smaller scale. Collecting donations for various charitable causes and for people in need is a very common front for fraudsters across the world – and this was exactly what she did at first. We were soon able to reconstruct one of these 'charity drives': During one of these high society festivities – a birthday in this case – it was announced that Dr Nicole Kaiser was collecting donations for children in Africa. A pickle jar, as one of the witnesses later described it, was passed around from table to table, and the guests were encouraged to put money inside. Since the pickle glass was transparent, everyone could see how much the other was donating – and who among the wealthy would want to come across as stingy in such illustrious company? Before long, the pickle jar was filled to the brim exclusively with large bills – €50 and mostly €100.

Kaiser's most profitable 'venture' appeared to be the construction of a hospital in Illeret, Kenya. Lothfels had donated large sums to have that hospital built, but no such project ever materialized in the real world.

In November 2016, we caught wind of the countess' newest project: To transport drinking water from Bhutan in the Himalayan Mountains to Africa with a specially modified plane. Bhutan's Queen Mother had supposedly given her approval already, and Elisabeth Lothfels had also promised to cover some of the transport costs. To me, this entire story seemed like a joke, but Dr Wassert was shocked and felt that we had to warn her friend Lothfels before she committed to the idea. I realized that now was the time to end our investigation and to finally act on it before we lost control over it, which would most likely happen once we told Lothfels about it. At this point we had already finished our forensic-linguistic investigation into the forgery and had also revealed Kaiser's true identity.

On 13 January 2017, we travelled to Munich to tell Lothfels what we had found out about her supposed friend and what had happened to projects she had been financing. Lothfels appeared to have been caught completely unaware, and our discussion was long and painful.

Contrary to our fears, we were able to convince Lothfels of her friends' duplicitous nature relatively quickly. After some consideration, Lothfels asked me not to pursue this matter any further and to cease our project altogether. I told her that this was not possible since we were dealing with an actual felony. Both I and the foundation I had been working with had incurred significant damage through the forgeries in the form of working time lost but also personnel, material and travel expenses. We had no choice but to file criminal charges. Elisabeth Lothfels was taken aback.

After thinking about it again, she came around and agreed to help us in solving the case, stressing that she herself had always acted in good faith. She then told us about other projects she had financed for Magdolna Kaiser. This was again a long list of 'classic' fraud cases. It turned out that Lothfels had not paid for one but two hospitals in

Kenya, in addition to another two wells there. There was also a host of 'small' ventures, which Lothfels asked us to investigate discreetly.

After some hesitation we agreed, and Elisabeth Lothfels promised me her full cooperation. On 13 January she provided me with plenty of documents regarding her dealings with Kaiser, which were supplemented by even more documents over the coming weeks. They included all kinds of material from proper documents to letters, all kinds of objects and even her SMS and WhatsApp messages, which included her correspondence with the 'Vatican', i.e. the forged correspondence with the popes and their confidantes. Lothfels also promised to answer all the questions I had. After all, it was now my task to evaluate everything we had from a legal point of view and to prepare to press criminal charges against Kaiser.

In one of our conversations, I asked Lothfels how she had been paying Magdolna Kaiser. She responded that she usually paid her in cash, although sometimes she also wrote her friend cheques if she did not have enough cash on hand. This was great news. Regardless of the bank, when a cheque is cashed the original is sent back to the bank of the person who issued it in the first place. I urged Lothfels to call her bank and to ask for copies of these cashed cheques. She did just that and had her secretary send me copies of these cheques.

In early March 2017, I then received the copies in the mail. This was exactly what I had been looking for. The cleared cheques were all issued by Lothfels between 2013 and 2016, and all of them were cashed by her friend Nicole. In total, I had at my disposal twenty-two different cheques, which I immediately added to a chart, adding both date of issue and clearing, as well as the sums and the intended use.

In every single cheque, the intended use box had apparently been filled out by Magdolna Kaiser herself. They included donations for refugees and hunger relief, as well as for hospitals in Africa and monasteries in Hungary. Curiously enough, they also included acquisition costs for personal items such as a stair lift, a wheelchair and even a massage table for the aged Pope Benedict XVI, as well as shoes and a birthday cake for Pope Francis I. The total amount of money transferred by cheque was nearly €440,000.

To confirm that it had indeed been Kaiser who had filled out the intended use boxes, I again sent samples to Professor Gruza, who analyzed the writing. Again, she was able to confirm, with a very high degree of certainty, that it was Kaiser's handwriting, although she did need the originals to confirm it without a doubt. At this point we had proven that Kaiser was not just a forger but a fraudster as well. The felonies kept piling up.

Aside from the cheques, Lothfels had given her friend large sums of money via cash or bank transfer. However, Lothfels did not know exactly how much cash she had paid Kaiser, just that it had been considerably more than what she had transferred by cheque.

As mentioned earlier, we had agreed to file criminal charges against Kaiser at our meeting in early January 2017. However, preparing everything took time and Kaiser was an avid traveller who could flee at any moment. We therefore decided to continue the approach that I had stuck to since I realized we were dealing with a forgery: We turned the tables on her.

While I was searching for further victims and collected and analyzed the evidence against her, we continued to pretend that everything was fine. We called her, sent her updates via texts and WhatsApp messages, and met with her as well. Lothfels told us that Kaiser was thoroughly fascinated by the idea of having a film made about Grósz Chorin and little Magda, as he had always called her. They had already talked about which actors they were going to cast, and how to pay for it. I already knew of it to some extent; the three women had talked about it previously in my presence. This gave me an idea: We could trick Kaiser into believing that we were about to start working on exactly this film project.

On 22 January 2017, Wassert sent her an e-mail:

> We have met regarding the project [...] and discussed several points, for example the implementation, further procedures, etc. ... The work and its contents are so unmatched that in the end Lisbeth came to the idea to write a screenplay based on the memoirs and the things you have told us. Bogdan could search for an author who could write a screenplay on our behalf. [...]

> Assuming your cooperation, the screenplay writer could then conduct an interview with you.

Kaiser was thoroughly elated. When we met with her a month later, she was nevertheless initially coy, before quickly coming around. She even suggested a name: László Nemes. The Hungarian director and screenplay writer had made headlines for his film *Son of Saul*, which won him multiple prizes, including the Oscar for the best foreign-language film. She agreed to contact him and, given the circumstances, we were perfectly fine with her handling this.

Furthermore, Kaiser revealed the 'existence' of another set of memoirs to us – that of Grósz Chorin's housekeeper Elly Ostertag. Ostertag had played an important role in Kaiser's stories from the beginning. Whenever Kaiser forgot some important details about her grandfather, she referred to Ostertag, whom Grósz Chorin had been very close to. Unfortunately, Elly Ostertag had died several decades ago, so only her daughter – who, confusingly, shared the same name as her mother – could provide the necessary information from the memoirs her mother had left to her. Thus far, however, all our efforts to get our hands on these records had come to naught, so we pretended to be excited by this turn of events. Kaiser was happy that we were happy and also promised to organize even more interviews with Holocaust survivors, not just in Hungary but also in the US. There was no end in sight.

The next month, on 26 March, we received the following email from her:

> I am on Lampedusa [to aid refugees and migrants arriving from Africa on behalf of Pope Francis I; B.M.], but on Wednesday I am back in Rome and then on 2 April I will meet Elly, there are three or four booklets – as Elly had told me – with records, very many names and addresses inside. She found this in her mother's room. In April, she will give me them. I will immediately send them to you.

And I was also active in the meantime.

> One of the surviving Mengele-twins is still alive in Budapest. […] He met very many doctors there [in Auschwitz] and also Dr Nyiszli and maybe also grandfather!!!!

We reacted with exuberant joy and agreed to travel to Budapest between 20 and 22 April, where she would arrange the interviews. We also decided to film the entire encounter because, after all, this would make great material for a documentary.

In early April, Isabel Wassert received the promised 'booklets' from Elly Ostertag. As with the earlier deliveries, they were notebooks and the entries were written in pencil, so we would again not be able to forensically determine the age of the documents. However, there were two major differences: First, the housekeeper – who naturally had a PhD – had written down her notes in very elaborate German, at a level far above what Kaiser was capable of. Secondly, the handwriting was clearly different as well. This strongly suggested that there was at least one other person working with Kaiser.

The booklets were accompanied by several other books, which – like with Grósz Chorin's supposed estate – were to give the illusion of it being part of a genuine private collection. Unfortunately for the forgers – and fortunately for us – they had missed one important detail. Some readers like to mark their books by writing their names on the book cut, and this is just what happened with one of the books. As it turned out, the former owner of the book was one of the victims of the false Vatican doctor, and as we learned later, Mengele's supposed suitcase had originally been his as well.

Kaiser prepared our trip to Budapest with her usual meticulousness: She arranged several meetings with survivors and even sent us a written itinerary ahead of time. Meanwhile, we contacted two cameramen from Kraków who I had worked with previously. Their job was to record the interviews but also the performance of the false countess. Furthermore, I instructed them to speak exclusively in Polish and not to show any sign of suspicions regarding Kaiser's outlandish stories. Given that she spoke Serbian very well, it was likely that she would be able to at least understand Polish, so they had to be careful.

For two days, on 21 and 22 April, we conducted interview after interview, each arranged by Kaiser. As always, she had done a great job: Unlike her, the survivors we managed to interview were genuine. She had even found a survivor of the twin experiments, who told us about his painful experiences in Auschwitz. This was very valuable for my next research project on the real prisoner-doctors in Auschwitz. While the Grósz Chorin publication project had been re-purposed to investigate the forgery in early 2016; the next project, the one about the prisoner-doctors in Auschwitz, remained in place.

This visit unexpectedly gave us another piece of evidence proving that Kaiser was not the person she was pretending to be. When I introduced the two cameramen to her on the first evening, I told her that one of them had worked with Steven Spielberg's Shoah Foundation, recording interviews with Holocaust survivors. Kaiser was thoroughly impressed and offered her own story: When Pope Francis I had visited Poland in July 2016, he took the tram in Kraków. Naturally, Kaiser had accompanied him on the tram, and she also shared some minor anecdotes as well. As soon as she left the room, one of the cameramen smirked. As it turned out, he had filmed the Pope's tram ride on behalf of the German public broadcaster ARD. The person who had just left the room had certainly not been present there.

Overall, it was a very enlightening trip. We left Budapest with the agreement that we would soon film an exclusive, detailed interview with Professor Kaiser, where she would talk about her grandfather at length. Naturally, we would respect her anonymity which was so dear to her, if she so wanted.

At this point, I filed criminal charges against her in Munich; I would later get directly involved in the complaint as a joint plaintiff. The prosecution quickly launched a proper investigation. The evidence of the fake countess' misdeeds we had gathered on our own apparently proved to be convincing enough and Kaiser was arrested on 17 August 2017.

Before her arrest, Kaiser tried to escape with what she could. Apparently, she had planned to escape to Switzerland and was in the process of transferring large amounts of money to Swiss banks – until her bank froze her accounts on suspicion of money laundering. It appears as if she hoped to escape justice by signing a notarized admission of guilt to Elisabeth Lothfels, after she and her lawyer had confronted Kaiser. However, this was not enough for us to relent.

Kaiser had previously stored away most of her possessions with her friends across southern Germany and Switzerland, whose houses were promptly searched. During the nearly simultaneous searches of her friends' houses and her apartment in Munich, the police found plenty of evidence, including forged documents and certificates, a backpack with around 3 kg of jewellery, as well as watches worth over €100,000.

On 14 May 2018, the trial against her began in Munich. She was charged with fraud in combination with the misuse of titles in twenty-three cases – damages were estimated to be at €438,500. Lothfels was the only injured party to come forward, while the Auschwitz Notes did not play a role in the trial for practical reasons – they were not worth the effort in the eyes of the prosecution.

Already on the second day, 18 May 2018, the court reached a verdict: Four years and six months in prison without parole. Initially, Kaiser told the press that she was guilty,[1] but then quickly changed her mind and appealed the verdict. A few months later, on 19 September 2018, the Federal Court of Justice in Karlsruhe found her appeal to be baseless and rejected it. The verdict was now legally binding.

Most of the facts we had found out during our initial investigations were confirmed by the police and during the trial. Later, however, the police investigation as well as our own investigation uncovered the missing pieces that completed the story of Magdolna Kaiser's criminal career.

Magdolna came to Germany in the 1970s, 1975 at the latest. That year, she met her future husband, a treasury officer from Saarbrücken, not a building cleaner as I had originally thought. She introduced herself as a medical student, and from 7 November 1975, Magdolna did indeed study medicine at Heidelberg University. The two soon became a couple and were married in a civil ceremony in Saarbrücken in the summer of 1976. A few days later, they had their church wedding

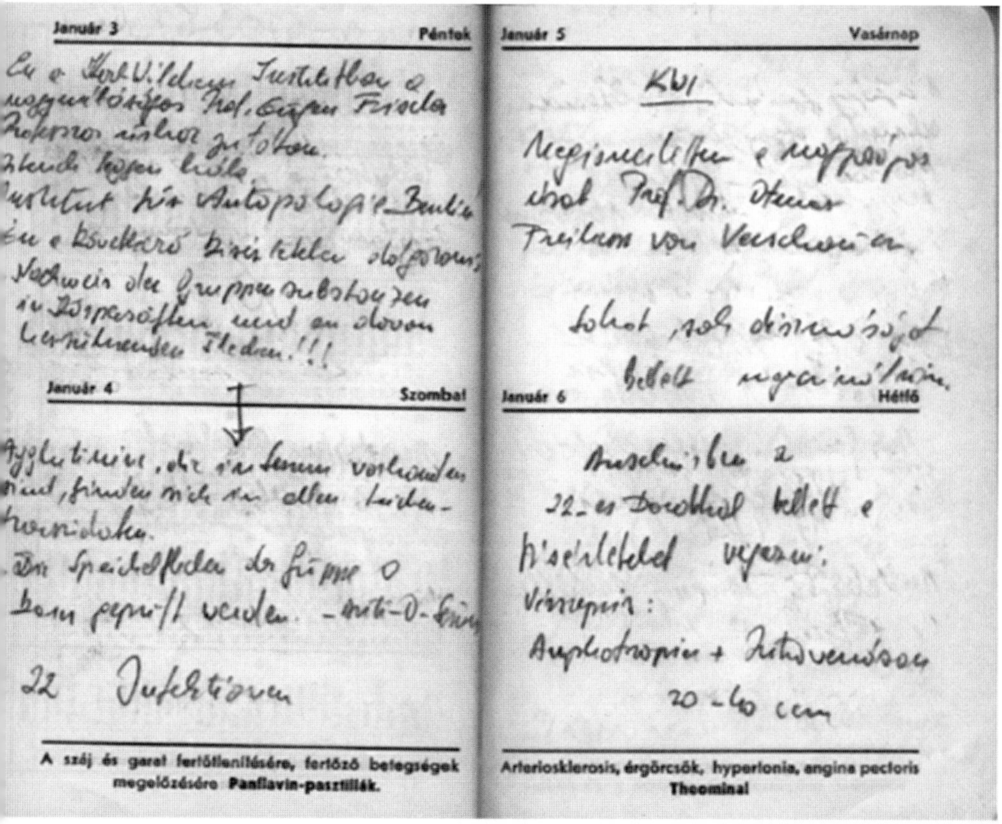

An excerpt from the handwritten Auschwitz Notes in the medical notebook from 1936.

The columns of numbers in the 'Trachoma' book have not been decoded.

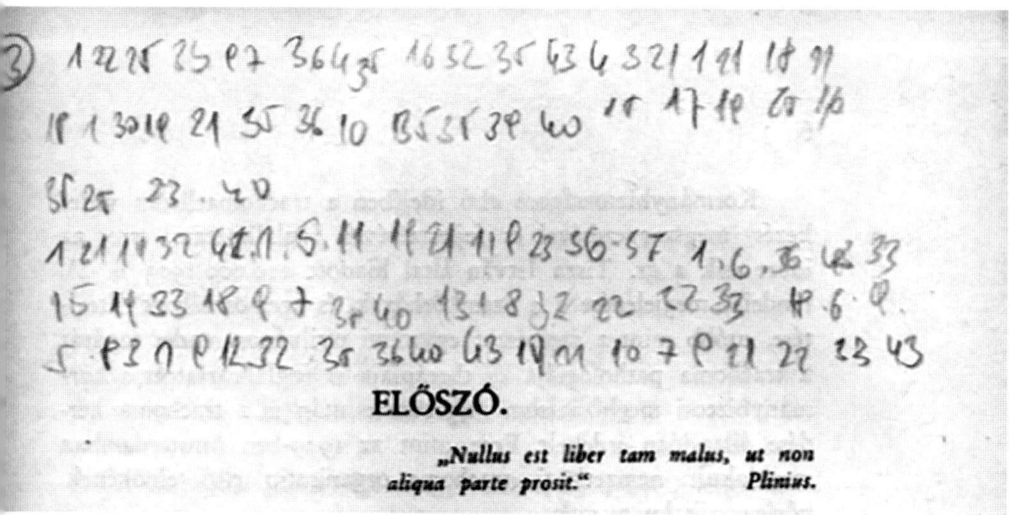

3. 'Hitler' in Auschwitz.

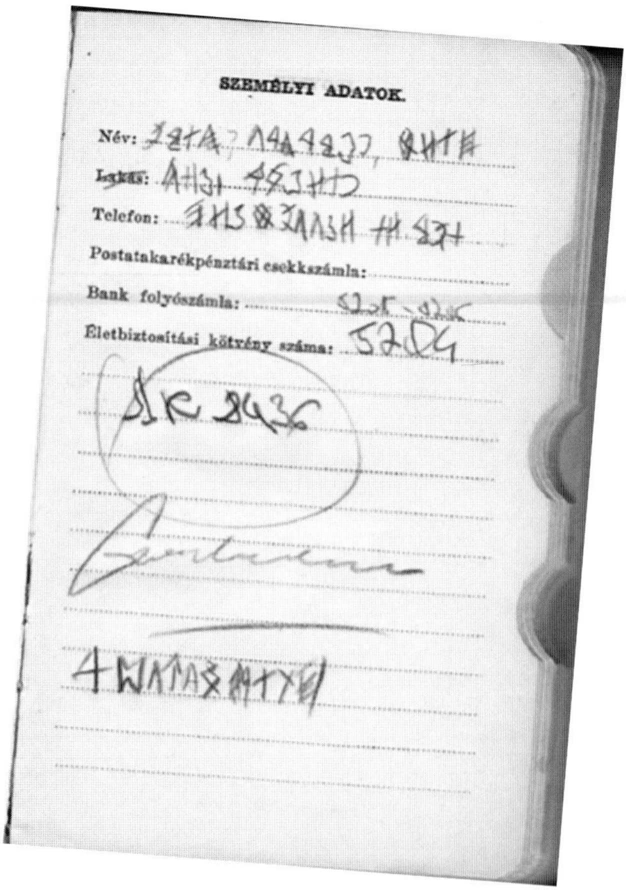

4. The cover sheet of the Auschwitz Notes filled with Old Hungarian runes.

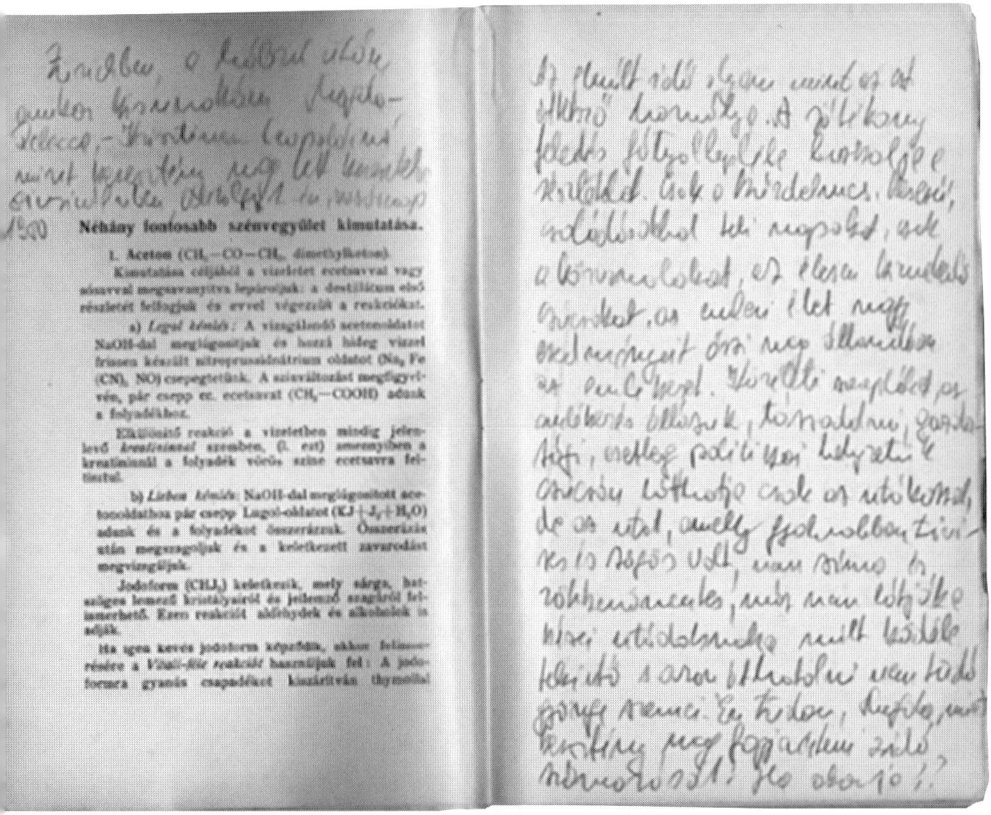

Néhány fontosabb szénvegyület kimutatása.

1. Aceton (CH_3—CO—CH_3, dimethylketon).

\n excerpt from the 'Central Piece'.

Ihe cover of Motorcza's book. The
ger assumed that the number on
cover belonged to Mengele, when
fact it belongs to the Auschwitz
ıseum.

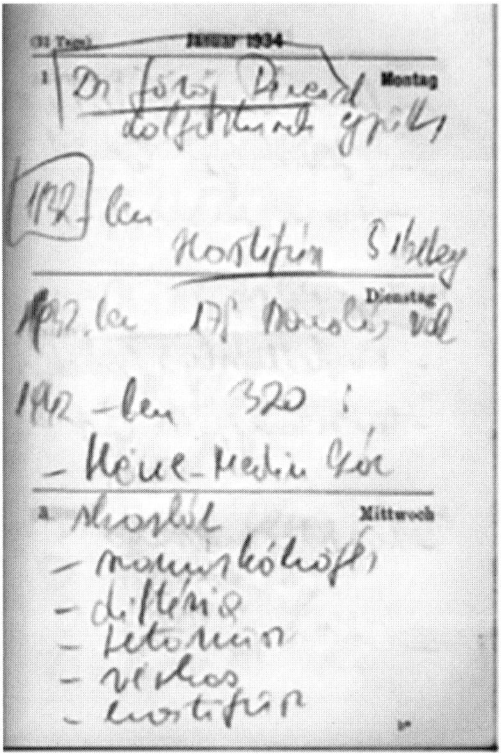

Dr Görög Dénessel dolgoztunk együtt 1932-ben	Mit Dr. Dénes Görög arbeiteten wir zusammen im Jahre 1932
Hastífusz 51 beteg	Bauchtyphus 51 Kranke
1932-ben 179 boncolás volt	1932 179 Obduktionen
1942-ben 320 :	1942: 320
- Heine-Medin kór	- Kinderlähmung
Skarlát - szamárköhögés - diftéria - tetanusz - vérhas - hastífusz	Scharlach - Keuchhusten - Diphterie - Tetanus - Ruhr - Bauchtyphus

7. The first page of the 1934 medical diary, with a transcription and translation.

8. Another page from the 1934 medical diary, with a transcription of the names mentioned in

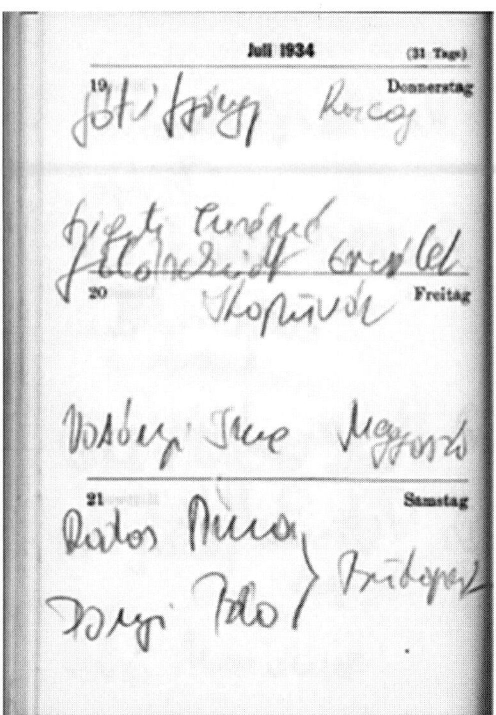

Gáti György Karczag

Szigeti Imréné
Goldschmied Erzsébet

Kapuvár

Varsányi Imre Megyaszó

Rados Anna

Budapest

Danyi Béla

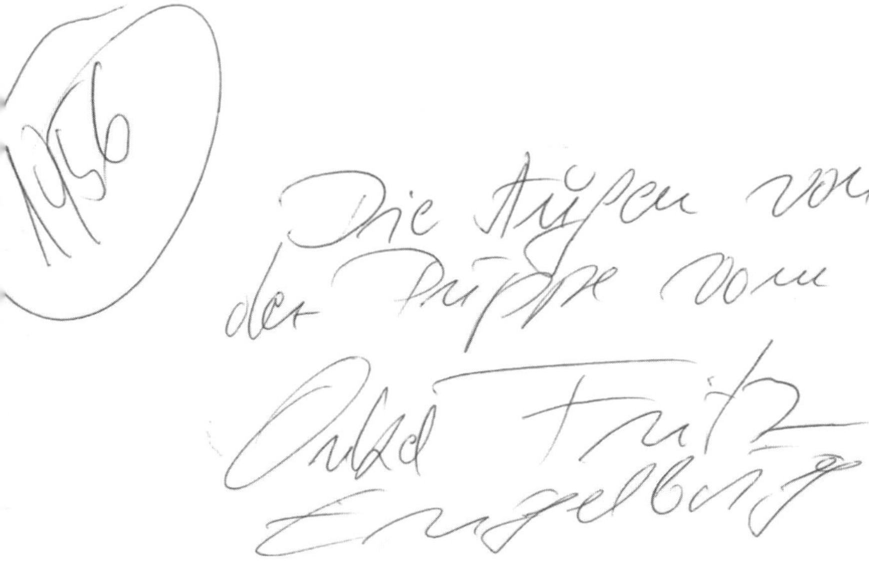

The eyes from Uncle Fritz's doll' - one of the handwriting samples used to prove the forgery.

& 11. An image of the book from the supposed estate (left) with the same annotations on the site www.antikvarium.hu (right).

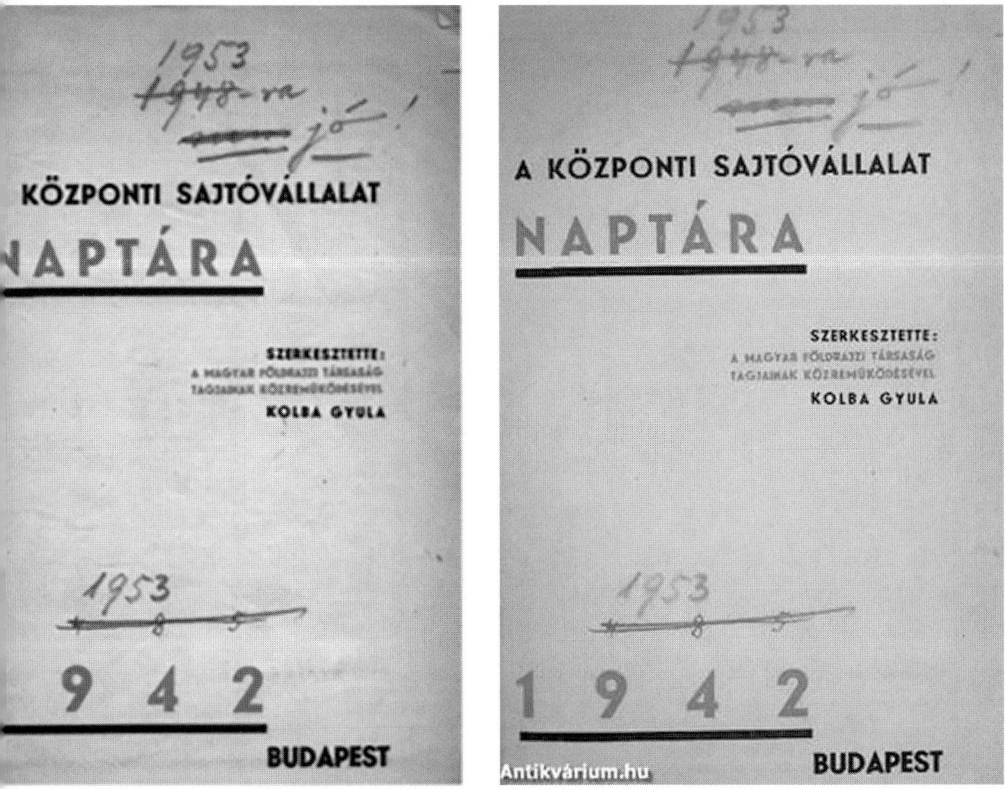

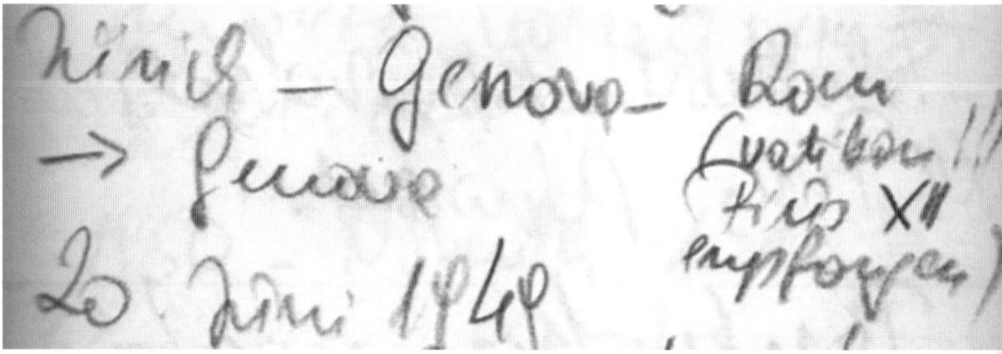

12. A greeting card from the countess used to compare handwriting samples with the Auschw
Notes.

13. Another greetings card with the countess' handwriting, this time sending Easter wisl
Although the text was in her hand, she had clearly forged the other signatures before signing
with her own name.

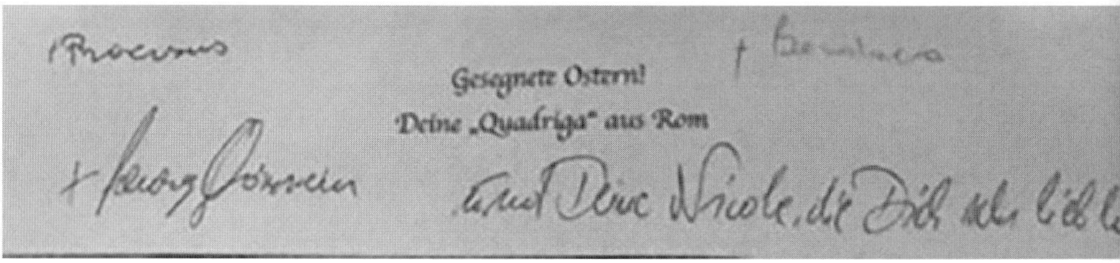

14. The capital 'D' in the half-sentence in this entry for 27 September in the Auschwitz Note
very similar to that used in the Easter greetings card (Plate 13).

15. A group of Jewish children kept alive at Auschwitz for use in Mengele's medical experiments, including twins Miriam Mozes and Eva Mozes (wearing knitted caps).

16. Dr Josef Mengele saw his time at Auschwitz as the perfect opportunity to conduct genetic research on the prisoners.

17. The site of one of the prison blocks at Auschwitz where Dr Mengele conducted his experiments on children, particularly twins.

18. The countess confidently strikes her trademark 'Mussolini pose'.

19. The countess and the author sitting next to each other at a reception.

in the Swiss town of Einsiedeln, a popular Catholic pilgrimage site. The newlywed couple then moved into an apartment in Saarbrücken.

Already at this point, Magdolna began to dramatize her past with made-up stories. For example, she told her husband that she was an orphan. Her biological parents – both supposedly university professors – had died in an accident. Her maternal aunt and her husband then adopted her. Years later, after her divorce, Magdolna 'revealed' to her new partner that 'I was an adopted child of my parents from the "Hungarian enclave". [...] My mother died during my birth. I am an "extramarital" and on top of that a "sin child", a "priest's child".'[2]

Shortly after her wedding, Magdolna broke off her medical studies after just two semesters and began – financed by her then-husband - training as a pharmaceutical sales representative in Bad Tölz. Her ex-husband testified in 2017 that she did indeed finish her training and then worked as a pharmaceutical sales representative afterwards.[3] In 1983, Magdolna became a German citizen. During this time, she commuted between Saarbrücken and Heppenheim and went on frequent work trips. According to her ex-husband, she continued to work at her pharmaceutical company until their eventual divorce in 1995, during which she received around 1 million Deutsche Marks. They did not have children and she moved away to Bad Homburg as early as 1993.

It is not entirely clear when Magdolna became a forger, but by the early 1990s, she already had several forged documents and certificates under her belt. Among them were:

A university diploma from the Karl-Marx University Leipzig in the field of medicine from 25 August 1978;

The certificate: 'License to practise medicine', issued by the German Democratic Republic, Leipzig District Office, 25 August 1978, in the name of Mrs Dipl. Med. Magdalena Kaiser née Beretka, born 20 July 1950 in Becej;

The certificate: 'License to practise medicine', issued by the District President in Gießen, 28 May 1986, in the name of Mrs.

Dipl. Med. Magdalena Kaiser née Beretka, born on 20 1950 in Becej;

Doctoral Certificate from the Faculty of Human Medicine of the Justius-Liebig University Gießen, 12 September 1989, in the name of Magdalena Kaiser, née Beretka. According to the forged certificate, she had been given the title Doctor of Medicine (Dr. med.);

According to a forged certificate dated 22 February 1994, the Saxon State Medical Association had given Frau Dr. med. Magdalena Kaiser, née Beretka the right to hold the title of 'specialist for internal diseases';

According to another forged certificate from the Saxon State Medical Association, 'Dr. med. Magdolna Kaiser née Beretka, born 20 July 1950' had become an 'expert for virology in internal medicine on 16 September 1994'.[4]

In February 1995, after separating from her husband, Magdolna met a wealthy entrepreneur from southern Germany. He was widowed and, sensing her chance, she introduced herself to him as a Hungarian countess, doctor of medicine and a scientist, as well as the daughter of a Hungarian-Jewish Holocaust survivor. As her story changed, her name did too and she now called herself Dr Magdalena N. Kaiser-Szentágothay, née Beretka-Szentágothay. Her date of birth had also changed by three weeks to 13 August 1950.

Magdolna and the entrepreneur became a couple in 1995 and Nicole, as she preferred to be called then, soon moved into his villa. However, both were extremely busy in their professional lives and travelled a lot, so their relationship was essentially limited to the weekends. Before long, Nicole met her partner's friends and family, whom she was mostly friendly with. The one exception was her partner's two adult children, who remained suspicious of her throughout, especially the daughter. This was not an issue, though, as their father told his children to stay out of his new relationship.

Shortly after she moved in with him, Magdolna (alias Nicole) announced that she had been made a 'professor at a university' by the Minister President of Hesse. As proof, she showed around a certificate dated 15 September 1995. To mark this auspicious occasion, she organized a party at their villa, where she and her achievements were duly celebrated. Naturally, the certificate of appointment was a forgery, and not even a good one at that, but it was enough to fool and impress non-academics.

Beginning in 1995, Magdolna Kaiser was now presenting herself as Professor Magdalena N. Kaiser-Szentágothay. At this point in time at the latest, she also began to make up the story of her being the granddaughter of a Jewish Auschwitz survivor. In the late 1990s, Magdolna travelled to Auschwitz together with her partner and his daughter to show them the place where her grandfather had worked as a prisoner-doctor and where many of her relatives had been murdered. A few years later, in the early 2000s, Magdolna then started telling people about the estate of her grandfather, which was being kept in a Swiss bank.

Originally, the safe was to be opened in January 2005. However, this date passed without anything occurring and the story remained dormant until 2014. At this point, Magdolna (alias Nicole) began to revisit the story and asked her friend to have it examined by a historian.

It is not entirely clear where Magdolna had worked in the 1980s and 1990s. Among her possessions, the police found a job reference from a pharmaceutical company from 24 July 2000 [it likely should have been 2001], according to which Dr Magdalena Kaiser MD had worked there between 1 January 1990 and 31 December 2000 [*sic*] as a research assistant in the business division 'Onkology [*sic*] and Immunology'. This job reference was clearly fake and someone sent it to the company's management, which sent 'Dr Magdalena Kaiser' a letter on 11 September 2001:

> Dear Dr Kaiser,
>
> We have a 'certificate' on our company paper dated 24 July 2000, in which, in poor German and with many spelling mistakes, it is

> confirmed that you worked in the business division 'Onkology and Immunology' until '31 December 2000'.
>
> The signature on the left is supposed to be the signature of the left signer but it is not identical to his signature. […] Before we forward this matter to the prosecution to review it from a criminal perspective, we want to give you the opportunity to respond until Monday, 17 September 2001.
>
> After this date, we will also contact the Justus-Liebig University Gießen and ask to be informed as to why the doctoral certificate dated 21 July 1993 only bears the signature of the dean.[5]

This letter suggests that Magdolna Kaiser was known to the company as Dr Kaiser MD and that she had likely worked there. The latter has been confirmed to me by witnesses who said that she had indeed worked for that company, albeit as a pharmaceutical representative. Additionally, the company also had her forged doctoral certificate from the Justus-Liebig University Gießen.

Unfortunately, it appears as if the company and the prosecution chose not to act upon this. As a result, she was able to walk free, lick her wounds and continue her work as a fraudster and forger for another decade and a half.

Nevertheless, it does appear as if this experience had humbled her to some extent. At the very least, there was not much information about her criminal activities over the next decade. This only changed ten years later, when she befriended Elisabeth Lothfels, and her career as a con artist and forger took off again.

Chapter 12

'This Little Wonder'

At the heart of every con artist's story lies the power of suggestion. Indeed, the first person a con artist has to convince is themself. The better this self-deception works, the less likely the person is to be startled by something unexpected and lose focus. By convincing oneself well enough, one can even prevent unconscious physical reactions that could potentially unravel the charade, such as blushing.[1]

Con artists are drawn to a wide range of identities: In Germany, the postman Ernst Postel successfully became the head of a psychiatric hospital in the late 1990s; while the Swiss Tom Kummer became a 'star reporter' fooling the German-speaking press with made-up, exclusive celebrity interviews. In the USA, Frank Abagnale committed cheque fraud and posed as a lawyer, doctor and even pilot in the late 1960s and early 1970s; he was so talented the FBI later contracted him to root out con artists. Naturally, con artists are often drawn to nobility as well. One of the most famous incidents was that of Harry Domela, who in 1920s Weimar Germany pretended to be Wilhelm of Prussia, a prince of the imperial Hohenzollern dynasty, and indeed the grandson of the last German emperor Wilhelm II.

In the last decade in America, the German-Russian Anna Sorokin reinvented herself as Anna Delvey, a rich heiress and socialite who defrauded her supposed peers for years. And who could forget the tales of Q, the anonymous agent who waged a great war against the President Donald Trump's enemies in the 'deep state' and whose supposed exploits inspired a genuine political movement.

Many of these cases have made their way into popular culture, such as Frank Abagnale's, who in 2002 became the subject of the successful Hollywood comedy-drama *Catch Me If You Can*. Anna Sorokin's exploits meanwhile were turned into a drama miniseries in 2022.[2] German impostors have likewise seen their exploits turned into popular novels and plays, the most famous being the cobbler Wilhelm Friedrich Voigt who, in 1906, after being expelled from Berlin for being a convicted criminal, bought himself parts of a captain's uniform, commandeered a unit of soldiers and led a coup in the nearby town of Köpenick. After looting its treasury, he ordered the soldiers to stand guard, changed into civilian clothing and disappeared. He was eventually caught after a former cellmate of his tipped off the police.

Academic titles, reputable careers, elite institutions, high nobility and exclusive networks: These were the things audiences in the long twentieth century valued and which they still value to this day, especially if they themselves become part of a greater story. People lie and cheat, but they are still believed because these impostors make dreams come true, both theirs and ours. 'Where the world wants to be deceived and where people want to deceive, there the con artist stages a *folie à deux* that everyone enjoys,' writes the social scientist Stephan Porombka. 'Sociologists and psychologists call this an auto suggestive closed system, in which all of the participants can hype themselves up to dizzying heights.'[3]

Magdolna Kaiser, the daughter of a small country official and the former wife of a provincial finance official from the Saarland, who had failed her medical studies, always dreamt of having an illustrious academic career, belonging to exquisite circles, and being showered with praise, riches and power. She had been deprived of her right to all of this, so she simply took it for herself through a remarkable mixture of manipulative skill, cunning, improvisational talent and cold-bloodedness.

Kaiser used her faked immediate proximity to the popes to cultivate the interest and adoration of her victims. For Catholics, the Pope is the deputy of God on earth, the person who bridges the chasm between us common mortals and the Kingdom of God. As the supposed papal personal physician, she was able to sell her victims the illusion that they too were part of this incredibly exclusive and indeed holy circle.

This prospect exerted an almost magical attraction on Kaiser's targets, who believed they were buying things like shoes for Pope Francis I or a cassock lined with ermine fur for Pope Emeritus Benedict XVI. When the latter had trouble walking, they bought 'him' a stair lift.

In most past and contemporary religions, the act of giving is seen as more virtuous than the act of taking. Therefore, Kaiser always made sure to 'give' more than she took: She worked for the WHO in Africa, helped refugees on Lampedusa and aided orphans in Romania, almost to the point of constant exhaustion. 'Oftentimes,' writes the critic, curator and publisher Roberto Ohrt, 'the con artist plays the role of a figure in front of the audience, which they want to be but do not dare to be; though they still want to be close to this extraordinary phenomenon.'[4]

This is why, one could add, many are willing to contribute to that financially. Wherever there was the opportunity, Kaiser held out her hand. During her charity drive with the pickle jar during a birthday party, she likely collected thousands of euros for 'African children in need'. Who could refuse to help starving children survive when one already had everything their heart desired? And who would do so in front of equally rich onlookers who saw exactly how much they donated?

In the grand scheme of things, the pickle jar incident had been very minor, but in general, 'Africa' remained a common fixture in her fraudulent projects. Lothfels personally donated hundreds of thousands of euros to build two hospitals and wells in Kenya on the belief that she was helping a Catholic clergyman and his flock.

The charitable Lothfels liked to help, especially since she received heartfelt letters thanking her for her generosity. To round it all off, the priest and his Catholic mission station in Illeret were very much real – unlike the hospitals, wells and the letters. But who could hold it against a priest with dyslexia[5] that he did not write the letters on his own and instead asked the papal secretary Gänswein or his equally kind-hearted 'sister Nicole Magdalena' to write them for him? And who in his right mind would demand receipts from the inexhaustible servant of God who was rushing from crisis to crisis, and then told her dear friend that 'here I had to help, with Your support'?[6]

The real person of the priest was only the façade around which Kaiser weaved her increasingly outlandish net of deception. The last project she was working on involved buying water from Bhutan in the Himalayas, and then transporting it thousands of miles by plane to draught-ridden regions of Africa, all in the name of the WHO. This entire arrangement was questionable if not absurd on its face, but by then, Lothfels had already become completely taken by Kaiser's stories.

As we found out later, it had all begun with a forged, heartfelt letter from the priest during a time of deep personal crisis for Lothfels. Several years prior, Lothfels' only son had been found unconscious. He was rushed to the hospital, where he was put into a coma, but he did not survive. For the family, his sudden death was a truly traumatic shock, especially for his mother. It was in this moment that Kaiser, who already knew Lothfels, appears to have sunk her hooks into her. She helped Lothfels grieve, brought spiritual support from the Vatican, where Pope Emeritus Benedict XVI supposedly held Masses for Lothfels' son after Kaiser told him about her plight. For his Catholic mother, this was a tremendous relief.

Furthermore, during the burial of Lothfels' son, something extraordinary happened. As the priest said the Holy Mass, a flock of white butterflies suddenly emerged and flew around to the amazement of everyone present. Kaiser took note of this and decided to use it for her purposes. She told Lothfels that the priest in Kenya had been praying for her son, but now she took it up a few notches by fabricating a truly extraordinary story, according to which the priest, after he had prayed for her son, had fallen asleep. As he awoke from his slumber, he found on his bedside table a dead butterfly – a symbol of transformation, in this case that of the transition from the earthly world to the afterlife. In this moment, he knew that Lothfels' son had died. When Kaiser returned from her next purported trip to Illeret, she brought with her a truly wondrous gift: The very same butterfly, framed and with a dedication from the Catholic priest. No wonder the grieving mother was more than willing to help the compassionate clergyman in his ever-expanding endeavours in Kenya.

'One of the tools utilized by unscrupulous scam artists is the social norm of reciprocity. Simply stated, the social norm of reciprocity is that we feel obligated to repay those who have provided a favor to us.'[7] Kaiser had given Lothfels an extraordinarily emotionally valuable gift, and Lothfels paid back the favour with great sums of money. More importantly, Lothfels gifted her something much more important – trust and validation. From then on, Lothfels fully believed anything Kaiser said, regardless of how bizarre it was.

According to Sonja Veelen, who studies the tricks of con artists and the way they interact with the audience, this kind of behaviour is rooted in our need for consistency. When first meeting a person, we decide very quickly whether to trust that person or not. Once we have made up our mind, we tend to stick to our initial judgement and will often rush to defend it if confronted with evidence to the contrary. That way, once an imposter has already earned our trust, we are more likely to believe and take increasingly greater steps in the direction we have already chosen. Doing otherwise would only trigger a backlash, both emotionally and reputationally. In many cases, this can go so far that the victims of an imposter rigorously deny everything if confronted with the truth.[8]

Kaiser, as we discovered during our investigation, had perfected the game of reciprocity. Again and again, I heard about her doing things that did not yield her any immediate gain, but still underpinned her persona and brought doubters back onto the path of trust. For example, she regularly made others appear in a positive light. In one of the most stunning incidents, she had managed to convince the Bavarian State Chancellery and the Bavarian Minister President to award Papal Secretary Georg Gänswein the Bavarian order of Merit, because Benedict XVI supposedly wished this to be done. Gänswein was completely surprised – he had not done anything in particular for Bavaria – but was still very flattered and naturally accepted the award. The Pope Emeritus shared both his surprise and delight.[9]

Kaiser also managed to leverage her impressive network in the medical community to help people by arranging immediate appointments with prestigious medical specialists. In return, the people she helped were much more likely to support her financially in her 'charitable' endeavours. It is not entirely clear how she managed to build up this network in the medical community, but she did study medicine for two semesters and then worked as a pharmaceutical representative for many years. Regardless, it was known that she was being addressed as 'Colleague' and 'Professor' in some of the clinics.

By successfully building a positive reputation like that, she created a fair amount of 'silent amplifiers' who reinforced her effect on the public by providing her with social proof. Humans, being social animals, like to orient themselves according to the actions of others, since they must be doing something right.[10] In other words: If A believes a person – in this case Kaiser – and B does as well, C is very much inclined to do so as well.

This also happened to me. Even though some of Kaiser's stories did seem rather outlandish from the start, I never doubted her claim that she was descended from Hungarian high nobility, worked for the Vatican and was both a doctor and a lecturer. She was introduced to me as a trustworthy person and continued to be treated as such in illustrious circles – including by the dean of a major Hungarian university.

Over the years, Kaiser was able to set up very elaborate chains of verification. Lothfels, whom Kaiser had got to know via Lothfels' sister, had been convinced by years of regular letters, greetings cards and messages via text and WhatsApp that she was in direct contact with Popes Francis I and Benedict XVI, Gänswein and 'Nicole' ('Your "quadriga" from Rome'). Wassert, meanwhile, was first convinced by the trust Lothfels had put in Kaiser, who then further manipulated Wassert by asking for her medical advice when 'treating' the ailments of God's representative on earth.

One time, when we met with Kaiser in a Swiss town, she arranged a meeting with the town mayor. He had met her via another prominent member of the community and was proud of the fact that she – the prestigious Vatican doctor – had agreed to become the godmother of one of his children. Her godchild was already an adult at that point, showing just how long she had worked on cultivating this particular persona and the chains of social verification that came with it.

To make others believe that you are who you claim to be lies at the heart of any successful con artist's career. Alfons Backes-Haase referred to this as an 'interpsychic power grab' in his analysis of the

Dadaist Walter Serner, who in 1927 published his book *Last Loosening: A Handbook for the Con Artist & Those Aspiring to Become On*.[11] A skilful manipulator is able to build up a great network of 'silent amplifiers' that magnify his or her own efforts. In addition to the tricks mentioned earlier, the liberal distribution of praise and compliments is key to building sympathy, while making oneself scarce is also very beneficial.

The literature also talks about how the mirage of authority and expertise can be further enhanced by the deliberate use of symbols.[12] Kaiser was an avid user of this technique as well, and she liked to gift small rosaries which had supposedly been blessed by Pope Francis himself. My personal highlight of Kaiser displaying her ties to the popes came in the summer of 2014, during the final of the Fifa World Cup in Brazil. I was with Lothfels as we watched the final between Germany and Argentina. Coincidentally, Pope Francis is from Argentina, while Pope Emeritus Benedict XVI was German. Kaiser took the opportunity to call her friend Lothfels and reported to her that the popes could not decide which side to pray for, so they simply went to sleep early. Only Gänswein was still up, and he – as a football expert – was explaining to her what was going on in the game. Lothfels was thoroughly delighted and turned up the volume so that I could listen to the conversation as well.

All this requires a great deal of personal effort, imagination, creativity, but also presence of mind, the willingness to take risks – and personal enjoyment. After all, con artists generally do not see themselves as common fraudsters and desperately try to avoid being seen as such. The educator Stefan Hopmann writes that these are 'characterizations that every conman of distinction must reject as insulting'. After all, 'simple fraud or deception is piecework, true conmanship meanwhile is an art'.[13]

If one looks at Kaiser's web of lies that she had spun over the decades, one cannot but agree. It is telling that she was particularly successful wherever she promised to heal emotional wounds, which rendered her victims vulnerable to her machinations. However, it must be noted that the desire for salvation was not unilateral in Kaiser's relationships.

'But now I look at this little wonder, my granddaughter Magda'.[14] This is how Kaiser introduces herself on page 49 of the memoir, the supposed 'heart' of her grandfather's writings. She had been referred to earlier, as the addressee of the work, but this was the first time she was mentioned in the main text. At this point, other aspects came into the foreground:

> *[Page 51]* Already at the peak of my life's pyramid, I have been tasked by the Creator to raise my little granddaughter. I lost my sons and my wife in Auschwitz.
>
> This little girl – this little Magda. The baby was still so young, when she was only a few hours old, she lost both her mother and Albert, my son, her father, who may have survived Auschwitz – a great thank you to Dr Mengele for this – but who could not find joy in raising his daughter anymore.
>
> I must finish this. I hope that our gracious God will give me enough strength and years that I can see Magda in her profession – I hope she does not become a doctor. And then I can close my eyes and up there I will meet my Rebecca [*sic*], and there I will [*page 53*] tell her everything. That I am not the monster who stood next to Dr Mengele – 50 metres behind his back – on the end station, on the ramp. And I can tell her too that Dr Mengele was not only a killer, but also that he saved the lives of our three sons. We have to thank Mengele that our little granddaughter Magda exists. What a great wonder it is that a human soul and body emerges from these ashes. My gracious God, how can I thank You for all of this. And I pray to You in the darkness of the night. And when I wake up and walk into the other room, the kids' room, then the sun shines onto me from little Magda. [*page 54*] You, my gracious God, I only ask that this tiny soul never learns what her father, grandfather and her grandmother, her family went through, what they had to go through because of this damned Nazi-Germany. I ask You, that she never learns of the existence of Auschwitz. I ask You, God, hear my prayers. Magda shall grow up amidst beauty, surrounded by truth, goodness and love. I beg You, beg You. […]

> [*Page 75*] But what I do not want is that my little Magda learns of everything [*that happened in Auschwitz*]. Now I go again in the kids' room, to look at my little Magda.
>
> [*Page 113*] My past is full of bloody memories and deep suffering, but my present is happy – because of Magda. I have promised her mother that I will raise her.
>
> [*Page 115*] I wander [...] around on the familiar street as if I was the unsteady shadow of myself. Only the sight of Magda takes me out of my deep lethargy. Silently I bear the pain of my illness. But I once again go to Magda, I look at her and imagine that Rebekka speaks to me: Will you take care of her?! Yes, now it makes sense to continue!! There is a for-whom and a why. I will work again. For Magda. It will be a good feeling to help people again, to help women bear children!

This little wonder, this delicate, vulnerable little being, the light in the dark that illuminated the life of her deeply traumatized grandfather. Magda was the reason that her grandfather recovered his will to live, to care for her was his purpose. Through her, he was able to make peace, even with his nightmare – Mengele himself. She was the innocent child that saved a tortured soul, protected against the demons of the past with a wall of silence. This was the stuff great dramas are made of.

Impostors construct these grandiose identities to claim for themselves what they feel they are missing: Money, fame, attention, admiration, but also compassion and love. Kaiser had achieved all of this in her role as a Vatican doctor. Financially, her fraudulent endeavours enabled her to lead a very comfortable life. Aside from the money she stole directly, one of her victims allowed her to live in one of her apartments in Munich. Another victim, meanwhile, allowed her to regularly use a chalet in Switzerland.

In all her roles, Kaiser remained in the background and did her best to limit the number of people who knew about her greatness. Her ostentatious insistence on discretion had so far protected her from detection, but it also prevented her from achieving fame in the wider world. It is very likely that the forgery was her way to break out of the self-imposed isolation, and as a skilled manipulator she had done her best to insert herself into the story as much as possible to get the greatest amount of attention.

Every society, every generation forges that which it cares about the most, surmised the authors of the symposium 'Fake', organized by the British Museum in 1990. One could add: And it forges that which is especially rare. History as a science rests on the analysis of documents. If there are only a few of them, every single piece of information that appears is of extraordinary importance. The reasons for a lack of sources are very diverse. Often, so much time has passed that there is very little contemporary material remaining. In other cases, such as Auschwitz, the documents detailing the crime were systematically destroyed to hide them from public view. In other cases, especially when it comes to testimonies, only very few people are physically and emotionally able to stand witness.

Naturally, forgers have exploited all of these circumstances. In the nineteenth century, the Greek forger Constantine Simonides wowed his philhellenic contemporaries by producing what everyone was dreaming of: Antique maps, drawings, multi-volume works of history from ancient authors whose works had been long lost. He did this with so much skill, weaving a labyrinth of cross-references and loose ends that those who uncovered his forgeries had to fear losing their reputation more than he did. To this day, even reputable museums, auction houses and libraries carry artifacts where it is unclear if they are genuine antiques or 'genuine Simonides'.[15]

In post-war Germany, the time of National Socialism and the Holocaust regularly evokes a great deal of interest. Newly surfaced documents are frequently discussed, a fact that has not escaped forgers. In the most famous case, the German illustrator-turned-criminal Konrad Kujau, wrote a grand total of sixty-two Hitler diaries, beginning in the mid-1970s. The German public fell for this scheme and both the newspaper *Stern* and its owner, the media conglomerate Bertelsmann, bought the rights to the diaries for at least 9.3 million

Deutsche Marks. This was a very high price to pay at the time, but it was dwarfed by the reputational damage done once the supposed diaries were revealed to have been a forgery in 1983.[16]

Kujau's exploits themselves became the stuff of legend and after he was released from prison, he was able to make a living selling 'original Kujau forgeries' of famous paintings. This in turn attracted the attention of forgers, and in 2010, a woman claiming to be his niece was found guilty of forging his forgeries.[17]

As a result of incidents like these, there has been a great deal of scepticism regarding documents that have somehow 'resurfaced'. Furthermore, the focus of public interest has since shifted. Today, even in Germany, it is the victims – or rather their stories – that are popular. The German-Jewish journalist Henryk Broder suspects that behind this stands the desire for 'heroic tales' as a sort of 'point' where the public can 'drop off its repentance'.[18] This may be part of the story, although Broder was specifically talking about another *faked* memoir here. In general, in the genuine stories of the victims, heroism usually does not play a big role. However, when being confronted with such stories, one usually identifies with the victims, and this appears to be very therapeutic for a lot of the perpetrators and especially the children of the perpetrators who are, grappling with their parents' crimes. Engaging with the victims in this way allows the descendants of the perpetrators to deal with their own very ambivalent feelings towards their parents' generation; the intense inner conflict is thus calmed.[19] In essence, this allows these people to switch sides.

This desire for redemption thus offers a great opportunity for forgers and impostors. Beginning in 1968, Karin Mylius, who was in truth the daughter of an SS Einsatzkommando member, pretended to be Jewish and defrauded the eastern German city of Jena for nearly twenty years. She even had her parents, including her father, who had directly participated in the mass murder of Jews, buried in the honorary grove of the local Jewish cemetery. The Jewish communities had known of her real identity very early on, but her communist party membership made her untouchable.[20]

In Pinneberg, near Hamburg, German Wolfgang Seibert had pretended to be the descendant of Holocaust survivors. Over the years, he managed to become the head of the local Reformed Jewish community, which he even represented at the Central Council of Jews in Germany. However, his story was likewise a lie; on the contrary, both his Protestant father and grandfather had fought in the Wehrmacht. Before claiming to be from a family of Holocaust survivors, Seibert had claimed to have been a 'Gypsy'.[21]

In another case, SS-man Günter Reinemer recast himself as a Jew named Hans Wagner after the war. He spied for the Americans, hunted Nazis and, after a series of further moves, identity and profession changes, eventually settled in Caracas, Venezuela, where he married a Jewish woman from Poland. He lived there for fifteen years as a supposed Holocaust survivor until his death and was a well-respected member of the Jewish community. He confessed to everything on his deathbed.[22] In fact, he confessed to more than everything; his participation in the mass murders at the Treblinka death camp, in particular, there is no evidence.[23] It appears as if he lied to make himself both the victim and the perpetrator.

In contrast to Reinemer, the historian Marie Sophie Hingst did produce evidence, albeit forged, in an attempt to have twenty-two of her supposed family members honoured as Holocaust victims at the Yad Vashem World Holocaust Remembrance Center in Israel. Nineteen of the people had been completely made up; the other three were real and indeed related to her, but they had been neither Jews nor did they fall victim to the National Socialists.[24]

In Berlin and elsewhere, Ernst Müller was active under the names Professor Marco von Lobkowicz, Professor Herbert von Gmachler, and Professor Roberto Sbogetoni. He claimed to have been a survivor of both Auschwitz and Theresienstadt and as such, he lectured at the House of the Wannsee Conference and the Moses Mendelssohn Center in Potsdam and was interviewed by Steven Spielberg's Shoah Foundation. Furthermore, he had made a name for himself as a professor of medicine and a trauma expert in psychiatric hospitals. He was also descended from Bohemian high nobility and was supposed to set up the World Health Organization representative office in eastern Germany after 1990.[25]

This is only a very cursory selection; there are countless other cases like these.[26]

Both the imposters and the victims are in large part motivated by deep-seated desires and emotional injuries. This also applies to the rest of the audience that likes to hear such stories and thereby creates the opening for the impostors. The most famous Holocaust imposter of this kind was Binjamin Wilkomirski,[27] who convinced countless people, first in Germany and Switzerland, then across the entire world, that as an infant he had survived two concentration camps, where he had witnessed unspeakable horrors. He had locked up his trauma throughout most of his life, but it was only with the help of an innovative Israeli psychotherapist that he was able to access these long-lost memories, about which he was then able to talk about freely. Wilkomirski even went on to publish a book titled *Fragments: Memories of a Wartime Childhood* that won several awards.

However, it soon emerged that Wilkomirski was not who he claimed to be. Instead of being born in a concentration camp, he had been born in 1941 in neutral Switzerland, as Bruno Grosjean. In 1945, he was taken in by a wealthy family from Zürich, which then fully adopted him in 1957. From that time, his last name was Dössecker.

Despite the many inconsistencies, people and even experts generally believed his story. His publisher, his agent, the media and the public thought he was genuine. One of the lowest points was his reunification with his supposed father, who was a genuine Holocaust survivor who believed that WIlkomirski was his long-dead son. This highly emotional event was truly harrowing, tearful – and was recorded by a professional camera crew. There were doubts about the veracity of his claim from the start, but most simply *wanted* to believe him.[28] The story was simply too good to be false.

In 1994, the Massachusetts-based publisher, Jane Daniel, got word of the tales of Misha Defonseca, a Holocaust survivor. Born as Misha Levy, her Jewish parents had been deported to Eastern Europe when she was just 7 years old. Little Misha then embarked on a grand journey across German-occupied Europe to find her parents, marching through the forests, sneaking in – and out – of the Warsaw Ghetto and even killing a German soldier in self-defence. At one point, she even joined a pack of wolves, and it was as part of this pack that she survived the Holocaust and the war.[29]

Jane Daniel immediately recognized the potential of this truly amazing Holocaust story and convinced Defonseca to write down her memories for her publishing house. To help Defonseca write the book, she convinced Professor Vera Lee from Boston to join the project as a co-author. In 1997, the supposed Holocaust autobiography was then published under the title *Misha: A Mémoire of the Holocaust Years*.[30]

The book was a commercial success in Europe and was translated into eighteen languages; it even became the basis of a French-language movie that made headlines. In the USA, however, the book failed to make a mark commercially, and Defonseca and the co-author sued the publisher for, among other things, failing to advertise the book properly. The courts eventually agreed with the authors, awarding Defonseca an eye-watering $22.5 million and her co-author a sum of $9.9 million as compensation.

Just several months later, in early 2008, the entire story was revealed to have been untrue. After some research it soon turned out that the supposed Holocaust survivor was, in fact, Monique Ernestine Josephine de Wael and had been born into a Catholic family in Belgium. While her parents had indeed been persecuted by the German occupiers, the persecution was due to their activity in the resistance. Her father was deported to a concentration camp, where he died, and Monique grew up with her grandmother in Brussels and later with her uncle. In 1973, she married her husband and together with him moved to the US in 1985.

After these revelations, Monique de Wael claimed that she did not in fact lie, but that she had been acting in good faith: 'It's not the true reality, but it is my reality. […] Ever since I can remember, I felt Jewish. There are times when I find it difficult to differentiate between reality and my inner world.'[31] In the end, she could not be proven to have committed a crime, but nevertheless, in 2014 she was forced to pay back the $22.5 million she had received from her former publisher.[32]

In 2005, American author Jean Goodwin Messinger published the life story of Holocaust survivor Rosemarie Pence under the title *Hannah: From Dachau to the Olympics and Beyond*. According to the book, Pence, a Jewish child from Germany, had been deported to the Dachau concentration camp as a 3-year-old. At Dachau, she had been subjected to medical experiments, but survived and after the war she was raised by Catholic nuns. These nuns also taught her how to ski so well that she was able to participate in the 1956 Winter Olympics at Cortina d'Ampezzo, where she competed for Germany. Afterwards, she moved to Israel to live in a kibbutz. She later married an American fighter pilot and moved to the US. Unfortunately, he was later shot down during a combat mission over Vietnam and had been missing ever since.

Messinger was completely taken by this story and decided to write it down and publish it – without properly verifying it first, however. Four years after the book's publication, it then emerged that Rosemarie Pence had made up her story. In reality, she was a Protestant German-American who had run into trouble with the law for a variety of offences, including cheque fraud.[33]

In 2019, the story of Peter Loth from Florida made headlines worldwide. Loth was likewise a Holocaust survivor and he appeared as a joint plaintiff and witness in the trial against Bruno Dey, who had been a SS guard in the Stutthof concentration camp. Loth appeared before the court on 12 November and talked about how he was from a Jewish-German family from Danzig (now Gdańsk). His mother was deported to Stutthof in March 1943; she was pregnant at the time and Loth was born in the camp. Both Peter Loth and his mother were subjected to medical experiments there. In 1945, Loth was separated from his mother and grew up in a Polish orphanage. It was not until he was 15 years old that he was reunited with his mother in West Germany; his mother had in the meantime married an American soldier and together with him they later moved to the US. Loth talked about his harrowing experiences of abandonment, sexual violence and discrimination. 'Especially painful [...] for him was the constant feeling of being an outcast and the painful questions about his own identity.'[34]

During the trial, something extraordinary happened. Loth asked the accused: 'How do you feel today? Do you regret something?' He replied that he did indeed regret everything that had happened.

> Then Loth asks the accused to look him in the eyes and asks: 'Would you forgive me? For the hate and the anger, which I temporarily felt against the German people?' 'Sure, I feel no hate', the accused responded. Then Loth goes around the table, says 'I forgive you too' and hugs D. [the accused]. Both men are in tears, they hold each other in their arms. 'Now I am free'. Loth says as he walks back to his seat. 'Through this I liberate myself.'[35]

'This story went around the world', the German news magazine *Der Spiegel* reported later 'but it was not true.'[36] It soon came out that Loth had completely invented his extraordinary story. According to civil records from Dortmund in West Germany, Loth came from a Protestant German family and had no ties to Judaism; his birth at the Stutthof concentration camp had been a complete lie. Prior to the trial, Loth had been cultivating this fake narrative for decades, and publicly talked about it in front of classrooms and on other occasions.[37] After the truth was revealed, Loth quickly withdrew his collateral action and apologized for what he had done. Nevertheless, he continued to claim that 'all the things I had said during the trial, are true according to the best of my knowledge.'[38]

Loth's false testimony did not derail the proceedings, however, and the SS-man was given a suspended sentence of two years in July 2020. Still, the damage Peter Loth had caused was immense. The international Christian-Jewish 'March of Life' charity wrote:

> The true victims of Peter Loth's story are the Holocaust survivors and the Jewish witnesses, especially the parties involved in the trial in Hamburg. They are victimized once again, because of the great

> deal of attention that is diverted to the Peter Loth incident from the actually relevant topic – the terrible Stutthof concentration camp and the guilt of the perpetrators.[39]

These stories of fake Holocaust survivors are just the tip of the iceberg. Saskia Baron, a British journalist and film producer, recently wrote in a review of a documentary about the case of Misha Defonseca:

> Over the decades there have been numerous instances of people claiming falsely to be Holocaust child survivors (Rosemarie Pence, Moshe Peter Loth, Rosemarie Koczy, Binjamin Wilkomirski). One could make a fascinating documentary about these delusional claimants, including Misha [Defonseca], and what prompts their lies – mental illness, financial gain, a desire to be loved as a victim, or a desperate craving for fame. One could make an equally fascinating documentary about why the public is so eager to eat up a story as wild as Misha's.[40]

Furthermore, these incidents show that even after the fraud is uncovered, it is very hard to bring these imposters to justice. Defonseca, for example, simply claimed that she genuinely believed the story she had been telling everyone. Bruno Dössecker, alias Binjamin Wilkomirski, claimed the same, while also denying others from seeing his birth certificate, which would have unravelled his scheme much earlier. It is fair to assume that Magdolna Kaiser had been following these cases closely and that she had learned from them. At the very least, she had been familiar with the Wilkomirski case as I ascertained during a conversation I had with her.

Aside from these 'classic' fraud tales, there are also the stories from genuine Holocaust survivors, who, for whatever reason, 'enriched' their fundamentally real experiences by adding made-up elements. The most famous cases of these were those of Jerzy Kosinski and Martin Gray. Jerzy Kosinski (1933-1991) survived the Holocaust in occupied Poland thanks to a forged birth certificate, and later emigrated to the US in the late 1950s. There, he became a writer and wrote among others his bestselling memoir *The Painted Bird* (1965), detailing his experiences during his time in hiding. It later came out that he had invented most of the events he talked about, but at its core, it was true – he did indeed survive the Holocaust hidden away in the Polish countryside.[41]

Martin Gray was a Franco-American writer of Polish-Jewish heritage. He was born in Warsaw in 1922 under the name Mieczysław Grajewski, survived the Holocaust in occupied Poland and then emigrated to the US in 1946. There, he found success as a businessman before moving to France together with his family. In 1971, he wrote his autobiography *Au nom de tous les miens* [For Those I Loved], which was translated into twenty-six languages and sold over 30 million copies. In it and its sequels, he wrote about his experiences as a Jew in German-occupied Poland, including his time in the Treblinka death camp. He claimed that he fled Treblinka and managed to join the partisans and later the Red Army.[42] However, the historian Gitta Sereny proved in 1979 that at the very least the story of his imprisonment at Treblinka had been invented. Likewise, his stories about him fighting for the partisans were very questionable too.[43]

Defonseca, Wilkomirski and the others carefully cultivated their supposed Jewish identity over decades before bursting into the spotlight. Kaiser likewise had been working on her legend as a second-generation Holocaust survivor for many years before contacting us. Complete moral authority, tales of gruesome crimes but also of incredible heroism – this was what the supposed countess was after. As we had ascertained during our investigation, Kaiser had been forging stories and medical certificates for years. The next logical step up was the story of Mengele, Auschwitz, human experiments, her supposed Jewish grandfather becoming an accomplice, and among it all, like a ray of light in the dark – little Magda.

For her Auschwitz memoirs, Kaiser mostly employed the same tried-and-true methods she had used to forge her correspondence with the Vatican. She plagiarized a great deal and relied a lot on the internet – without considering that her victims could access the same information she did, however. Kaiser also knew how to fuse together the various plagiarized texts with her own texts to create something relatively coherent. It is likely that she had help given the sheer volume of the fabricated material, as well as the detailed historical knowledge needed for it. She certainly did have a wide-ranging network of friends across multiple countries who we never found out much about, and Elly Ostertag's diary was clearly written by someone else. Nevertheless, what is clear is that she personally forged most of what she showed us.

Kaiser likely counted on the fact that none of the people involved initially – Wassert, Lothfels and I – spoke Hungarian, allowing her to plagiarize Hungarian texts to her heart's content. After all, Hungarian stands isolated as the sole spoken, Finno-Ugric language in Central Europe, and is thus completely incomprehensible to us. Without Kemény, who as a native Hungarian-speaker was able to catch the subtleties and linguistic inconsistencies in the texts he was translating, knew the subject as a historian and also knew where to search online, it would have taken much longer for us to confirm that we were dealing with a forgery. Kaiser had immediately realized the danger he he posed to her scheme and demanded that we not work with him, offering to translate these texts on her own instead. Her mistake was to believe that we had indeed discontinued his services; another one was to believe that she would be able to control the direction of our research project via Wassert, or at least monitor it.

Above all, she clearly did not imagine the kinds of problems a proper historical investigation posed for her. Kujau's Hitler Diaries had been preceded by other forged Hitler documents, which the Hitler expert Professor Eberhard Jäckel had published in 1980. Because of this, the first Kujau forgeries had thus been certified to be real by some of the foremost experts in the field. While there were doubts regarding the authenticity of these documents from the start, the demand was there and *Stern* was unable to resist.

It is very probable that Kaiser was familiar with this story. After all, she did insist on Lothfels' idea to get a historian – in this case me – on board. Publishing the first edition of the Grósz Chorin documents as part of a scholarly edition promised not only historical fame, but would also verify her forgeries and, just as importantly, set the stage for further projects. That she had plenty in store for us was evident, and throughout our project she was continuously teasing us with even more 'discoveries', which she undoubtedly sought to profit from as well. She likely would have been safe too; who in his right mind would question the stories of a second-generation Holocaust victim who is backed by history itself?

The aura of truth is essential for any con artist – but also for a historian like me. When I first heard of the presence of these documents, I was skeptical. I still vividly remembered the downfall of my colleague Jäckel in the 1980s, but also the case of the historian Werner Maser. In the late 1970s, he had proudly presented to the world Hitler's supposed son Jean Loret – without presenting conclusive proof. As a result, I was very cautious. I simply could not proceed without first ascertaining the veracity of the original documents beyond a shadow of a doubt, confirming the internal consistency and credibility of the claims made in the ever-expanding 'estate'.

However, the original documents were lacking. Even the death certificate she had promised us right from the beginning was still missing years later. Kaiser's own birth certificate was not there as well. When I asked about the land register entry confirming the transfer of her grandfather's apartment to Kaiser, she simply broke out in tears – this all was still too painful for her and she did not wish to be pushed around like that. Research into the Hungarian side of her family, the venerable Batthyány – was *verboten* [forbidden] on emotional grounds. This sort of emotional deflection is one of the main emergency maneuvers impostors like to use.[44] In this case, it did work to some extent, and I relented for the time being. Wassert was going to look into this later while writing about the countess' family history anyway. Not following through immediately was my mistake.

It was only when Lothfels, Wassert and I were talking about Kaiser's deceptions after unveiling her web of lies that we recognized how well she had played us off against one another. She had essentially been securing the backstage through targeted avoidance strategies that succeeded in dividing the different audiences to such an extent that she was never caught playing conflicting roles at the same time.[45] For me, she was the granddaughter of a prisoner-doctor who was promising to hand me a historical sensation, for Wassert, she was a friend and colleague whose family history she wanted to learn about, while Lothfels knew her as a conduit to the Vatican and a close confidante who had helped her immensely in the past and now needed help herself. Each of us knew a different Kaiser, and each of us was interested in different things.

Despite significant differences, Kaiser's Auschwitz forgeries showed several parallels to Kujau's faked Hitler Diaries. I therefore think that it is likely she was at least inspired by them. For example, she made sure to not repeat Kujau's mistake of writing with modern ink on modern paper. When the paper Kujau had been using was forensically analyzed, it emerged it had been bleached with materials that had only been in use since 1955, proving the diaries to be forgeries.[46] Later, the ink was analyzed as well and were also found to contain materials that only began to be added after the war.[47] Kujau had been completely oblivious to the possibility that such things could even be tested.[48] Magdolna Kaiser did not make this mistake and exclusively wrote on paper from the 1930s and 1940s, with pencils and copy pens, whose composition had not changed since the nineteenth century.

While she had seemingly learned from his mistakes, she apparently learned from his successes too, and the preparation and popularization of her forgeries was very similar to the way Kujau had done it earlier. Initially, Kujau had sold individual forged documents from Hitler to various people, including collectors and businessmen. In 1975, he produced his first Hitler diary covering the first half of 1935, which he loaned to a businessman, while retaining full ownership himself. Kujau used an alias – Konrad Fischer – and added a fake doctoral degree to his name as well.[49]

In 1978, Professor Dr August Priesack and Professor Eberhard Jäckel, both renowned experts in the field, were given some of the individual documents for appraisal. Both believed them to be genuine. Afterwards, 'Konrad Fischer' (i.e. Kujau) handed Professor Jäckel seventy-six Hitler documents for publication, completely free of charge. It was only in September 1979 that Professor Jäckel saw the first Hitler diary (from 1975). Like the previous documents, he believed it to be real and indeed a breakthrough for historiography.[50]

In autumn 1980, Jäckel and his colleague Kuhn published the document collection *Hitler: Sämtliche Aufzeichnungen 1905–1924* [Hitler: Complete Records 1905-1924] with the Deutsche Verlagsanstalt in Stuttgart. Among the published documents were the seventy-six Hitler documents Konrad Kujau had forged.[51] They had thus passed all scrutiny and were accepted into the historical mainstream as genuine. In the introduction, the publishers praised the Kujau forgeries in particular, singling them out as 'especially precious pieces of writing' and wrote 'of fifty, in part, particularly revealing documents from private collections.'[52]

In October 1980, the German magazine *Stern* printed excerpts from Jäckel's and Kuhn's book. This was a very notable occurrence; popular magazines such as *Stern* rarely pay this much attention to editions of historical documents like they did here.

The publication of the seventy-six Hitler documents in a reputable historical edition and the popularization thereof electrified Kujau. Now that public interest had been sufficiently stoked – and he had been given the coveted academic seal of authenticity – Kujau returned to writing more Hitler diaries. Beginning in early 1981, he went on to produce a flurry of new diaries, which – according to him – had been hidden away in the vaults of a Swiss bank. Notably, this was the exact same narrative Kaiser had presented us with regarding Grósz Chorin's documents. In the end, Kujau authored a grand total of sixty-two Hitler diaries and sold them all to *Stern* for 9.3 million Deutsche Marks. In April 1983, *Stern* then published the first of these Hitler diaries accompanied by great media hype. However, this only lasted for a few days. It very quickly emerged that the diaries had been forged – a complete disaster for the magazine and everyone involved.

Like Kujau, Kaiser had transferred the first batch of forged documents – via Lothfels – to me, a historian, completely free of charge. This seemed to prove to us that she did not have any material interest in the story, otherwise she would have demanded money or insisted on retaining the rights. Once we had published the first batch of documents, giving them the seal of authenticity, much of the academic and public attention would have inevitably fallen upon Kaiser herself. Only then could she finally capitalize on her scheme by receiving substantial fees from film rights, public appearances and perhaps even her own autobiography. If successful, this bonanza could possibly go on for years if not decades.

Aside from the substantial material benefits, Kaiser would also have received generous media attention, as well as wide social recognition, which she evidently craved. This would likely even merit a place for her in the history books. Until then, her greatness was very much limited and she was only able to play the role of a high-born professor in the service of the Vatican in front of a relatively small group of people.

Kujau simply wanted to become rich. Wilkomirski and many others wanted to become either famous or have their faked identity accepted as real. Meanwhile, Magdolna Beretka from Bečej wanted both riches and fame.

Regardless of their motives, con artists are extremely dangerous. They wreak havoc in the lives of individuals, parasitizing people and ruining the reputations of experts and even entire media publishing houses. In the context of the history of the Second World War, they also cause immense societal damage. Not only do they muddy history until they are eventually unmasked, but they also draw into question all the true things we know about the Third Reich and the Holocaust in particular. This way, they fuel Holocaust denial. In cases like Wilkomirski's and Kaiser's, where they abused the stories and memories of real victims, they furthermore abuse the victims a second time.

Wieland Schwanebeck calls imposture a 'cultural practice' in the introduction of his anthology *Über Hochstapelei* [On Imposture].[53] How can we detect imposters and con artists? The authors of one of the articles provide us with a list of nineteen indicators with which the constructs of imposters can be tested. However, even with such a complex and standardized procedure, the authors lament that the rate of error is still high – up to 35%. Con artists are at their most effective when they can underpin their lies with forged documents. Only through the discovery of such falsifications is it possible to uncover such impostors beyond a doubt.[54] Even Simonides had not been spared this fate.

Magdolna Kaiser wanted to make it big as a fraudster, impostor and forger. And indeed, she had already achieved a lot. Just using our limited means, we found that she had managed to steal millions.

Looking at it from a distance, it seems like she lost control the moment her craving for recognition got the better of her and she began to aggressively insert herself into her story. Beforehand, she had successfully cultivated an aura of utter selflessness, which she broke by redirecting all the attention onto herself, little Magda, her grandfather's infant saviour. As soon as 'this little wonder' stepped onto the scene and was validated, her otherwise impeccable social instincts began to fail, and she was unable to recognize that we had long seen through her deception.

But is this truly the end of the story? Shortly before her arrest, Magdolna (alias Nicole), confessed to us that she was in fact not the biological granddaughter of Grósz Chorin. On the contrary, she was now telling us that she was in fact the secret daughter of Cardinal Jean-Marie Lustiger, Archbishop of Paris, who had died in 2007. He had grown up as Aron Lustiger, a Polish Jew, and was the cousin of historian and Holocaust survivor Arno Lustiger. Aron survived the war in hiding and converted to Catholicism in Orléans.

According to the philologist Thomas Rahn, 'the confession of the impostor is the hidden telos of the impostor's career [...]. The crime is the preparation for a great story.'[55] This makes one wonder: what was going to be her finale? And who would she be at that point?

Imposters like her have sprung up regularly in the past and it is only a matter of time until the next imposter bursts into the public spotlight. Chances are that they are already walking among us.

Jan Philipp Reemtsma: Promises of Glamour and Invented Darkness

This is the story of an unusually bizarre fraud, a con story. And the story of its exposure. The discovery of this impostor by the Polish-German historian Bogdan Musial is intimately tied to the particularly peculiar and strange side of this story. A Hungarian countess that is not one, who among other things collects money for African hospitals that do not exist and instead pockets the money for herself, a woman claiming to be the personal physician of not one but two popes, which is a lie, who also says she is the descendant of an Auschwitz survivor, who never existed. To make this part of her invented story believable, she seeks out a historian whom she likewise manipulates and who is to help her manipulate the astonishment-gripped public. But it went wrong.

The first time I met Bogdan Musial was during the confrontations around the first exhibition on the crimes of the German Wehrmacht, which I was the patron of as the founder and then-head of the Hamburg Institute for Social Research.[1] There, Musial had earned himself a reputation for his very careful, accurate presentation of sources that reached beyond his profession.

The Hamburg Foundation for the Promotion of Science and Culture, which I likewise founded and led, later supported Musial's work *Sowjetische Partisanen 1941-1944: Mythos und Wirklichkeit* [Soviet Partisans 1941-1944: Myth and Reality] (Paderborn 2009). Now, half a decade later, Musial spoke to me regarding a very interesting story that had been brought to his attention. A certain Dr Kaiser, a personal doctor of the Pope, who was descended from the Hungarian branch of the Batthyány family, and who was engaged in all kinds of endeavours – including in the funding of an exchange programme for Bhutanese students at the Szent István University in Budapest[2] – had contacted him regarding the story of her late grandfather. He, a Jewish doctor, had been deported to Auschwitz, where he was forced to work for none other than Josef Mengele. That very same Mengele had saved her grandfather's life, an act which he repaid by helping Mengele hide away after the war. Her grandfather had left a diary – and Musial was the one to publish it. Musial asked me if the foundation would support the research necessary to publish such an edition financially. I said yes.

Someone who already knows that this was a fraud may frown upon this story. Hungarian countess, plus Vatican doctor, plus international philanthropist, plus Jewish Auschwitz-survivor grandfather – and Mengele is also in the mix? This is all a bit much, indeed. But this is how a lot of the stories told by con artists work: They are barely believable, otherwise it would not make sense to even tell them, and that they are believed is, among other reasons, rooted in the fact that nobody thinks anyone would make up such a clearly unlikely story.

There was also more, which will be discussed later. On top of that, unlikely is a very relative term. By definition, in the moments of history where something very extraordinary happens, what *does* happen is virtually unthinkable in more normal times. Where social rules and dynamics change, because the nature of power and the way it is exerted have changed, one will find events and people that would otherwise be impossible. In a place like Auschwitz, where this happened on a scale and in forms seen in no other place, the usual rules of what is humanely possible and what is not, do not apply. 'This cannot be real, nobody would do that' – this does not work when it comes to Auschwitz. Yet, one also has to remain careful when confronted with newly discovered documents. A historian needs to exercise caution – not out of general distrust, but because they need to verify and analyze each source they are working with. What kind of source is it? How was it preserved? How did it emerge? These and many more questions like them need to be answered. It was precisely this kind of research that I was talking about with Musial.

What did we expect from this diary? Virtually every newly discovered source about any historical place can potentially add to the already existing body of knowledge. Regarding Auschwitz and the prisoner-doctors in particular, there was at the time some knowledge of the details, but rather little in the way of systematic knowledge. Given the large gaps, every new detail uncovered could add to the overall picture, if not change it completely. This is doubly true for this case, where a man purportedly lived a kind of dual existence: That of a guardian angel of the prisoners – and at the same time that of henchman of a mass murderer, who set up his own personal version of hell into which he sent defenceless prisoners in the name of 'medical science'. In this context, there is no normal, not only in the moral sense – whatever that means.

And in a life that is highly extraordinary in the first place – a member of a venerable noble family and medical service for a very special group – another factor comes into play that under normal circumstances is highly extraordinary as well, does not make the entire story much less likely. Probabilities do not add up, after all. Winning the lottery does not render one immune to other, equally improbable events such as contracting an exceedingly rare illness, for example.

Indeed, it was the entire cluster of improbabilities that imbued the story with an air of believability – nobody in his or her right mind would make up something as unlikely. The conclusion of the story is banal. The imposter – exposed, the diary – a forgery. Some of her victims were mentioned in the press, and she was sent to prison. Still, the story itself is in a way 'good', gripping but also interesting as well – since con stories in general are nearly always gripping and what makes them gripping always gives a great anthropological insight into how humans, as social and cultural creatures, work. In this specific case, it offers us a deep glimpse into the workings of the cultural functioning of the Central European person in the latter half of the twentieth century and the early twenty-first century.

Let us now turn to another case. The name Karl May is a household name in the German-speaking world and his tales of the Wild West are still read to this day and people still watch the movies based on them. However, before he became 'Karl May', he was a small-time fraudster and impostor. And once he became 'Karl May', he turned into – a great impostor?

At any rate, in 1864, before his success as an author, he lied about being an ophthalmologist by the name of 'Dr Heilig MD',[3] went to a tailor and – after confirming his fake identity by issuing a medical prescription – had himself given a fresh set of new clothing – without paying for it. As 'seminary leader Lohse', he showed a great interest in expensive furs, before stealing several and running away. As music copyist 'Hermin', he tried the same but only managed to evade justice for a short time.[4] He was soon arrested and sent to prison. After his release, he went around posing alternatively as a 'police lieutenant' or 'secret policeman', seizing supposedly counterfeit money. He was again arrested, and during a search of his possessions, the police found the passport of a fictitious American consul-general by the name of Burton. Still, he managed to run away, finding refuge with a certain Malwine Wadenbach, to whom he posed as a writer from Dresden. He moved on but was eventually caught sleeping in an attic. The investigators were confronted with a truly fantastical story: He now claimed to be Albin Wadenbach, the son of a planter from Orby, Martinique, who was touring Europe together with his younger brother to visit their family. Unfortunately, however, the two brothers had become separated recently, and the brother had accidentally taken Albin's identification documents with him. This story convinced the investigators and he was able to keep up the façade for four weeks, writing letters to various made-up people whom he asked to help. In the end, his story fell apart when he contacted Malwine Wadenbach and the police began investigating the author whom she had sheltered previously. May was sentenced to five years in prison.

So far, so strange – or perhaps not. Regardless of how much one wants to tie May's history of imposture with his later life as a writer (in his autobiography, he described his flight from the police as follows: 'I broke […] my fetters and disappeared.'), one has to admit that it is only this later life as a strange but important author that elevates his earlier history of petty crime. On the other hand, however, even the pettier con stories can be fascinating on their own, be it due to the creativity of the story, or because they make their victims look exceedingly foolish. The cases themselves appear as unbelievable as the lies the impostors come up with. The apparent mystery lies in both.

But back to Karl May. He became increasingly famous as the author of a series of supposed travel stories; some of his readers understood the 'I' in his stories about Old Shatterhand and Kara ben Nemsi as what it was – as the voice of the narrator in the first-person present-tense, a common occurrence in Western literature – but others believed it to be May himself. This does happen frequently. Many readers of the East German author Stephan Hermlin[5] likewise believed the protagonist of his novels to be a literarily over-shaped, but still fundamentally autobiographical figure. How much empirical 'I' lies within Alfred Andersch's *The Cherries of Freedom: A Report*?[6] This all depends on how much the reader of these books who values the 'I' is empirically 'correct'. And it decisively depends on whether the author, through his books or life story, sanctions such identifications – or not. Karl May made his readers an offer, some (many) took it up – and in turn made him the offer to play this role in public as well. This soon turned into a breathtaking circus. He went on tours, he filled halls.

One newspaper reported that 'in the dining hall of a hotel' he was giving 'the most nonsensical answers to the equally nonsensical question … He claimed, among other things, that he spoke around 1,200 languages and dialects, that he had succeeded Winnetou as the commander of the Apache and that he used to have 35,000 warriors under his command, and that he had recently been to Mecca.'[7] What was this? 1,200 languages and dialects? Is one supposed to say that this is so unlikely that one *had* to believe it because one *could only believe* it? Surely, if someone claims to speak languages other than English, like German, French or Spanish – this is not that uncommon. If one also speaks Russian and Mandarin – that's remarkable. Even more? Then one says to oneself: He is exaggerating, his Slovene – well, that will surely be just a few words and phrases, a 'good morning' and 'thank you'. Alternatively, one thinks that it is *so* unlikely that someone would speak so many languages, that it would be *completely unlikely* that one would brag about something like that. It could happen that one tends to simply believe a person's outlandish claims because one does not want to believe that this person would lie so brazenly. One does not want to believe brazenness, but even more, one does not want to believe that the other person believes one to be so foolish as to fall for such nonsense.

This is especially true when one has already gone some way to accommodate the other person. If one chooses to not believe the other today, one would have to admit that one should not have believed the other yesterday as well. To not be foolish today, one has to admit that one had been foolish yesterday. The people who saw their Karl May come up with the most outlandish stories on the fly were the ones who had believed the 'I' in his books to have genuinely been him, and who now wanted to see him in person, this man who was rather meek and short in stature – how did he 'break his fetters'? How did he kill a Grizzly with a knife? Knock out a giant Native American with a single punch? Others had been annoyed with the exceedingly boastful first person narrator of the novels and had set aside the books because of this; others were annoyed but chose to set aside their misgivings to enjoy his entertaining and colourful stories. But for those who had believed the tiny Saxon to have completed all these feats of heroism across the world, the man who was still kind of one of them at heart, who was well-versed in philosophy and knew the *Qur'an* so well that he was able to embarrass any Muslim scholar – why not believe his exceptional linguistic feats as well? After all, when one has already begun to believe, it is very hard to stop believing, because you believe it 'gives you something'. If Jesus walked across water, as it is said, why would He not be able to return from the dead?

When David Hume examined the question of wonders, he came to the conclusion that there *could* of course be wonders, but one *never* has any reason to *believe* in any specific wonder. The likelihood that we simply do not know enough to fully explain an event is always larger than the likelihood that it is a genuine wonder. Even most people who have not read Hume should know this intuitively.

And yet many parents put amber necklaces around their infants to soothe their teething pains. They believe in the effectiveness of this remedy because others do so too, because people they see as credible told them to, instead of saying 'These people are nice and all, and what they are saying is good and nice, but: Amber necklaces? Oh dear!' This is not merely a question of credibility but of whether one wants to let in the extraordinary into one's life. Especially *because* one does not know how exactly an amber necklace is supposed to help with the aching jaws of a teething infant, it is nice to imagine oneself to be part of a great unfathomable whole, into which one is granted a small, yet unusual insight. Thus, there stands 'Dr Karl May (the title 'Dr' was his too, legally even, after an obscure institution had given him one) and not only outshines the many who have come to listen to him, but indeed everyone else; in the presence a of a true *Übermensch* like him, everyone else pales in comparison. Like all believers, the worshippers debase themselves in order to elevate themselves as his chosen ones. It is like in the Monty Python movie *The Life of Brian*: 'He has given us – a shoe!' 'It's a sandal!' Or as it is in the Gospel of John, which the parody references: He lived among us.

In cases like this, Thomas Mann's titular figure Felix Krull is often referenced. However, he was no impostor in the classical sense, he did not even want to be one; he only did a noble a favour: The noble's family demanded the noble go on a world tour, but he much preferred to remain in Paris with his mistress. Krull then agreed to switch identities out of kindness, but also because he thought he could play the role of count better than the count himself.

This is probably not that difficult. It is sometimes quite baffling what kind of people families with great and ancient names produce, eccentric only in stupendous banality. But why is one baffled? Who is baffled too much has already fallen for the deception to some extent. Did one expect that just because someone is a Prince So-and-So of Whatever he is less likely to be an idiot or freak than someone from among the normals? The name of the family does not matter that much, what matters more are the numbers, and with a very high likelihood, there are one or several of that kind. After all, one still wants the unlikely. In the eighteenth century, there were countless works on why people believed in ghosts. These people wanted proximity to the radiance of the exceptional, because who is shined upon in such a way is not in the dark anymore, but stands in the light, even if it is rather pale.

Borrowed light. Krull was somebody whose mere presence was radiant, even before he began his travels as a count. His company was pleasant, and even if he simply blessed a liftboy with the right gesture or an appropriate smile, he lit up his day. Indeed, if someone wants to have success as a con artist, one needs to be *able to be one*. Mann made his Krull look handsome, but this was not necessary. May did not look like Old Shatterhand, but he still managed to do it. Hitler looked like an inferior copy of Charlie Chaplin's Tramp, but very few took issue with that. Projection – one sees what one wants to see – is too little; one sees what one desires to see. No Fata Morgana looks like an oasis on its own.

Had the story described in this book been an ordinary con story – always taking into account that such stories would not exist if they did not touch upon the extraordinary, and that even 'ordinary' con stories are thus extraordinary in their own special way – the book would not have to be written. What makes this story so special, special even by the standards of the already by definition extraordinary con stories, is the combination of highly volatile elements – ancient nobility, high-profile charity, practising medicine at a highly unusual place – and the appropriation of some of the most horrific events in human history.

Why did Mrs Kaiser, Countess Batthyány, with everything she was pretending to be, need to add a grandfather who was a prisoner-doctor in Auschwitz? Why did she pour so much energy into this part of her invented biography, even though she could have simply dropped a remark about a Jewish family member here and there, and then said, 'I could not find a trace of him, please do not ask…'? On the contrary, she forged a whole series of documents, and instead of seeking some accomplice, she went to a historian who was to attest to the authenticity of the forgery – what a supreme display of confidence in her skills!

She further stoked his professional curiosity by hesitantly giving out more pieces of information here and there. She exaggerated a bit, sure, but all con artists exaggerate – it is in their nature. Indeed, many con artists' careers are, in fact, ruined by themselves when they try to exceed their already extraordinary successes. If the previous tricks succeeded, why not the next one, and the one after that too? This can turn into a veritable maelstrom in which both the impostor and audience get trapped. The forger Kujau produced one Hitler diary after another and on top of that promised additional paintings and even operas.

But in general, most such people stay true to what they are used to. Perhaps an impostor playing the role of a prince whose ancestors were frequent guests at Versailles goes on to invent a story of a long-lost cousin who in the sixteenth century was married off to a Great Khan as a favour to a Russian tsar? The image becomes more colourful, and who can even verify it?

An invented Jewish grandfather who was also an Auschwitz survivor (with all the accessories the impostor had made up herself to appropriate an even darker history) does not seem to fit into this pattern at first glance. Some speculation may clarify how it happened that Mrs Kaiser-Batthyány became the first to combine a venerable pedigree and glamorous philanthropy with that which one can only talk about in hushed voices (but that which could still perhaps make for good content for a talk show on the theme of 'How did you feel when you learned that your grandfather…?').

Until the second half of the twentieth century, having become the victim of a crime (or having family ties to victims of historical crimes) was usually seen as something less-than-honourable and was therefore often downplayed. Today, however, this has been turned into something that can attract positive attention.[8] What once meant pain and danger – and shame – was transmuted into something that could bestow respect. Both are irrational.

Whoever has become the victim of a crime of course does not have to feel shame about this, but at the same time, there is little reason to be proud of it. But then came a time in which it was treated as a reason for pride. A similarly strange and illustrative proof for this is the case of Wilkomirski. In 1995, a book was published by the Swiss author Binjamin Wilkomirski, in which he wrote – thanks to psychotherapy – about his reclaimed past as a child who survived German concentration and death camps. The descriptions were filled with gruesome details; readers were left speechless. The book became famous, the author too, and he received prizes. There were doubts, but the doubters – renowned historians among them – remained silent, until the Swiss journalist Daniel Ganzfried uncovered the fraud – or was it just a case of autosuggestion?[9] Wilkomirski was, in fact, Bruno Dössecker and he surely did experience a difficult and unhappy childhood in an adoptive Swiss family in Switzerland. But why did he invent one that was much worse?

In his 1909 essay 'Der Familienroman der Neurotiker' [The Family Romances], Sigmund Freud wrote about the regularly occurring phenomenon of people claiming to be of 'more noble background' than they actually are, perhaps one who had been fathered by a prince with a prestigious-sounding name.[10] The case of Wilkomirski gives us an example of such fictitious ancestry that could not possibly be more terrible.

We can still joke about someone who lies about noble heritage, but in such a case we cannot: And why should we? After all, 'Wilkomirski' did not brag about his supposed fate, he only spoke about it and the respect grew up around it. By the way, his book won literary prizes too, and he was praised for his vivid description of the horror he had supposedly faced. Once the swindle – be it deception or self-deception – had been uncovered, the literary value of his book fell to the ground.

In our case, being 'Countess Batthyány' was not enough, neither was Bhutan (which, oddly enough, was real, though the ties had been acquired through deception), the Vatican, nor the charity in Africa. She needed – how can I put it – to 'get Auschwitz' too. The difficulty in finding the right words here is the problem. It feels like blasphemy. Of course it is not. Auschwitz, the German death camp near the Polish town of Oświęcim, is no holy site. The Auschwitz Memorial was built at the site of a horrific mass crime, and it commemorates mass murder, torture, hunger – and informs the public about it. When visiting this place, or even talking about it, one must show reverence. And yes, an invented Auschwitz survivor is irreverent, just like the relatives of a German supposedly murdered there, who tried to make herself more interesting for a blog, whose assumed identity as a sexual therapist did not seem to be notable enough for her.[11]

'Irreverent' may feel too weak for many, but stronger terms such as 'blasphemy' certainly miss the mark. The murder does not sanctify the murdered, and just like it is wrong to say that mass murder becomes 'just a statistic' at a certain point, the opposite is wrong too: It does not become a sacred event. We cannot force the horrible and unusual into the ordinariness of what can be grasped with numbers, just like we cannot borrow a sacral routine to cope with it emotionally. Certainly, we should not even try to do this. But the latter does happen. Banal life seeks out sacred evil, to get something from it: Dark glamour. In this case a second word fits next to 'irreverent' as well: Perverse. In the case of Kaiser-Batthyány, we are dealing with an impostor and a woman whose addiction to attention topples over into outright perversion.

Notes

Chapter 1

1. Real name changed by the editor. This also applies to the documents in which she is mentioned.
2. Real name changed by the editor. This also applies to the documents in which she is mentioned.
3. The transcript – including the errors – is what I received.
4. Cf. for example: Gerald L. Posner and John Ware, *Mengele. Die Jagd auf den Todesengel*, Berlin 1988; Karl Heinz Roth, 'Die wissenschaftliche Normalität des Schlächters – Josef Mengele als Anthropologe', in: *Dokumentationsstelle zur NS-Sozialpolitik, Mitteilungen I*, 1985, pp.1–10; recently in great detail: David G. Marwell, *Mengele. Unmasking the 'Angel of Death'*, W.W. Norton & Company, New York 2020; Marwell writes, among others, about the 'Mengele Effect' pp.76-8.
5. Regarding the destruction of evidence, cf. among others: Andrej Angrick, *'Aktion 1005'. Spurenbeseitigung von NS-Massenverbrechen 1942–1945. Eine 'geheime Reichssache' im Spannungsfeld von Kriegswende und Propaganda*, 2 Vols., Göttingen 2018, Vol.2, pp.1093f.
6. Benoît Massin, 'Mengele, die Zwillingsforschung und die ›Auschwitz-Dahlem Connection‹;' in: *Die Verbindung nach Auschwitz. Biowissenschaften und Menschenversuche an Kaiser-Wilhelm-Instituten. Dokumentation eines Symposiums*, published by: Carola Sachse, Göttingen 2003, pp.201–54, here p.238.
7. The following description of events relies on Massin's 'Mengele'; in the beginning, I first consulted this – in my opinion, very good – article as well as the anthology *Die Verbindung nach Auschwitz* which it is part of, to get a basic overview.
8. Josef Mengele, *Rassenmorphologische Untersuchung des vorderen Unterkieferabschnitts bei vier rassischen Gruppen*, Diss. phil., München 1937; Josef Mengele, 'Sippenuntersuchungen bei Lippen-Kiefer-Gaumenspalte', in: *Zeitschrift für menschliche Vererbungs- und Konstitutionslehre* 23 (1939), pp.17–42; his papers were published among others in the journal *Der Erbarzt*, cf. Year 4 (1937), pp.140f., Year 4 6 (1938), p.17, Year 4 8 (1940) pp.59f. and Year 4 116, as well as Year 4 (1941), p.213f.

9. This was not a novel phenomenon; in the early twentieth century, German researchers sent thousands of skulls and specimens from the colonies to Germany. This included specimens acquired from victims of genocide; one collection at the Charité – Berlin University of Medicine, was found to include twenty skulls from the genocide of the Nama and Herero people in mid-1900s Namibia; they either 'stem from the period of the liquidation of the Herero' or the internment of survivors in the Shark Island concentration camp. Among the latter group, several were found to have suffered from malnutrition caused by the poor conditions within the camp. Upon their death, they were dissected by German colonial doctors, most likely at the military hospital there, preserved and sent to Germany, where the German anthropologist and anatomist Paul Bartels, along with two of his doctoral students, conducted research on the facial muscles of the dead.

   The skulls were handed over to a Namibian delegation on 30 September 2011. Since then, there have been several other repatriations of specimens from the colonial era.

   Cf. Restitution of Namibian skulls in 2011, in: Charité, https://anatomie.charite.de/ueber_den_faecherverbund/human_remains_projekt/restitution_of_namibian_skulls_2011/ (accessed April 2023).
10. Massin, 'Mengele', p.222.
11. Ibid., p.238.
12. Vera Trnka and Heinrich Stephan Nolte, *In den Grauzonen der Geschichte. Der Prager Kinderarzt Berthold Epstein (1890-1962)*, Berlin 2022.
13. Paul J. Weindling, 'Akteure in eigener Sache. Die Witness Aussagen bei der Überlebenden und die Verfolgung der medizinischen Kriegsverbrechen nach 1945', in: *Die Verbindung nach Auschwitz. Biowissenschaften und Menschenversuche an Kaiser-Wilhelm-Instituten. Dokumentation eines Symposiums*, published by: Carola Sachse, Göttingen 2003, pp.255–82, here: pp.274–7.
14. Bogdan Musial, *Deutsche Zivilverwaltung und Judenverfolgung im Generalgouvernement. Eine Fallstudie zum Distrikt Lublin 1939-1944*, Wiesbaden 1999; Bogdan Musial, *'Aktion Reinhardt'. Der Völkermord an den Juden im Generalgouvernement 1941-1944*, Osnabrück 2004.

Chapter 2

1. *Die Auschwitz-Hefte. Texte der polnischen Zeitschrift 'Przeglad lekarski' über historische, psychische und medizinische Aspekte des Lebens und Sterbens in Auschwitz*, published by: Hamburger Institut für Sozialforschung, Vol.2 and supplementary volume, Hamburg 1994.
2. The original files for the Höss trial are held in the main Warsaw branch of the IPN Archive (AIPN) under the call number GK 196/82-103; the original files concerning the investigation against Josef Mengele are held in the IPN Archive in Kraków under: Akta Główne Prokuratora S 51/05/Zn.

Chapter 3

1. E-Mail from the law firm to Prof Dr Kaiser-Batthyány/Szentágothay, 1 July 2014 (private archive).
2. E-mail from the law firm to Prof Dr Kaiser-Batthyány/Szentágothay, 15 December 2014 (private archive).
3. E-mail from the law firm to Prof Dr Kaiser-Batthyány/Szentágothay, 15 December 2014, 17:15, Subject: Appointment on 27 January 2015 in Zürich (private archive).
4. E-Mail from the law firm to Lothfels, 18 December 2014, 09:48, Subject: Regarding Kaiser (private archive).
5. E-Mail from the law firm to Lothfels, 19 December 2014, 11:38, Subject: Regarding Kaiser (private archive).

Chapter 4

1. Cf. Weindling, 'Akteure', p.258f., p.266 and p.271f.
2. 'Biuletyn Informacyjny, 8.10.1942, Nr.39 (143)', in: *Biuletyn Informacyjny*, Vol.2: *Przedruk roczników 1942-1943*, Warsaw 2002, pp.1096-1105, here p.1098; Danuta Czech, *Kalendarium der Ereignisse im Konzentrationslager Auschwitz-Birkenau 1939-1945*, 2nd ed., Reinbek bei Hamburg 2008, p.162.
3. Czech, *Kalendarium*, p.42f.
4. ADDED: I.G. Farben was founded after the merger of several German chemical industrial giants in 1925; after the war, it was split up again into its constituent parts, which continued to dominate the German chemical industry, including BASF, Agfa and Bayer.
5. Bernd C. Wagner, *IG Auschwitz. Zwangsarbeit und Vernichtung von Häftlingen des Lagers Monowitz 1941-1945*, München 2000, p.259.
6. Franciszek Piper, *Die Zahl der Opfer von Auschwitz. Aufgrund der Quellen und der Erträge der Forschung 1945 bis 1990*, Auschwitz 1993, pp.151-69.
7. Aleksander Lasik, 'Die Personalbesetzung des Gesundheitsdienstes der SS im Konzentrationslager Auschwitz-Birkenau in den Jahren 1940-1945', in: *Hefte von Auschwitz* 20 (1997), pp.290-368.
8. Witness statement by Prof Jan Olbrycht, 13 November 1946: AIPN, GK 196/89, pp.166-89, here: p.183.
9. Witness statement by Dr Steinberg during the Nuremberg Trials (excerpts), in: André Lettich, *Trente-Quatre Mois dans les Camps de Concentration. Témaignage sur les crimes 'scientifiques' commis par les médecins allemands*, Tours 1946, pp.42-74.
10. Interrogation protocol of Johann Paul Kremer, 30 July 1947: AIPN, Gl. 196/142, pp.226, here p.24; 'Tagebuch: Johann Paul Kremer [Auszüge]', in: *Auschwitz in den Augen der SS: Rudolf Höss, Perry Broad, Johann Paul*

Kremer, published by the Auschwitz-Birkenau State Museum, Auschwitz 1997, pp.140-207.

11. Interrogation protocol of Dr Władysław Tondos (former prisoner-doctor), 15 July 1947: AIPN, GK 196/142, pp.53-8, here p.56f.
12. Letter from Viktor Brack to Reichsführer of the SS and the German Police Heinrich Himmler, 23 June 1942 (copy): AIPN, GK 196/119, p.4f.
13. Letter from Himmler to Brack, 11 August 1942 (copy): AIPN, GK 196/119, p.6.
14. Witness statement by Dr Tadeusz Paczuła, 23 December 1966: HHStA Wiesbaden, 631a/548; Questioning of Dr Horst Schumann, 17 November 1966: Ibid., 631a/462, pp.529-36.
15. Danuta Czech, 'Die Rolle des Häftlingskrankenbaulagers im KL. Auschwitz II', in: *Hefte von Auschwitz* 15 (1975), pp.5-112, here: p.57.
16. Witness statement by Ludwig Gehr, 14 August 1964: HHStA Wiesbaden, 631a/541. Gehr had been the head of the Siemens bureau in Gleiwitz at the time and set up both 'x-ray bombs'.
17. Interrogation protocol of Rudolf Höss, 9 January 1947: AIPN, GK 196/103, pp.124–41, here: p.132f.
18. *Der Dienstkalender Heinrich Himmlers 1941/42*, edited, commented and with an introduction by Peter Witte et al., Hamburg 1999, pp.162 (entry from 27 May 1941, Fn. 28).
19. Letter from Prof Dr C. Clauberg MD to the Reichsführer-SS Heinrich Himmler, 30 May 1942 (copy): AIPN, GK 196/119, pp.8–10, here: p.10.
20. Interrogation protocol of Rudolf Höss, 9 January 1947: AIPN, GK 196/103, pp.124-41, here: p.132.
21. Dorota Lorska, 'Block 10 in Auschwitz', in: *Die Auschwitz-Hefte,* Vol.1, pp.209–12, here: p.209f.
22. Interrogation protocol of Dr Adelheid Hautval, 2 July 1956: LASH, Abt. 352.3, No.16459 (without pagination); Questioning of Dr Horst Schumann, 7 June 1968: HHStA Wiesbaden, 631a/463, pp.748-53.
23. Letter from the Führer's Chancellery (signature unreadable) to the Reichsführer-SS and Chief of the German Police Heinrich Himmler, 29 April 1944: AIPN, GK 196/119, p.7.
24. Interrogation of Dr Horst Schumann, 7 June 1968: HHStA Wiesbaden, 631a/463, pp.748-53, here: p.749f.
25. Interrogation of Rudolf Höss, 20 March 1947 20.3.1947: AIPN, GK 196/109, pp.94-100, here: p.95.
26. Witness statement by Felicja Pleszowska, 4 December 1947: AIPN, GK196/164, pp.181-93, here: p.190; Witness statement by Dr Alina Brewda,19 November 1946: Ibid., GK 196/99, pp.59-67, here: p.63; Witness statement by Dr Janina Kowalczykowa, 20 March 1947: Ibid., GK 196/109, pp.36-96, here: p.62. Cf. also Micheels, Louis J., *Doctor #117641: a Holocaust Memoir*, Yale University Press, New Haven 1989.

27. 'Secret Report by Dobrosława Klein (after the war: Dorota Lorska), prisoner-doctor in Block 10, regarding medical experiments in Block 10 to the Polish underground, undated, late 1943', in: *Grypsy z Konzentrationslager Auschwitz Józefa Cyrankiewicza i Stanisława Kłodzińskiego*, edited and with an introduction by Irena Paczyńska, Kraków 2013, pp.225–30. Regaring the dating of the report and its origin, cf. Lorska, 'Block 10'.
28. Quoted according to Hans-Walter Schmuhl, *Grenzüberschreitungen. Das Kaiser-Wilhelm-Institut für Anthropologie, menschliche Erblehre und Eugenik 1927-1945*, Göttingen 2005, p.320.
29. Ibid., pp.320-4, quote on p.323.
30. Report of the director Eugen Fischer on the activities of the KWI für Anthropologie, 4 December 1940: APMG, Abt. Rep. 1A, Nr.2400, pp.159-79, here: p.163.
31. Massin, 'Mengele', p.204f.
32. Ibid., pp.211–14.
33. Report of the director Eugen Fischer on the activities of the KWI für Anthropologie, 4 December 1940: APMG, Abt. Rep. 1A, Nr.2400, pp.159–79, here: p.194.
34. Regarding the evolution of the twin research of the KWI, cf. Massin, 'Mengele', pp.211–17.
35. Cf. Nikolaus Wachsmann, *KL. Die Geschichte der nationalsozialistischen Konzentrationslager*, München 2015, pp.532-4.
36. There, the research assistant Karin Magnussen conducted studies into the topic of heterochromia (variation in eye colour in a single individual); in early 1943, while still in Dahlem, she had examined the Melchau family, in which this condition had occurred at a high frequency – three pairs of twins had heterochromia. Cf. Massin, 'Mengele', p.242f. Regarding Magnussen, also cf. Schmuhl, *Grenzüberschreitungen*, pp.482–502; regarding research on 'gypsy and dwarf twins' conducted by the KWI doctoral candidate Georg Wagner cf. ibid., p.469f., as well as Massin, 'Mengele', p.235.
37. Mieczysław Kieta, 'Das Hygiene-Institut der Waffen-SS und Polizei in Auschwitz', in: *Die Auschwitz-Hefte*, Vol.1, pp.213–18.
38. Massin, 'Mengele', p.219.
39. Ibid., p.209f. and p.220.
40. Report of the Hessian State Criminal Police Office, 14 February 1980 concerning the criminal investigation against Josef Mengele, including biographical information, signed by Schaffert: HHStA Wiesbaden, 461/37976, Vol.212 (no pagination).
41. Regarding the ties between Liebau, Verschuer, members of the KWI and Mengele, cf. Massin, 'Mengele', pp.224-8; Schmuhl, *Grenzüberschreitungen*, p.476f. and p.480.
42. Dr med. Erwin von Helmersen, curriculum vitae, 20.9.1945: IPN Kraków, Kr 502/1396, p.52f. However, von Helmersen did not mention his affiliation

with the KWI here and in the interrogations. Cf. also Massin, 'Mengele', p.228f.; Schmuhl, *Grenzüberschreitungen*, p.481f.
43. Progress reports from the KWI for Anthropology to the DGF, research semester 1.10.1943-31.3.1944, keyword specific protein complexes, BA Koblenz, R 73/15342, p.64, quoted according to Massin, 'Mengele', p.232.
44. Regarding the project on the specific protein complexes, cf. ibid., pp.229-33, as well as Schmuhl, *Grenzüberschreitungen*, p.479 and pp.502-22. The concentration camps in the Old Reich had been declared 'Jew-free' by November 1942, and 'gypsy-free' by spring 1943.
45. Thus concludes Massin, 'Mengele', pp.236-40.
46. Interrogation protocol of Rudolf Höss, 9 January 1947: AIPN, GK 196/103, pp.121-41, here: p.140.
47. This is the assessment of Schmuhl, *Grenzüberschreitungen*, p.478f.
48. Affidavit by Horst Fischer, 16 May 1966: BStU, MfS, HA IX/11, ZUV Nr.84, Vol.2, Part 1, pp.113-20, here: p.117.
49. Robert Jay Lifton, *Ärzte im Dritten Reich*, comprehensive edition, Berlin 1998, p.409. Lifton anonymized Münch as Ernst B.
50. According to the witness statement by the former prisoner-doctor Janina Kościuszko, 13 March 1947 during the Höss Trial: AIPN, GK 196/106, pp.41-66, here: p.55: 'This was the time when there [in Auschwitz-Birkenau] Dr Mengele had set up an anthropological research institute and where he studied twins in particular.'
51. Massin, 'Mengele', p.236.
52. Interrogation protocol of Wilhelm Brasse, 10 July 1972: IPN Kraków, S 51/05/Zn, Vol.16, pp.3017-21 (old file). The Polish prisoner Brasse had been a photographer at the identification service and took pictures of Jewish women, twins, triplets and people with dwarfism on Mengele's orders.
53. Helena Kubica, 'Dr Mengele und seine Verbrechen im Konzentrationslager Auschwitz Birkenau', in: *Hefte von Auschwitz* 20 (1997), pp.369-455, here: p.381.
54. Ibid, pp.381-4.
55. Massin, 'Mengele', p.244.
56. Miroslav Kárný, 'Das Theresienstädter Familienlager (BII-b) in Birkenau (September 1943 – July 1944)', in: *Hefte von Auschwitz* 20 (1997), pp.133-7.
57. Massin, 'Mengele', p.235.
58. Both witness statements cited according to Lifton, *Ärzte*, p.392.
59. Interrogation protocol of Martina Puzyna, London, 31 October 1972: HHStA Wiesbaden, 461/37976, Vol.13, pp.12-19, here: p.16.
60. Kubica, 'Mengele', p.386.
61. Report by Dr Otto Wolken, 17 April 1945: AIPN, GK 196/88, pp.131-303, here: p.277.
62. Massin, 'Mengele', p.235f.
63. Kárný, 'Familienlager', p.191.

64. Miklós Nyiszli, *Im Jenseits der Menschlichkeit. Ein Gerichtsmediziner in Auschwitz*, published by Friedrich Herber, second edition edited by Herber; third edition edited by Herber and Andreas Kilian, Berlin 2011, pp.94-7.
65. Interrogation of Dr Rudolf Vitek (Weißkopf), 8 May 1967: IPN Kraków, S 51/05/Zn, Vol.20, pp.3896-906, here: p3897 (old files).
66. Witness statement by Dr Rudolf Vitek (Weißkopf) during the trial against Dr Horst Fischer in March 1966: BStU, MfS, HA IX/11, ZUV Nr.84, Vol.169, pp.114-24, here: p.115.
67. Cf. the notes of Dr Rudolf Vitek (Weißkopf) following the interrogation from 8 May 1967: IPN Kraków, S 51/05/Zn, Vol.20, pp.3907-17, here: pp.3909-12.
68. Witness statement by Professor Berthold Epstein, 7 April 1945: AIPN, GK 196/99, pp.23-36, here: p.35.
69. Regarding the murder of twins with heterochromia, cf. the interrogation protocol of Erich Muhsfeldt, 19 August 1947: AIPN, GK 196/144, pp.80-7, here: p.85f.; Nyiszli, *Im Jenseits*, p.47f.; Massin, 'Mengele', p.243. Regarding the cooperation between Magnussen and Mengele cf. ibid., pp.247-52.
70. Schmuhl, *Grenzüberschreitungen*, p.479.
71. Massin, 'Mengele', p.238.
72. Regarding the selection of people with physical deformities, cf. Nyiszli, *Im Jenseits*, pp.125-30; regarding the practice of abortion, cf. the interrogation protocol of Dr Gisella Perl, New York, 9 March 1973 (German translation): HHStA Wiesbaden, 461/37976, Vol.15, pp.222-6.
73. Massin, 'Mengele', p.237f.
74. Weindling, 'Akteure', p.260.
75. Lifton, *Ärzte*, p.409.
76. Massin, 'Mengele', p.237.
77. Affidavit by Dr Horst Fischer, 16 May 1966: BStU, MfS, HA IX/11, ZUV Nr. 84, Vol.2, Part 1, pp.113-20, here: p.117: 'As SS camp doctor, he [Mengele] mostly concerned himself with racial research in the gypsy camp and with studies on twins.'
78. Thomas A., quote according to Lifton, *Ärzte*, p.406.
79. This is from the testimony of Teresa W. in Lifton, *Ärzte*, p.415f. The pseudonym probably stands for Martina Puzyna. Cf. also the witness statement by Stanisława Rachwał, 25 August 1945: AIPN, GK 196/84, pp.87-152, here: p.138. Rachwał, who had been interned in Auschwitz since 13 October 1942, had worked for the Political Department, intake division, as a prisoner office worker since 1943 and was thus able to observe how Mengele was hiding his twin research documents from his fellow SS men.

Chapter 5

1. In the Łódź Ghetto for example, a copy of the novel *Les Vrais Riches* by François Coppée was used to write down autobiographical notes in four

languages. Cf.: Hanno Loewy and Andrzej Bodek (pub.), *'Les Vrais Riches' - Notizen am Rand. Ein Tagebuch aus dem Ghetto* Łódź *(Mai bis August 1944)*, analyzed and commented by Jan Philipp Reemtsma, audio edition, München 1999. Regarding examples from Auschwitz, cf.: *Grypsy z Konzentrationslager Auschwitz*.

2. Henry Petroski, *Der Bleistift. Die Geschichte eines Gebrauchsgegenstands. Mit einem Anhang zur Geschichte des Unternehmens Faber-Castell*, Basel/Boston/Berlin 1995.

Chapter 6

1. Regarding Eva Kor's gesture and its aftermath, cf.: Jochen Buchsteiner, 'Ein Opfer hat das Recht, frei zu sein', in: *Frankfurter Allgemeine Zeitung* 24 April 2015; Malte Lehming, 'Keiner muss sich für sein Verzeihen rechtfertigen', in: *Der Tagesspiegel*, 27 April 2015; 'Überlebende streiten über Versöhnungsgeste', in: *Spiegel Online*, 27 April 2015, http://www.spiegel.de/panorama/justiz/auschwitz-prozess-versoehnungsgeste-von-eva-kor-sorgt-fuer-streit-a-1030852.html [accessed 11 July 2019].
2. The link to the English-language coverage of the event has since been deleted.

Chapter 7

1. Witness statement by Dr Jan Grabczyński, 30 June 1946: AIPN, GK 196/85, pp.170-3, here: p.172: 'Pańszczyk also conducted surgeries even though he had nothing to do with the medical profession.' The Polish prisoner Mieczysław Pańszczyk worked as a nurse in the infirmary of what would later become the main camp from June 1940. Cf. Oszkár Betlen, *Leben auf dem Acker des Todes*, Berlin 1962. Betlen, a Hungarian 'wire-shoemaker' (i.e. an electrician) by trade, arrived at the infirmary in Auschwitz-Monowitz as a prisoner-nurse in early 1943: 'I apply bandages, give injections, cut open boils. Some patients refer to me as "doctor".' (p.99). Cf. also the interrogation of Dr Stefan Buthner (Budziaszek) MD, 22 July 1971: Fritz Bauer Institut, 4 Js798/65, Vol.7, pp.1270-92. The former prisoner-doctor described this situation as 'unacceptable' (p.1272).
2. Witness statement by Dr Stanisław Suliborski, 21 January 1947: AIPN, GK 196/161, pp.307-308. Dr Suliborski, prisoner in Auschwitz from 15 August 1940, first became a prisoner-nurse in September 1940, before becoming a prisoner-doctor in the main camp until his release on 10 February 1942.
3. Interrogation of Professor Dr Vito Jurivic, 16 October 1973: HHStA Wiesbaden, Sign. 461/37976/18, pp.2-4; Ota Kraus / Erich Kulka, Die Todesfabrik Auschwitz, Berlin 1991, pp.107-18, here: p.107.

4. Kieta, 'Hygiene-Institut', p.213 [emphasis in the quote].
5. Comparison of Deaths in the Concentration Camps in the Second Half of the Year 1942 and the First Half of the Year 1943, SS Main Economic and Administrative Office, Amt D/III, Oranienburg, 22 September 1943 (copy): AIPN, GK 196/117, p.124.
6. The evaluation of the remaining books with the prisoner numbers during the evening count between 10 January 1942 and 19 August 1942: AIPN, GK 196/92, pp.1-118, here: pp.91-7.
7. Letter to the First Camp Doctors of the Concentration Camps (including AU = Auschwitz), 28 December 1942, SS Main Economic and Administrative Office, Amtsgruppe B, SS-Brigadeführer and Generalmajor of the Waffen-SS [Georg Lörner] (copy): AIPN, GK 196/94, p.142f.
8. Ibid.
9. Report by Dr Stefan Buthner (Budziaszek), 2 and 3 February 1974, written down by Tadeusz Iwaszko: APMO, Oświadczenia, Vol.88a, pp.1-61.
10. Ibid; Interrogation of Stefan Budziaszek, 5 March 1948: AIPN, GK 164/179/4, pp.29-40. Cf. also Ewa K. Bacon, *Saving Lives in Auschwitz. The Prisoners' Hospital in Buna-Monowitz*, West Lafayette 2017, pp.51-72.
11. Professor Dr Berthold Epstein, statement under oath, 3 March 1947 (copy): AIPN, GK 151/460, pp.358-63, here: p.359; Report by Berthold Epstein, 11 March 1945 (Russian translation): GARF, f.7021, op.108, d.46, pp.36-40, here: p.36.
12. Report by Dr Stefan Buthner (Budziaszek), 2 and 3 February 1974, written down by Tadeusz Iwaszko: APMO, Oświadczenia, Vol.88a, pp.1-61.
13. Interrogation of Dr Otto Wolken, 24 November 1972: HHStA Wiesbaden, 461/37976, Vol.12, pp.210-13, here: p.210 back page.
14. Witness statement by Władysław Fejkiel, 10 October 1946: AIPN, GK 196/89, pp.17-28, here: p.17f.
15. Interrogation protocol of Dr Horst Fischer, 11 August 1965: BStU, MfS, HA IX/11, ZUV No.84, Vol.4, pp.219-22, here: p.222.
16. KL Auschwitz, Prisoner Personnel Card of Roman Zenkteler [*sic*] (copy). Zenkteller, between 1914 and 1918 field doctor in the German Army, was interned in the Officer Camp Neu-Brandenburg (as First Lieutenant in the Polish Army); on 5 September 1941, he was sent to Auschwitz on the orders of the Stapo [State Police] Schwerin, reason: '(intelligentsia-Pole) polit. Pole': AIPN, BU-VI-55141-51(2)/15.
17. Viktor E. Frankl, ... *trotzdem Ja zum Leben. Ein Psychologe erlebt das Konzentrationslager*, with an introduction by Hans Weigel (June 1977), EBooks, Kösel.
18. Kieta, 'Hygiene-Institut', p.213.
19. Czech, *Kalendarium*, p.347; Witness statement by Professor Berthold Epstein, 17 April 1945: AIPN, GK 196/99, pp.23-36; in detail in Trnka and Nolte, *In den Grauzonen der Geschichte*.

20. Lucie Adelsberger, *Auschwitz. Ein Tatsachenbericht*, 2nd, corrected edition, Bonn 2005, p.49.
21. Witness statement by Professor Berthold Epstein, 7 April 1945: AIPN, GK 196/99, pp.23-36, here: p.25.
22. Witness statement by Karel Minc during the trial of Dr Horst Fischer in March 1966: BStU, MfS, HA IX/11, ZUV Nr.84, Vol.169, pp.76-94, here: p.93.
23. Witness statement by Dr Rudolf Vitek (Weisskopf) during the trial of Dr Horst Fischer in March 1966: BStU, MfS HA IX/11 ZUV Nr.84, Vol.169, pp.114-24, here: p.115.
24. Interrogation protocol of Dr Rudolf Vitek MD, 20 January and 10 March 1966: BStU, MfS, HA IX/11, ZUV No.84, Vol.17, pp.114-24 and pp.125-30; notes by Dr Rudolf Vitek MD following the interrogation on 8 May 1967: IPN Kraków, S 51/05/Zn, Vol.20, pp.3907-17 (old location).
25. Interrogation protocol of Dr Rudolf Vitek (Weisskopf) MD, 8 May 1967: IPN Kraków, S 51/05/Zn, Vol.20, pp.3896-906, here: p.3889 (old location).
26. Notes by Dr Rudolf Vitek MD following the interrogation on 8 May 1967: IPN Kraków, S 51/05/Zn, Vol.20, pp.3907-17, here: p.3909 (old location).
27. Tadeusz Szymański, Danuta Szymańska and Tadeusz Śnieszko, 'Das "Spital" im Zigeuner-Familienlager in Auschwitz-Birkenau', in: *Die Auschwitz-Hefte*, Vol.1, pp.199-207, here: p.205.
28. Interrogation protocol of Martina Puzyna, London, 31 October 1972: HHStA Wiesbaden, 461/37976, Vol.13, pp.12-19.
29. Quote: Ibid, p.14. Cf. also: Interrogation protocol of Dr Katarzyna Łaniewska MD, 17 August 1966: IPN Kraków, S 51/05/Zn, Vol.17, pp.3287-92, here: p.3291 (old location). At the time, Łaniewska was the block doctor in Block 23 in Birkenau's women's infirmary.
30. Interrogation protocol of Martina Puzyna, London, 31 October 1972: HHStA Wiesbaden, 461/37976, Vol.13, pp.12-19, here: p.14f.
31. Ibid, p.15.
32. Ibid, p.16.
33. Ibid, p.18.
34. This is according to Protocol 32, recorded on 28 July 1945 in the office of the National Commission for the Welfare of Deported Hungarian Jews. Dr Miklós Nyiszli, doctor from Nagyvárod (German translation): HHStA Wiesbaden, 461/37976, Vol.13, pp.57-62, here: p.57f. A copy of the Hungarian original can be found at ibid, p.52-6. In the memoir he published in 1946, Nyiszli did not mention his work in the concrete commando and claimed that Mengele had already been waiting at the ramp, looking for doctors who had studied in Germany and who could conduct dissections when Nyiszli arrived. According to him, he was the only one of fifty doctors in his transport who had reported in. Nyiszli's memoirs are not without contradictions. Nevertheless, Dr Otto Wolken, who had been a

prisoner-doctor in Birkenau between July 1943 and January 1945, said in his witness statement from 1972 that 'The core of the aforementioned account [regarding Mengele's activities at Auschwitz-Birkenau] is correct in my opinion'. Interrogation protocol of Dr Otto Wolken, Vienna, 24 November 1972: HHStA Wiesbaden, 461/37976, Vol.12, pp.210-13, here: p.213. Regarding Körner: Czech, *Kalendarium*, p.684 (Körner's prisoner number 169840 had been given on 20 December 1943); Ernst Klee, Auschwitz. *Täter, Gehilfen, Opfer und was aus ihnen wurde. Ein Personenlexikon*, 2nd edition Frankfurt a. M. 2015, p.227.

35. Protocol 32, recorded on 28 July 1945 in the office of the National Commission for the Welfare of Deported Hungarian Jews. Dr Miklós Nyiszli, doctor from Nagyvárod (German translation): HHStA Wiesbaden, 461/37976, Vol.13, pp.57-62, here: p.57f. Cf. also the interrogation protocol of Erich Muhsfeldt 16 August 1947: AIPN, GK 196/144, pp.66-76. According to his own testimony, Muhsfeldt (p.75) was in charge of Crematoria I and II; Nyiszli thought only Crematorium I was under his command.
36. Nyiszli, *Im Jenseits*, p.77.
37. Ibid, p.27-9.
38. Ibid, p.29.
39. Protocol 32, recorded on 28 July 1945 in the office of the National Commission for the Welfare of Deported Hungarian Jews. Dr Miklós Nyiszli, doctor from Nagyvárod (German translation): HHStA Wiesbaden, 461/37976, Vol.13, pp.57-62, here: p.58.
40. Interrogation protocol of Erich Muhsfeldt, 19 August 1947: AIPN, GK 196/144, pp.80-7, here: p.86.
41. Nyiszli does not mention Brandt in either his memoir or his witness statement from 28 August 1945; the name does not appear in other witness statements either. Muhsfeldt meanwhile mentions 'Brand' a second time in the witness statement cited here: 'Mengele, Brand, Thilo and others' did the selections for the incoming transports. This 'Brand' was likely Günther Brandt (1898-1973), a doctor of medicine and an anthropologist, who had been an assistant at the KWI for Anthropology between 1931 and 1933. In 1934, he joined the SS and became a staff leader at the SS Race and Settlement Office. During the war, Brandt served in the navy, after the war he became a medical specialist. Cf. Ernst Klee, *Das Personenlexikon zum Dritten Reich*, Frankfurt a. M. 2003.
42. Interrogation protocol of Erich Muhsfeldt, 19 August 1947: AIPN, GK 196/144, pp.80-7, here: p.85f., quoted according to the German translation of the Polish original: HHStA Wiesbaden, 461/37976, Vol.44, pp.2-10, here: p.8. Regarding this dissection, cf. Nyiszli, *Im Jenseits*, pp.43-6.
43. Interrogation protocol of Dr Gisella Perl, New York, 9 March 1973 (German translation): HHStA Wiesbaden, 461/37976, Vol.15, pp.222-6.
44. Ibid, p.226.
45. Report by Dr Otto Wolken, 17 April 1945: AIPN, GK 196/88, pp.131-303, here: p.277 and p.246.

46. Witness statement by Dr Otto Wolken, 22 June 1945 in the presence of Jan Sehn: AIPN, GK 196/88, pp.79-97, here: p.92.
47. Interrogation protocol of Dr Hajdu Arpad (Armin Sreter), 4 May 1972: HHStA Wiesbaden, 461/37976, Vol.26, pp.36-9, here: p.37.
48. Ibid, p.38.
49. Witness statement by Dr Alina Brewda, 19 November 1946: AIPN, GK 196/99, pp.59-67, here: p.59f.
50. Cf. Czech, *Kalendarium*, p.407; Entry for Ludwik Fleck in: *Stanford Encylopedia of Philosophy*, https://plato.stanford.edu/entries/fleck/ [accessed 23 June 2019].
51. Witness statement by Professor Géza Mansfeld, undated (April 1945): AIPN, GK 196/86, pp.12-23.
52. Interrogation of Henri Limousin, 18 December 1946: AIPN, GK 196/99, pp.1-12.
53. Nyiszli, *Im Jenseits*, p.48.
54. Cf. Angrick,'*Aktion 1005*', Vol.2, pp.1095-7.
55. Appeal to the International Public, 4 March 1945, signed by Professor Géza Mansfeld, Professor Berthold Epstein, lecturer Dr Bruno Fischer, Professor Henri Limousin: GARF, f.7021, op.108, d.46, pp.8-11.
56. Ibid.
57. Protocol of the interrogation of Professor Berthold Epstein, 7 April 1945: AIPN, GK 196/99, pp.23-36, here: p.35.
58. Interrogation of Tadeusz Joachimowski, 18 April 1972: IPN Kraków, S 51/05/Zn, Vol.11, pp.2110-18; Ulrich Völklein, *Josef Mengele. Der Arzt von Auschwitz*, Göttingen 1999/2000, p.134f.
59. Nyiszli, *Im Jenseits*, p.155f.
60. Statement by Dr Miklós Nyiszli, Nagyvárod, in March 1946, published in: Ibid., *Im Jenseits,* U4.
61. Adelsberger, *Auschwitz*, p.178, Fn. 40.
62. Cf. https://web.archive.org/web/20131217204523/http://bulovka.cz/o-nemocnici/sedmdesatpet-let-nemocnice-na-bulovce [last time accessed 1 May 2019]. Cf. also: Trnka and Nolte 'In den Grauzonen der Geschichte', pp.167-228.
63. Lucie Adelsberger to Fritz Weinschenk, Attorney-at-Law, 29 March 1970: Fritz Bauer Institut, Ermittlungsakten 4 Js 798/64, Vol.4, p.694.
64. Cf. the report from 11 December 1973 regarding the case of Zenkteller, former prisoner-doctor in the Auschwitz camp, Main Commission of the Investigation of Hitlerist Crimes (signature unreadable): AIPN, BU 2188/225, p.57f.

Chapter 8

1. Letter from Kazimierz Smoleń, director of the Auschwitz-Birkenau State Museum, 7 May 1981, Main Commission of the Investigation of Hitlerite Crimes in Poland: AIPN, GK 165/368, p.1; Klee, *Auschwitz*, p.398.

2. Interrogation protocol of Eugen Reach (born in 1877), 21 February 1945: GARF, f.7021, op.108, d.3, pp.104-107.
3. Interrogation protocol of Géza Mansfeld (born in 1882), 21 February 1945: GARF, f. 7021, op.108, d.3, pp.108-10.
4. Klee, *Auschwitz*, p.411; report by Dr med. Erwin Valentin (born in 1883), 17 February 1945: GARF, f.7021, op.108, d.33, pp.22-9.
5. Sari J. Siegel, 'Treating an Auschwitz Prisoner-Physician: The Case of Dr. Maximilian Samuel', in: *Holocaust and Genocide Studies* 28, H.3 (Winter 2014), pp.450-81.
6. Cf. Hans-Joachim Lang, *Die Frauen von Block 10. Medizinische Versuche in Auschwitz,* Augsburg 2011.
7. In more detail: Cf. Ibid.
8. Cf. 'Secret Report', p.226. Regarding the state of health of the three women, cf. the witness statement by Dr Alina Brewda, Tel Aviv, 6 April 1967: HHStA Wiesbaden, 631a/539 (no pagination).
9. Siegel, 'Treating', pp.464-7, believes his death to have been in 1943; the Yad Vashem Center assumes so as well, cf. http://yvng.yadvashem.org/nameDetails.html?language=de&s_lastName=&s_firstName=&s_place=&itemId=11622901&ind=0&winId=1670565279013487007 [accessed 12 July 2019], as does the information on the 'Stolperstein' in Cologne: https://museenkoeln.de/ns-dokumentationszentrum/default.aspx?s=2523&sfrom=1196&stid=1808&buchstabe=S [accessed 12 July 2019]. Other witnesses claimed that he died in 1944: Witness statement by Felicja Pleszowska, 24 October 1946: AIPN, GK 196/89, pp.76-85, here: p.82; witness statement by Isaack Mandelbaum, 27 October 1945: Ibid, GK 196/148, pp.80-4; To the International Public, 4 March 1945, signed by Professor Géza Mansfeld (Hungary), Professor Berthold Epstein (Prague), lecturer Dr Bruno Fischer (Prague), Professor Henri Limousin (France): GARF, f.7021, op.108, d.46, pp.8-11. According to his former assistant, Pleszowska, there was a rumour he had been killed in May 1944 following an argument with an SS man; Mandelbaum indicates that his murder happened in the early summer of 1944. Epstein, Fischer and Limousin recall that Samuel was sent to Birkenau in late July/early August, where he was shot in order to eliminate him as a potential witness.
10. United Nations War Crimes Commission, Staffs of the German Concentration Camps. N. I Auschwitz-Birkenau, November 1945: AIPN, GK 196/118, pp.18-42, here: p.35.
11. List of Perpetrators, Auschwitz Concentration Camp, War Crimes Group (US) APO 633: AIPN, GK 196/118, pp.43-129, here: p.103.
12. Witness statement by Erna Fleig, 12 January 1955: LASH, Abt.352.3, No.16459 (no pagination).
13. Cf. Eric Friedler, Babara Siebert and Andreas Kilian, *Zeugen aus der Todeszone. Das jüdische Sonderkommando in Auschwitz,* Lüneburg 2005.

14. Assessment by Professor Jan Olbrycht, 26 March 1947: AIPN, GK 196/111, pp.206-47, here: p.234.
15. Camp Order No.25/44 of the Camp Commander of the Auschwitz Concentration Camp I, 11 May 1944: AIPN, GK 196/121, p.120f.
16. *Lost Album of Auschwitz. The 116 Images of Photographic Album of Karl Höcker, Commander in Auschwitz*, published by Javier Gómez Pérez, 2014.
17. Interrogation protocol of Rudolf Höss, 31 January 1947: AIPN, GK 196/131, pp.159-65.
18. Regarding the runes, http://www.timediver.de/Altungarische_Szekler_Kerbschrift_Rov%E1s%EDr%E1s.html [accessed 12 July 2019] and http://www.obib.de/Schriften/AlteSchriften/Runen/Ungarisch/Runen.html [accessed 12 July 2019].

Chapter 9

1. Cf. Hermann Langbein, *Menschen in Auschwitz,* Wien 1987, p.187, p.257 and p.386; Interrogation protocol of Arthur Paschek, 11 December 1955: LASH, Abt.352.3, No.16459 (no pagination).
2. Interrogation protocol of Dr Jan Grabczyński, 30 September 1946: AIPN, GK 196/85, pp.170-3; Witness statement by Dr Jan Grabczyński in the trial against Rudolf Höss, 20 March 1947: Ibid, GK 196/109, pp.12-35.
3. I examine this issue in more detail in my book about the prisoner-doctors in Auschwitz.
4. Witness statement by Felicja Pleszowska, 24 October 1946: AIPN, GK 196/89, pp.76-85, here: p.81.
5. Assessment by Profesor Jan Olbrycht, 26 March 1947: AIPN, GK 196/111, pp.206-47, here: p.234.
6. Adelaide Hautval, 'Médecine et crimes contre l'humanité – Témoignage'. Translated into German by: Hermann Unterhinnigshofen, Manuskript 1996, p.46, quoted according to: Ernst Klee, *Auschwitz, die NS-Medizin und ihre Opfer,* revised edition, Frankfurt a. M. 2001, p.443.
7. 'Secret Report', p.226.
8. Langbein, *Menschen in Auschwitz,* p.262f.

Chapter 10

1. Eugeniusz Gołębiewski, 'Historia "Numeracji" w polskiej sieci telefonicznej', Warsaw, 8 October 2006: https://archiwum.uke.gov.pl/files/?id_plik=1198 [accessed 12 July 2019].
2. Attila Kirády, *Emberkisérletek a náci haláltáborokban,* Pécs 2015, p.237.
3. Simon Wiesenthal, *Az igaszág malmai… Emlékezések,* Budapest 1991. English edition: *Justice, Not Vengeance*, New York 1989.

4. Imre Kertész, *Fatelessness,* Evanston, Illinois, 1992. The Hungarian original was first published in 1975.
5. István Örkény, *Lágerek népe,* Budapest 1947.
6. Available at: http://www.multesjovo.hu/hu/aitdownloadablefiles/download/aitfile/aitfile_id/2479/ [accessed 12 July 2019].
7. Stefánia Mándy, *Az ellopott történelem. Versek 1944–1992,* Budapest 1992.
8. Handwriting analysis by Professor Dr Ewa Gruza, 28 January 2016 (in Polish). Original in possession of the author. Because Gruza only received scans initially, she had qualified her assessment 'with probability bordering on certainty'. Once she received the originals, she dropped this qualification.
9. There, it was mostly the book *Világfájdalom* [World Pain] by János Martosi Mórocz, Budapest 1940, that was plagiarized as well as the protocols of the Hungarian National Aid Committee (DEGOB) from 1945/46. The protocols are available online on: www.degob.hu [accessed 12 July 2019]; the same is true for other publications from where the forger had lifted pages of text, including: http://archivum.kanizsaujsag.hu/hirek/23272/dr-papp-attila-a-vatikan-es-a-magyar-holokauszt [accessed 12 July 2019] and https://library.hungaricana.hu/hu/view/KalocsaiPuspoksegKozlemenyei_1944/?pg=0&layout=s [accessed 12 July 2019]. Again, around 70% of the text had been either copied or paraphrased from other works.
10. Ferenc Garzuly, *'Fekete víz, örvénylő idő': szombathelyi patológiai jegyzőkönyvek üzenete, 1920–1956*, Vasszilvágy 2006.
11. Ibid., 'A múlt ányai: A szombathelyi patológia jegyzőkönyveinek üzenete (1920-1946)' [The Shadows of the Past: The Message of the Autopsy Reports of the Coroners in Szombathely (1920-1946)], in: *Vasi Szemle* 2004, http://www.vasiszemle.hu/2004/03/garzuly.htm [accessed 12 July 2019].
12. Translation: 'We can understand the abdominal typhoid epidemic, which broke out in the lunatic ward in 1932, thanks to the letter by Dr Dezső Tanka. [...] Into the "observation room" of the division, 51 patients had been crammed, 25 fell ill, seven of them died.'
13. Translation: 'In 1937, the number of autopsies is 179, in 1938, it falls again to 107, then it gradually rises, in 1942, the maximum is reached, 406 autopsies, but also in 1943, the number is high, 320 [...] Again, there emerge [cases of] polio, scarlet fever, whooping cough, diphtheria, tetanus, dysentery, abdominal typhoid fever.' Had the forger copied the text correctly in the medical diary, the first year would have been 1937.
14. Had the forger copied the text correctly, the number should have been 406; the number of 320 autopsies is for the year of 1943, not 1942.
15. 'Augen, die die Hölle auf Erden sahen', in: *Süddeutsche Zeitung*, 27 January 2015.
16. 'Fotók: akik túlélték a haláltáborokat', in: *HVG*, 27 January 2014.
17. This is evidently a very cynical and tasteless reference to Mengele's eye experiments in Auschwitz.

18. Kempinski Hotel Corvinus Budapest, Hotel Reservation Confirmation Number 2806946/54, 27 January 2016.
19. Nyiszli, *Im Jenseits*, pp.43-6.
20. Ibid, pp.125-30.
21. Complementary and extended handwriting analysis by Professor Dr Ewa Gruza, 7 April 2016. Original in possession of the author.
22. Hautval, 'Médecine', p.46, cited according to: Klee, *Auschwitz, die NS-Medizin und ihre Opfer*, p.443.

Chapter 11

1. Cf. 'Abzocke im Namen des Papstes', in: *tz München*, 15 May 2018.
2. Interrogation of Hans-Jürgen K., 22 November 2017: StA München I, Call No.255 Js 141599/17, pp.839-42; letter from Magdolna Kaiser to G.M., 28 November 2017, copy in the author's private archive.
3. Cf. diverging information regarding her places and periods of employment in the judgement of the Munich District Court, 17 May 2018: StA München I, Sygn. 255 Js 141599/17, p.1012f.
4. Copies of the forged certificates are in the private archive of the author as well as in: 255 Js 141599/17, pp.763-73.
5. Certificate of Dr Magdolna Kaiser MD, 24 July 2000 (copy). Private archive; letter to Dr Magdalena Kaiser, 11 September 2001, ppa B.T. (Director of Human Resources and Legal), ppa H.E., Head of Legal Department (copy). Private archive [ppa = by procuration].

Chapter 12

1. Thomas Rahn, 'Der Lügner als Autor, der Autor als Lügner. George Manolescus Memoiren und die Psychologie des Hochstaplers', in: Hartmut Eggert and Janusz Golec (pub.), *Lügen und ihre Widersacher. Literarische Ästhetik der Lüge seit dem 18. Jahrhundert. Ein deutsch-polnisches Symposion*, Würzburg 2004, pp.55-71, here: p.63.
2. *Anna Delvey is keeping busy during house arrest* (2023) *Town & Country*. Available at: https://www.townandcountrymag.com/leisure/arts-and-culture/a38962970/where-is-anna-delvey-today/ (accessed 31 May 2023).
3. Stephan Porombka, *Felix Krulls Erben. Die Geschichte der Hochstapelei im 20. Jahrhundert*, Berlin 2001, p.51.
4. Roberto Ohrt, 'Herr Ubu mit blonden Zähnen', in: *Kultur & Gespenster*, H. 8: *Hochstapler I/II*, Spring 2009, pp.51-71, here: p.64, Fn.7.
5. Regarding Father Florian and Illeret, including his struggle with dyslexia: http://www.illeret.org/ueber-pater-florian [accessed 11 July 2019].

Furthermore, cf.: Florian von Bayern, *Weil es etwas Größeres gibt. Mein Leben in Afrika,* recorded by Christian Weisenborn, Freiburg/Basel/Wien 2010.

6. Forged letter from Father Florian, 19 April 2015 (private archive).
7. Drehmer, Charles E., 'Reciprocity: An Antecedent to Fraud Compliance and Unethical Behavior' (2021). DePaul University, Chicago, *College of Science and Health Theses and Dissertations*, p.390. https://via.library.depaul.edu/csh_etd/390; Vgl. Auch Sonja Veelen, *Hochstapler. Wie sie uns täuschen. Eine soziologische Analyse,* Marburg 2012, p.79f.
8. Ibid,p.80f. Cf. also: Harald Nicolas Stazol, 'Impostors Revisited – oder warum Hochstapler hochstapeln', in: *Kultur & Gespenster*, H.9: *Hochstapler II/II*, Autumn 2009, pp.79-87. In this context, Stazol writes about the 'unconditional willingness' of the victims 'to have so much wool pulled over their eyes that they go blind' (p.83).
9. Press release of the Bavarian State Government, 9 October 2015: http://www.bayern.de/terminhinweis-ministerpraesident-seehofer-verleiht-bayerischen-verdienstorden-an-38-persoenlichkeiten-seehofer-besondere-ehre-fuer-herausragendes-engagement-ordenstraeger-stehen-fuer-zu/?seite=1579 [accessed 12 July 2019]. Cf. also 'Bayerischer Verdienstorden für Erzbischof Georg Gänswein', *kathnews* 14 October 2015, in: http://www.kathnews.de/bayerischer-verdienstorden-fuer-erzbischof-georg-gaenswein [accessed 12 July 2019].
10. Veelen, *Hochstapler*, p.81f.
11. Alfons Backes-Haase, 'Über topographische Anatomie, psychischen Luftwechsel und Verwandtes'. *Walter Serner – Autor der 'Letzten Lockerung'*, Bielefeld 1989, p.102. Cf. also Walter Serner, *Letzte Lockerung. Ein Handbrevier für Hochstapler und solche die es werden wollen,* reprint München 1981.
12. Veelen, *Hochstapler*, pp.82-4.
13. Stefan Hopmann, 'Über Hochstapler und andere Pädagogen', in: *Neue Sammlung. Vierteljahres-Zeitschrift für Erziehung und Gesellschaft* 33 (1993), H.3, pp.421-36, here: p.432.
14. Highlighted in the 'original', both here and in the following excerpts.
15. Regarding Simonides' work and impact, cf. the very well-worth reading biography by Rüdiger Schaper, *Die Odyssee des Fälschers. Die abenteuerliche Geschichte des Konstantin Simonides, der Europa zum Narren hielt und nebenbei die Antike erfand,* München 2011. The aforementioned exhibition catalogue from London is cited according to p.116.
16. Regarding the scandal surrounding the Hitler Diaries, cf. Manfred Bissinger, *Hitlers Sternstunde. Kujau, Heidemann und die Millionen,* Hamburg 1984; Günter Kunert, 'Die Tagebücher Hitlers', in: Karl Corino (pub.), *Gefälscht! Betrug in Politik, Literatur, Wissenschaft, Kunst und Musik,* new edition, Frankfurt a. M. 1990, pp.128-36.
17. 'Art dealer convicted of forging forger's forgeries'(2010) *The Guardian,* available at: https://www.theguardian.com/artanddesign/2010/sep/10/forgeries-conviction-kujau (accessed 31 May 2023).

18. Irene Diekmann and Julius H. Schoeps (pub.), *Das Wilkomirski-Syndrom. Eingebildete Erinnerungen oder Von der Sehnsucht, Opfer zu sein,* Zürich/München 2002, p.349f.
19. Ulrike Jureit, 'Opferidentifikation und Erlösungshoffnung: Beobachtungen im erinnerungspolitischen Rampenlicht', in: Ulrike Jureit and Christian Schneider, *Gefühlte Opfer. Illusionen der Vergangenheitsbewältigung,* Stuttgart 2010, pp.17-103, here: p.26f. Cf. also Stefan Mächler, 'Aufregung um Wilkomirski. Genese eines Skandals und seine Bedeutung', in: Diekmann and Schoeps (pub.), *Wilkomirski-Syndrom,* pp.86-131, in particular p.110f.
20. Lothar Mertens, 'Eine Christin als "Rabbinerin": Karin Mylius', in: Diekmann and Schoeps (pub.), *Wilkomirski-Syndrom,* pp.262-72.
21. Regarding Seibert and his elaborate tales, cf. in particular the detailed report by Martin Doerry and Moritz Gerlach, 'Der gefühlte Jude', in: *Der Spiegel,* 20 October 2018.
22. Egmont R. Koch, *Wagners Geständnis. Wie sich ein SS-Mann als Jude tarnte,* München 2001.
23. Thomas Gehringer, '"Wagners Geständnis": Der Wahrheit dritter Teil', in: *Der Tagesspiegel,* 12 March 2001. Gehringer talks about the doubts expressed by Stefan Aust.
24. Martin Doerry, 'Die Historikerin, die 22 Holocaust-Opfer erfunden hat', in: *Der Spiegel,* 31 May 2019. Her story ended tragically; several weeks after her forgeries were revealed, she was found dead in her apartment on 17 July 2019. The police ruled out the possibility of foul play. Cf. Christian Vooren, 'Sie glaubte ihre eigenen Lüngen', in: *Tagesspiegel,* 27 July 2019: https://www.tagesspiegel.de/kultur/bloggerin-marie-sophie-hingst-gestorben-sie-glaubte-ihre-eigenen-luegen/24845010.html [accessed 15 July 2022].
25. Regarding Müller, cf. Avraham S. Weinberg, *Wilkomirski & Co. – im Land der Täter, im Namen des Volkes,* Berlin 2003, pp.36-9; Michal Bodemann, 'Ernst Müller, geb. 1918', in: *Der Tagesspiegel,* 7 December 2000.
26. For more examples, cf. Weinberg, *Wilkomirski & Co.,* p.35, pp.45-56 and pp.65-71; Diekmann and Schoeps (pub.), *Wilkomirski-Syndrom,* pp.216-61 and pp.288-300.
27. The term Wilkomirski Syndrome refers to the forgery and appropriation of Jewish stories of persecution by non-Jews.
28. Regarding Wilkomirski and the ensuing debates, cf. the previously mentioned anthology by Diekmann and Schoeps (pub.), *Wilkomirski-Syndrom,* but also the monograph by Daniel Ganzfried, ... *alias Wilkomirski. Die Holocaust-Travestie. Enthüllung und Dokumentation eines literarischen Skandals,* Berlin 2002, as well as the authors' reflections in Jureit and Schneider, *Gefühlte Opfer,* pp.23-5.
29. A genealogist reveals the painful truth about three Holocaust memoirs: they're fiction, in: *Bostonia,* Summer 2009: http://www.bu.edu/bostonia/summer09/hoax/ [accessed 3 July 2022].

30. David A. Kluft, '$22.5 Million Verdict In Copyright Registration Case Vacated Due To Fake Holocaust Memoir,' 6 May 2014, MFoley Hoag LLP, mondaq blog: https://www.mondaq.com/unitedstates/copyright/311406/$225-million-verdict-in-copyright-registration-case-vacated-due-to-fake-holocaust-memoir [accessed 3 August 2022].
31. 'Author of fake Holocaust memoir must repay £13.3m', in: *Jewish News*, 13 May 2014; https://www.jewishnews.co.uk/author-fake-holocaust-memoir-author-must-repay-13-3m/ [accessed 3 August 2022].
32. David A. Kluft, '$22.5 Million Verdict in Copyright Registration Case Vacated Due to Fake Holocaust Memoir,' 6 May 2014, in: https://www.mondaq.com/unitedstates/copyright/311406/225-million-verdict-in-copyright-registration-case-vacated-due-to-fake-holocaust-memoir [accessed 20 October 2022].
33. Susan Greene, 'Holocaust survival tale took in many,' in: *The Denver Post*, 16 September 2009: https://www.denverpost.com/2009/09/16/greene-holocaust-survival-tale-took-in-many/ [accessed 19 October 2022]; Katherine Popowski, 'Heroic WWII tale proves false,' in: https://archive.ph/20140823035726/http://archive.9news.com/rss/story.aspx?storyid=123532 [accessed 19 October 2022]; 'The incredible life of Rosemarie Pence,' 1 December 2018: https://www.deceptology.com/2012-02/incredible-life-of-rosemarie-pence.html [accessed 20 October 2022].
34. Report: Auschwitz-Committee in the Federal Republic, seventh day of hearings, Tuesday, 12 November 2019, recorded on 12 November 2019: https://www.auschwitz-komitee.de/1048/7-verhandlungstag-dienstag-12-11-2019/ [accessed 22 October 2022].
35. Julia Fischer, 'Emotionale Geste bei Prozess gegen Ex-SS-Wachmann in Hamburg,' 12 November 2019, in: https://www.evangelisch.de/inhalte/162455/12-11-2019/emotionale-geste-bei-prozess-gegen-ex-ss-wachmann-hamburg [accessed 22 October 2022].
36. Moritz Gerlach, 'Die leider falsche Geschichte von der großen Vergebung,' 27 December 2019, in: *Spiegel* 1/2020. https://www.spiegel.de/politik/kz-prozess-die-grosse-vergebung-leider-falsch-a-00000000-0002-0001-0000-000168667162 [accessed 22 October 2022].
37. Ibid; 'Nebenkläger mit falschem Lebenslauf', 27 December 2019, in: Ibid; Samira Aikas, Erinnern and Vergeben. 14 FSJkler*innen treffen einen Überlebenden des KZ Stutthof [Moshe Peter Loth], in: https://www.spiegel.de/politik/kz-prozess-die-grosse-vergebung-leider-falsch-a-00000000-0002-0001-0000-000168667162 [accessed 22 October 2022].
38. Moritz Gerlach, 'Nebenkläger mit falschem Lebenslauf zieht sich aus dem KZ-Prozess zurück,' 13 January 2020: https://www.spiegel.de/panorama/kz-stutthof-prozess-nebenklaeger-mit-falschem-lebenslauf-zieht-sich-

aus-prozess-zurueck-a-9818889e-e1c8-4277-8887-87df7a421cff [accessed 22 October 2022].

39. Statement of the March of Life regarding Peter Loth (undated): https://marschdeslebens.org/stellungnahme-zu-peter-loth/ [accessed 22 October 2022].
40. Saskia Baron, 'Misha and the Wolves review – tricksy documentary about a child survivor,' 5 September 2021, in: https://theartsdesk.com/film/misha-and-wolves-review-tricksy-documentary-about-child-survivor [accessed 23 October 2022].
41. Cf. James Park Sloan, *Jerzy Kosinski: A Biography*, by James Park Sloan, Dutton, 1996; *Jerzy Kosinski: A Biography*, reviewed by D.G. Meyers, in: *Books in Review*, October 1996, pp.58-64; http://www.leaderu.com/ftissues/ft9610/myers.html [accessed 24 October 2022].
42. Pol Schock, 'Schriftsteller Martin Gray ist tot,' in: *Luxemburger Post*, 25 April 2016, https://www.wort.lu/de/kultur/schriftsteller-martin-gray-ist-tot-571e04831bea9dff8fa76ad1 [accessed 25 October 2022].
43. Gitta Sereny, 'The Men Who Whitewash Hitler,' in: *The New Statesman*, Vol.98, No.2537, 2 November 1979, pp.67-73; Jacek Stachiewicz, 'Kim jest Martin Gray? Wywiad z majorem Wacławem Kapisto,' in: *Nowiny Rzeszowskie*, No.163, 1990, 2 November 1990, p.9.
44. Veelen, *Hochstapler*, pp.73-7, in particular p.75. The psychotherapist Martha Stout describes the 'crocodile tears on demand' as a 'trademark' of manipulators. Cf. Stout, *Der Soziopath von nebenan. Die Skrupellosen: ihre Lügen, Taktiken und Tricks,* Wien 2006, p.113.
45. Veelen, *Hochstapler*, p.63ff.
46. Michael Hagmann, 'FH, der Fälscher Hitlers', in: *EmpaNews*, Year 6/No.24/ December 2008, http://oldweb.empa.ch/plugin/template/empa/*/78799/---/Empa-News-Nr-24.pdf [accessed 22 September 2016].
47. Ibid, p.268.
48. Michael Seufert, 'Der Skandal um die Hitler-Tagebücher,' Frankfurt am Main 2011, p.94.
49. Ibid, pp.25-31, 82 (forged doctorate).
50. Karl-Heinz Janßen, 'Drei Zeugen in Not. Wie schwer es ist, den Ruf zu bewahren,' in: *Die Zeit*, 9 November 1984; Chronik, in: *Hamburger Abendblatt*, 3 March 2018; http://www.abendblatt.de/kultur-live/article108990488/Chronik.html (accessed 23 September 2016).
51. *'Hitler: Sämtliche Aufzeichnungen 1905–1924'* published by Eberhard Jäckel, Axel Kuhn, Stuttgart 1980; Eberhard Jäckel and Axel Kuhn, 'Neue Erkenntnisse zur Fälschung von Hitler-Dokumenten,' in: *Vierteljahreshefte für Zeitgeschichte*, Year 32 (1984), Vol.1, pp.163-9, here: p.163f.
52. Karl-Heinz Janßen, Unternehmen 'Grünes Gewölbe', in: *Die Zeit*, 1 June 1984; http://www.zeit.de/1984/23/unternehmen-gruenes-gewoelbe/komplettansicht [accessed 24 September 2016].

53. Wieland Schwanebeck (pub.), *Über Hochstapelei. Perspektiven auf eine kulturelle Praxis*, Berlin 2014, pp.9-21.
54. Roland Pfister et al, 'Lässt sich ein guter Hochstapler als solcher entlarven? Wenn ja, wie?', in: Ibid, pp.63-72.
55. Rahn, 'Lügner', p.69.

Epilogue

1. Musial had publicly criticized the exhibition, triggering a debate that soon took a more political and scholarly tone. The exhibition director Hannes Heer's treatment of Musial had been unfair, as I realized too late. As the overall director of the institute, I ultimately bore responsibility for this.
2. This programme was indeed real and had been inaugurated in the presence of the Queen Mother of Bhutan.
3. 'Heilig' means holy in German and is very closely related to the word for healing, which makes this name exceedingly silly. However, it is concerning that in his autobiography, Karl May talks about having suffered from years-long blindness as a child.
4. Helmut Schmiedt, *Karl May oder Die Macht der Phantasie*, München 2011, p.53. My description of events follows the narrative in that section.
5. Stephan Hermlin (1915-1997) was one of East Germany's most famous authors, mostly known for his stories, essays and works of poetry.
6. Alfred Andersch (1914-1980) was a German author. Despite being a communist, he left the party following Hitler's rise to power and went into internal exile, eventually divorcing his Jewish wife and fighting in the Wehrmacht as a conscript.
7. Schmiedt, p.144.
8. In more detail, cf. Jan Philipp Reemtsma, 'Opfermemoiren', in: Ibid., *Mord am Strand. Allianzen von Zivilisation und Barbarei*, Hamburg 1998, and Winfried Hassemer and Jan Philipp Reemtsma, *Verbrechensopfer. Recht und Gerechtigkeit*, München 2002.
9. Cf. Daniel Ganzfried, 'Die geliehene Holocaust-Biographie', in: *Die Weltwoche,* No.35, 27 September 1998, p.45f., and Stefan Mächler, *Der Fall Wilkomirski. Über die Wahrheit einer Biographie*, Zürich 2000.
10. The main character in Jean Paul's novel *Der Komet*, Nikolaus Markgraf, a son of a pharmacist who believes himself to have been fathered by Margrave Nikolaus. He then embarks on a search for his supposed father, and this search turns into a sort of pilgrimage for everyone who believes this story. Even the protagonist's father feels honoured by the fictitious affair of his deceased wife.
11. Cf. Martin Doerry, 'Die Historikerin, die 22 Holocaust-Opfer erfunden hat', in: *Der Spiegel*, 31 May 2019, pp.112–15.

Words of Thanks

Many have contributed to the uncovering of this forgery. Not all want to be named, but they all have earned my deepest gratitude. In particular I would like to thank the Hamburg Foundation for the Promotion of Science and Culture, without the support of which none of this would have been possible. The Foundation stood on my side at the moment dreaded by every researcher: The realization that they have fallen for an impostor. For their unwavering support until the completion of this book, my heartfelt thanks goes out to the Foundation and in particular its benefactor, Jan Philipp Reemtsma.

Archives and Literature

Archives

Archive of the Institute of National Remembrance, Warsaw: (AIPN)
Investigation and court files regarding Rudolf Höss and the SS personnel of KZ Auschwitz
Investigation files regarding Josef Mengele, Stefan Budziaszek, Roman Zenkteller, Władysław Dering
Archive of the Max-Planck-Society, Berlin (AMPG) Files of the KWI
Federal Commissioner for the Records of the State Security Service of the former German Democratic Republic, Berlin (BStU)
Investigation and court files regarding Horst Fischer
Fritz Bauer Institute (library), Frankfurt a. M.
Investigation files regarding Stefan Buthner (Budziaszek)
Hesse Main State Archives, Wiesbaden (HHStA Wiesbaden)
Investigation proceedings against Josef Mengele, Horst Schumann
Frankfurt Auschwitz Trial
Archive of the Institute of National Remembrance, Kraków (IPN Kraków)
Prosecution: Investigation files regarding Josef Mengele
Schleswig-Holstein State Archives, Schleswig (LASH)
Investigation proceedings against Carl Clauberg
State Archive of the Auschwitz Museum, Oświęcim (AMPO)
Oświadczenia (Reports)
State Archive of the Russian Federation, Moscow (GARF)
Extraordinary State Commission for the Establishment and Investigation of the Atrocities of the German Fascist Invaders and Their Accomplices

Literature

'Abzocke im Namen des Papstes: Sie betrog die Schwiegermutter von Heino Ferc', in: *tz München*, 15 May 2018.

Adelsberger, Lucie, *Auschwitz. Ein Tatsachenbericht*, 2nd corrected version, Bonn 2005.

Angrick, Andrej, *'Aktion 1005'. Spurenbeseitigung von NS-Massenverbrechen 1942–1945. Eine 'geheime Reichssache' im Spannungsfeld von Kriegswende und Propaganda*, 2 volumes, Göttingen 2018.

'Augen, die die Hölle auf Erden sahen', in: *Süddeutsche Zeitung*, 27 January 2015.

Die Auschwitz-Hefte. Texte der polnischen Zeitschrift 'Przegląd lekarski' über historische, psychische und medizinische Aspekte des Lebens und Sterbens in Auschwitz, published by the Hamburger Institut für Sozialforschung, 2 volumes and a supplementary volume, Hamburg 1994.

Backes-Haase, Alfons, 'Über topographische Anatomie, psychischen Luftwechsel und Verwandtes'. *Walter Serner – Autor der 'Letzten Lockerung'*, Bielefeld 1989.

Bacon, Ewa K., *Saving Lives in Auschwitz. The Prisoners' Hospital in Buna-Monowitz*, West Lafayette 2017.

Bavarian State Government, press release, 9 October 2015: http://www.bayern.de/terminhinweis-ministerpraesident-seehofer-verleiht-bayerischen-verdienstorden-an-38-persoenlichkeiten-seehofer-besondere-ehre-fuer-herausragendes-engagement-ordenstraeger-stehen-fuer-zu/?seite=1579.

'Bayerischer Verdienstorden für Erzbischof Georg Gänswein', *kathnews*, 14 October 2015, in: http://www.kathnews.de/bayerischer-verdienstorden-fuer-erzbischof-georg-gaenswein.

Bayern, Florian von, *Weil es etwas Größeres gibt. Mein Leben in Afrika*, aufgezeichnet von Christian Weisenborn, Freiburg/Basel/Wien 2010.

Betlen, Oszkár, *Leben auf dem Acker des Todes*, Berlin 1962.

Bissinger, Manfred, *Kujau, Heidemann und die Millionen*, Hamburg/Zürich 1984.

Bodemann, Michal, 'Ernst Müller, geb. 1918', in: *Der Tagesspiegel*, 7 December 2000.

'Biuletyn Informacyjny, 8.10.1942, Nr.39 (143)', in: *Biuletyn Informacyjny*, Vol.2: *Przedruk roczników 1942-1943*, Warsaw 2002, pp.1096-1105.

Buchsteiner, Jochen, 'Ein Opfer hat das Recht, frei zu sein', in: *Frankfurter Allgemeine Zeitung*, 24 April 2015.

Corino, Karl (pub.), *Gefälscht! Betrug in Literatur, Kunst, Musik, Wissenschaft und Politik*, durchges, new edition, Frankfurt a. M. 1990.

Czech, Danuta, *Kalendarium der Ereignisse im Konzentrationslager Auschwitz-Birkenau 1939-1945*, 2nd ed., Reinbek bei Hamburg 2008.

Ibid., 'Die Rolle des Häftlingskrankenbaulagers im KL. Auschwitz II', in: *Hefte von Auschwitz* 15 (1975), pp.5-112.

Diekmann, Irene and Julius H. Schoeps (pub.), *Das Wilkomirski-Syndrom. Eingebildete Erinnerungen oder Von der Sehnsucht, Opfer zu sein*, Zürich/München 2002.

Der Dienstkalender Heinrich Himmlers 1941/42, edited, commented and with an introduction by Peter Witte et al, Hamburg 1999.

Doerry, Martin, 'Die Historikerin, die 22 Holocaust-Opfer erfunden hat', in: *Der Spiegel*, 31 May 2019.

Ibid. and Moritz Gerlach, 'Der gefühlte Jude', in: *Der Spiegel*, 20 October 2018.

Eggert, Hartmut and Janusz Golec (pub.), *Lügen und ihre Widersacher. Literarische Ästhetik der Lüge seit dem 18. Jahrhundert. Ein deutsch-polnisches Symposion*, Würzburg 2004.

'Fotók: akik túlélték a haláltáborokat', in: *HVG*, 27 January 2014.

Frankl, Viktor E., ... *trotzdem Ja zum Leben. Ein Psychologe erlebt das Konzentrationslager*, with an introduction by Hans Weigel (June 1977), EBooks Kösel.

Friedler, Eric, Babara Siebert and Andreas Kilian, *Zeugen aus der Todeszone. Das jüdische Sonderkommando in Auschwitz*, Lüneburg 2005.

Ganzfried, Daniel, ... *alias Wilkomirski. Die Holocaust-Travestie. Enthüllung und Dokumentation eines literarischen Skandals*, Berlin 2002.

Garzuly, Ferenc, 'A múlt ányai: A szombathelyi patológia jegyzőkönyveinek üzenete (1920-1946)' [The Shadows of the Past: The Message of the Autopsy Reports of the Coroners in Szombathely (1920-1946)], in: *Vasi Szemle* 2004, http://www.vasiszemle.hu/2004/03/garzuly.htm.

Ibid., *'Fekete víz, örvénylő idő': szombathelyi patológiai jegyzőkönyvek üzenete, 1920-1956*, Vasszilvágy 2006.

'Secret Report by Dobrosława Klein (after the war: Dorota Lorska), Prisoner-doctor in Block 10, Regarding Medical Experiments in Block 10, to the Polish Underground, undated, late 1943', in: *Grypsy z Konzentrationslager Auschwitz Józefa Cyrankiewicza i Stanisława Kłodzińskiego*, edited and with an introduction by Irena Paczyńska, Kraków 2013.

Gehringer, Thomas, '"Wagners Geständnis": Der Wahrheit dritter Teil', in: *Der Tagesspiegel*, 12 March 2001.

Gołębiewski, Eugeniusz, 'Historia "Numeracji" w polskiej sieci telefonicznej', Warsaw, 8 October 2006: https://archiwum.uke.gov.pl/files/?id_plik=1198.

Hopmann, Stefan, 'Über Hochstapler und andere Pädagogen', in: *Neue Sammlung. Vierteljahres-Zeitschrift für Erziehung und Gesellschaft* 33 (1993), H.3, pp.421-36.

Jäckel, Eberhard and Axel Kuhn (Hg.), *Hitler. Sämtliche Aufzeichnungen: 1905-1924*, Stuttgart 1980.

Ibid., 'Zu einer Edition von Aufzeichnungen Hitlers', in: *Vierteljahrshefte für Zeitgeschichte* 29 (1981), p.304f.

Jureit, Ulrike and Christian Schneider, *Gefühlte Opfer. Illusionen der Vergangenheitsbewältigung*, Stuttgart 2010.

Kárný, Miroslav, 'Das Theresienstädter Familienlager (BII-b) in Birkenau (September 1943 – Juli 1944)', in: *Hefte von Auschwitz* 20 (1997), pp.133-237.

Kertész, Imre, *Roman eines Schicksallosen*, Berlin 1996.

Kieta, Mieczysław, 'Das Hygiene-Institut der Waffen-SS und Polizei in Auschwitz', in: *Die Auschwitz-Hefte*, Vol.1, pp.213–18.

Kirády, Attila, *Emberkisérletek a náci haláltáborokban*, Pécs 2015.

Klee, Ernst, *Auschwitz. Täter, Gehilfen, Opfer und was aus ihnen wurde. Ein Personenlexikon*, 2nd ed. Frankfurt a. M. 2015.

Ibid., *Auschwitz, die NS-Medizin und ihre Opfer*, revised new edition, Frankfurt a. M. 2001.

Ibid., *Das Personenlexikon zum Dritten Reich*, Frankfurt a. M. 2003.

Klinger, Judith, and Gerhard Wolf (pub.), *Gedächtnis und kultureller Wandel. Erinnerndes Schreiben – Perspektiven und Kontroversen*, Tübingen 2009.

Koch, Egmont R., *Wagners Geständnis. Wie sich ein SS-Mann als Jude tarnte*, München 2001.

Kubica, Helena, 'Dr Mengele und seine Verbrechen im Konzentrationslager Auschwitz Birkenau', in: *Hefte von Auschwitz* 20 (1997), pp.369-455.

Kultur & Gespenster, Hochstapler #I/II und *#II/II*, H.8 (Spring 2009) and H.9 (Autumn 2009).

Kunert, Günter, 'Die Tagebücher Hitlers', in: Corino (Hg.), *Gefälscht!*, pp.128-36.

Lang, Hans-Joachim, *Die Frauen von Block 10. Medizinische Versuche in Auschwitz*, Augsburg 2011.

Langbein, Hermann, *Menschen in Auschwitz*, Vienna 1987.

Lasik, Aleksander, 'Die Personalbesetzung des Gesundheitsdienstes der SS im Konzentrationslager Auschwitz-Birkenau in den Jahren 1940-1945', in: *Hefte von Auschwitz* 20 (1997), pp.290-368.

Lehming, Malte, 'Keiner muss sich für sein Verzeihen rechtfertigen', in: *Der Tagesspiegel*, 27 April 2015.

Lettich, André, *Trente-Quatre Mois dans les Camps de Concentration. Témaignage sur les crimes 'scientifiques' commis par les médecins allemands*, Tours 1946.

Lifton, Robert Jay, *Ärzte im Dritten Reich*, unabridged edition, Berlin 1998.

Loewy, Hanno and Andrzej Bodek (pub.), *'Les Vrais Riches' - Notizen am Rand. Ein Tagebuch aus dem Ghetto Łódź (Mai bis August 1944)*, evaluated and commented by Jan Philipp Reemtsma, audio edition, München 1999.

Lorska, Dorota, 'Block 10 in Auschwitz', in: *Die Auschwitz-Hefte*, Vol.1, pp.209–12.

Lost Album of Auschwitz. The 116 Images of Photographic Album of Karl Höcker, Commander in Auschwitz, pub. by Javier Gómez Pérez, 2014.

Mächler, Stefan, *Der Fall Wilkomirski. Über die Wahrheit einer Biographie*, Zürich 2000.

Mándy, Stefánia, *Az ellopott történelem. Versek 1944-1992*, Budapest 1992.

Marwell, David G., *Mengele: Unmasking the 'Angel of Death'*, W.W. Norton & Company, New York 2020.

Massin, Benoît, 'Mengele, die Zwillingsforschung und die "Auschwitz-Dahlem Connection"', in: *Verbindung nach Auschwitz*, pp.201–54.

Mengele, Josef, *Rassenmorphologische Untersuchung des vorderen Unterkieferabschnitts bei vier rassischen Gruppen*, Diss. phil., München 1937.

Ibid., 'Sippenuntersuchungen bei Lippen-Kiefer-Gaumenspalte', in: *Zeitschrift für menschliche Vererbungs- und Konstitutionslehre* 23 (1939), pp.17–42.

Micheels, Louis J., *Doctor #117641: A Holocaust Memoir*, Yale University Press, New Haven 1989.

Mórocz, János Martosi, *Világfájdalom* [World Pain], Budapest 1940.

Musial, Bogdan, *Deutsche Zivilverwaltung und Judenverfolgung im Generalgouvernement. Eine Fallstudie zum Distrikt Lublin 1939-1944*, Wiesbaden 1999.

Ibid. (pub.), *'Aktion Reinhardt'. Der Völkermord an den Juden im Generalgouvernement 1941-1944*, Osnabrück 2004.

Nyiszli, Miklós, *Im Jenseits der Menschlichkeit. Ein Gerichtsmediziner in Auschwitz*, published by Friedrich Herber, 2nd edition edited by ibid. and Andreas Kilian, 3rd ed., Berlin 2011.

Ohrt, Roberto, 'Herr Ubu mit blonden Zähnen', in: *Kultur & Gespenster*, H.8, pp.51-71.

Örkény, István, *Das Lagervolk. Roman*, Frankfurt a. M. 2010.

Petroski, Henry, *Der Bleistift. Die Geschichte eines Gebrauchsgegenstands. Mit einem Anhang zur Geschichte des Unternehmens Faber-Castell*, Basel/Boston/Berlin 1995.

Piper, Franciszek, *Die Zahl der Opfer von Auschwitz. Aufgrund der Quellen und der Erträge der Forschung 1945 bis 1990*, Auschwitz 1993.

Porombka, Stephan, *Felix Krulls Erben. Die Geschichte der Hochstapelei im 20. Jahrhundert*, Berlin 2001.

Posner, Gerald L. and John Ware, *Mengele. Die Jagd auf den Todesengel*, Berlin 1988.

Rahn, Thomas, 'Der Lügner als Autor, der Autor als Lügner. George Manolescus Memoiren and die Psychologie des Hochstaplers', in: Eggert and Golec (pub.), *Lügen und ihre Widersacher*, pp.55-71.

Roth, Karl Heinz, 'Die wissenschaftliche Normalität des Schlächters – Josef Mengele als Anthropologe', in: *Dokumentationsstelle zur NS-Sozialpolitik, Mitteilungen I*, 1985, pp.1–10.

Rühle, Alex, 'Wie man Wahrheit kontaminiert', in: *Süddeutsche Zeitung*, 8 June 2019.

Schaper, Rüdiger, *Die Odyssee des Fälschers. Die abenteuerliche Geschichte des Konstantin Simonides, der Europa zum Narren hielt und nebenbei die Antike erfand*, München 2011.

Schmuhl, Hans-Walter, *Grenzüberschreitungen. Das Kaiser-Wilhelm-Institut für Anthropologie, menschliche Erblehre und Eugenik 1927-1945*, Göttingen 2005.

Schwanebeck, Wieland (pub.), Über Hochstapelei. Perspektiven auf eine kulturelle Praxis, Berlin 2014.

Serner, Walter, *Letzte Lockerung. Ein Handbrevier für Hochstapler* [Ibid., Das gesamte Werk, Vol.7], published by Thomas Milch, München 1981.

Siegel, Sari J., 'Treating an Auschwitz Prisoner-Physician: The Case of Dr Maximilian Samuel', in: *Holocaust and Genocide Studies* 28, H.3 (Winter 2014), pp.450-81.

Stazol, Harald Nicolas, 'Impostors Revisited – oder warum Hochstapler hochstapeln', in: *Kultur & Gespenster*, H.9, pp.79-87.

Stout, Martha, *Der Soziopath von nebenan. Die Skrupellosen: ihre Lügen, Taktiken und Tricks*, Wien 2006.

Tadeusz Szymański, Danuta Szymańska and Tadeusz Śnieszko, 'Das "Spital" im Zigeuner-Familienlager in Auschwitz-Birkenau', in: *Die Auschwitz-Hefte*, Vol.1, pp.199-207.

'Tagebuch: Johann Paul Kremer [Auszüge]', in: *Auschwitz in den Augen der SS: Rudolf Höß, Perry Broad, Johann Paul Kremer*, published by the Auschwitz-Birkenau State Museum, Auschwitz 1997, pp.140-207.

Trnka, Vera and Nolte, Heinrich Stephan, *In den Grauzonen der Geschichte. Der Prager Kinderarzt Berthold Epstein (1890-1962)*, Berlin 2022.

'Überlebende streiten über Versöhnungsgeste', in: *Spiegel online*, 27 April 2015, http://www.spiegel.de/panorama/justiz/auschwitz-prozess-versoehnungsgeste-von-eva-kor-sorgt-fuer-streit-a-1030852.html.

Veelen, Sonja, *Hochstapler. Wie sie uns täuschen. Eine soziologische Analyse*, Marburg 2012.

Die Verbindung nach Auschwitz. Biowissenschaften und Menschenversuche an Kaiser-Wilhelm-Instituten. Dokumentation eines Symposiums, published by Carola Sachse, Göttingen 2003.

Völklein, Ulrich, *Josef Mengele. Der Arzt von Auschwitz*, Göttingen 1999/2000.

Wachsmann, Nikolaus, *KL. Die Geschichte der nationalsozialistischen Konzentrationslager*, München 2015.

Wagner, Bernd C., *IG Auschwitz. Zwangsarbeit und Vernichtung von Häftlingen des Lagers Monowitz 1941-1945*, München 2000.

Weinberg, Avraham S., *Wilkomirski & Co. – im Land der Täter, im Namen des Volkes*, Berlin 2003.

Weindling, Paul J., 'Akteure in eigener Sache. Die Aussagen der Überlebenden and die Verfolgung der medizinischen Kriegsverbrechen nach 1945', in: *Die Verbindung nach Auschwitz*, pp.255–82.

Wiesenthal, Simon, *Az igaszág malmai… Emlékezések*, Budapest 1991.

Index